THREE COMEDIES FOR THE SCREEN

APOCALYPSE LATER

DÉJÀ VU DÉJÀ VU

HOOSIER DADDY

Screenplays written by

Pat Mulligan

authorHOUSE®

AuthorHouse™
1663 Liberty Drive, Suite 200
Bloomington, IN 47403
www.authorhouse.com
Phone: 1-800-839-8640

First published by AuthorHouse 1/20/2009

ISBN: 978-1-4343-6379-4 (sc)

Printed in the United States of America
Bloomington, Indiana

This book is printed on acid-free paper.

Dedications: To environmentalists. To time travelers and alcoholics. Also, to people in the service industry, athletes and strippers.

Table of Contents

APOCALYPSE LATER. A farcical spin on the environmental crisis. It's a story of a modern day savior who has gone astray. His plan to save the world backfires when he and his disciples kidnap the children of two corporate moguls. Their companies are staunch contributors to global warming. Ostensibly, the plan works but, the kids prove to be a handful and rival factions enter into play. It's a tale of the tail wagging the dog.

DÉJÀ VU DÉJÀ VU. Two Eighties yuppies lose their shirts in the crash of '87. They are also being studied by students in another dimension. In an experiment they catapult our heroes on a time travel adventure. They start their trek at Woodstock in 1969. Eighties yuppies who were once hippies become disillusioned. Now, they have to go back to the future the old fashioned way - one day at a time.

HOOSIER DADDY. A black youth, brought up in rural Indiana by his white coach/dad, develops a promising basketball career. He comes of age and decides to search for his biological father, only to find out his daddy is now his momma. He/she is now an exotic dancer in Vegas.

INTRODUCTION

Screenplays have their own format which include SLUG LINES, CHARACTER HEADINGS and STAGE DIRECTIONS. Slug Lines indicate place (interior or exterior) and time (day or night). These are necessary for a shooting script which the director needs to set up shots for a film. Another abbreviation used in scripts is (V.O.) or (O.S.) These are used when a character is narrating or is off stage during their speech. Here is an example of a screenplay format.

FADE IN:

SUBTITLE: LOS ANGELES, CALIFORNIA 1998

EXT. COURTHOUSE - ESTABLISHING - DAY

INT. COURTHOUSE - DAY

THE JUDGE (V.O.)
Welcome to justice, L.A. style.

The BAILIFF swears in JOHN PALMER. John seems to be uneasy. The JUDGE nods to the PROSECUTING ATTORNEY to proceed.

PROSECUTING ATTORNEY
Mr. Palmer, did you kill Jill Dikonbery?

JOHN PALMER
That depends on what you mean by kill.

PROSECUTING ATTORNEY
Did you cause her to stop breathing?

JOHN PALMER
She was on a respirator and it stopped working.

PROSECUTING ATTORNEY
You were also her benefactor. You'd be the recipient of a million dollars if she died.

JOHN PALMER
(cries out)
But, she was terminal. It was euthanasia!

PROSECUTING ATTORNEY
I rest my case.

DISSOLVE TO:

INT. JURY ROOM - DAY

The JURY mull about as they reach their verdict...etc.

Again, this format would be necessary for a shooting script, but would be an impediment for the average reader, visually, interrupting the flow. I will present to you three screenplays sans slug lines, employing titles instead to set up the year, place or event. Character headings will be used and of course, stage directions. In other words, it will be presented as if you were seeing it.

PROLOG

In the darkest days of the Bush Administration in 2008, our world and our country had become a precarious place. During Bush's watch we experienced 9/11, and the unnecessary and destructive Iraq War, a war that is bankrupting our country. The sad irony is, before we took out Saddam we had him by the "short and curlys". He in turn had his people (Sunnis, Shia and other unenlightened Islamic groups) by their respective "short and curlys." It was a win-win. The occupation became a huge baby sitting job that's wasted the lives of thousands of Americans and countless thousands of innocent Iraqis.

Also during Bush's watch, we saw oil prices, energy costs, food and travel expenses sky-rocket. There was the Katrina fiasco, countless administration scandals and the implosion of our financial institutions. That collapse was brought about by imprudent financial policies. This in turn lead to the gluttony known as the Sub Prime Lending Rate. The end result was a Wall Street meltdown. We saw an exponential wave of jobs leave our country. The border crisis and the immigration debacle unfolded during Bush's watch as well.

G.W. was elected twice by narrow margins. His first election was fixed, thanks to a brother in high places and the skewed ruling of Supreme Court Justice, William Rehnquist. There were some "fuzzy numbers" moved about in Ohio for that second election.

In the meantime, other "dark forces" were at work. **Corporate greed**. This is a tale of what could have happened if the "forces of good" took control. But, as you'll see, even those forces were susceptible to corruption.

We have a new President and a new administration. Let's hope that we can dig ourselves out of this hole. The events of this story came to a climax in 2008.

APOCALYPSE LATER

Pat Mulligan

FADE IN:

MUSIC - Jimi Hendrix's, *MANIC DEPRESSION*

1989 - PRINCE WILLIAM SOUND

Oil drenched birds flounder on shore.

1991 - KUWAITI DESERT

Torched oil wells spew billows of smoke into the atmosphere which blocks out the sun. A tattered poster of SADDAM HUSSEIN rustles in the wind.

1993 - WACO TEXAS

The BRANCH DAVIDIAN COMPOUND goes up in flames.

1995 - OKLAHOMA CITY

Smoke emanates from the remains of the ALFRED P. MURRAH BUILDING.

2001 - THE WORLD TRADE CENTER

The plane plunging into the SECOND TOWER.

2003 - BAGHDAD

The "Shock and Awe" bombs destroy the city.

2006 - OVAL OFFICE

> GEORGE BUSH
> Stay the course.

THUNDER

> GOD (O.S.)
> This guy made Nixon look like an amateur. This is getting out of hand. I've sent you a new Savior.

2007 - ACADEMY AWARDS

AL GORE smiles as *An Inconvenient Truth* wins the Oscar for Best Documentary Feature.

> GOD (O.S.)
> It's not him. He's good, but he's still
> a politician.

BETHLEHEM PENNSYLVANIA - Thirty three years ago

LATE NIGHT, OUTSIDE, on a wet intersection. Suddenly, an old beat up FORD speeds across the intersection.

> GOD (O.S.)
> The first Savior saved your souls. This
> one's going to try and save your hides.
> Good luck, kid.

A BOLT OF LIGHTNING strikes the Ford, causing it to spin out of control. Coming the other way a CADILLAC tries to avoid the Ford. The Ford then skids onto the sidewalk, stopping just short of a religious paraphernalia shop. Inside the DISPLAY WINDOW a crucifix with a configuration of Jesus nailed to it is jostled by the commotion.

> GOD (O.S.)
> He was born in the back seat of an
> old Ford.

The Cadillac comes to a stop. INSIDE the Ford, from the radio, The Doobie Brothers, *JESUS IS JUST ALRIGHT* is blasting. The driver, JOE, turns to his wife, MARY, who is sweating profusely and is about to give birth in the back seat.

> JOE
> Mary, we're almost at the hospital!

> MARY
> It's funny, but I think this is where
> we conceived. Ahhh! Now, Joe!

Joe scrambles into the back seat to assist his wife.

> GOD (O.S.)
> His mother was no virgin and his father,
> a mechanic. To keep with some tradition,
> I've sent the Three Wise Men.

4

From the Cadillac, THREE MEN looking very Italian and dressed in pin-stripe suits pile out and run over to the Ford. One of the men wipes the window and looks inside.

MAN # 1
Minga! Look, a baby just popped out.

MAN # 2
Madonna. Now, da guy is wrappin' da little bambino in swaddling clothes.

MAN # 3
What the frick is swaddling clothes?

Man # 1 knocks on the window. Joe rolls it down.

MAN# 1
Eh, is dere anyting we can do?
(to Man # 2)
Go get dose gifts.

He runs to the Cadillac.

INSIDE the Ford, Joe and Mary are caught up in the joy of the moment. Man #2 comes running back with some gift wrapped boxes. Man # 1 pops his head in.

MAN # 1
Sorry to intrude folks. We was just on our way to my godson's circumcision party. Please take deeze gifts. I hope it's a boy.

As Mary lifts the baby up, the swaddle drops, exposing his little doodle.

MAN # 3
Is he Jewish?

MAN # 1
What are you a wise guy?

MAN # 3
Yeah, as a matter of fact, I am.

CLOSE UP of the baby.

> GOD (O.S.)
> His name is Jerry Collins. They, who
> come to know him will call him J.C.

MORNING - INSIDE of a SCHOOL SHOP CLASS

> GOD (O.S.)
> He's got the messiah gene. I tried to
> eliminate the martyr chromosome.

J.C. at age thirteen. He wears a Greenpeace T-shirt. A head band holds back his shoulder length hair. He is at a lathe, putting the finishing touches on a LARGE CROSS.

> GOD (O.S.)
> Oh, Jeeze.

LATE AFTERNOON - OUTSIDE OF CAMPUS - UC AT BERKELEY

J.C., a freshman at Berkeley, has the look of a prophet. His entourage of three, MATTHEW, MARK and JUDE, follow him to a hillside where hundreds of STUDENTS wait for his arrival. J.C. addresses the crowd.

> J.C.
> Does anyone here believe in re-
> incarnation?

> VOICE FROM CROWD
> Yeah!

> J.C.
> Welcome back.

LAUGHTER from the crowd.

> J.C.
> There's an enemy. It's our complacency.
> Oil, corporate greed and global warming
> are killing us.

About a half an hour has passed. Two students, SEAN YOUNG and KIRK MANWARING, wearing "Young Republicans" T-shirts, speak out.

> SEAN
> J.C. You have filled the voids in our
> empty heads with propaganda.

6

KIRK
But how 'bout filling the void in our
empty stomachs with chow?

J.C.
Ah, Sean and Kirk. Matthew, Mark,
Jude. Do we have any bread?

MATTHEW
We're broke.

J.C.
Patience is a virtue. But, as we've seen,
patience can be the enemy of change. So,
I must ask you. Do you have any change?
Mark, pass the hat. Collect the bread and
it will multiply.

MARK
And where shall we go for food?

J.C.
Fish 'n' Chips.

FOUR YEARS LATER

HIGH NOON on the PACIFIC OCEAN

A GREENPEACE BOAT tries to intercept a WHALING SHIP, to no avail. The whaling
ship bumps the Greenpeace boat. A raft with FOUR JAPANESE MEN is lowered
from the whaling vessel. They are armed. The Japanese intercept and board the
Greenpeace boat. J.C., the captain, addresses his two new disciples: MAGDELIN,
a young black woman and STUKE, a young Asian man.

J.C.
Magdelin, Stuke, radio in our findings.

Matthew, Mark and Jude approach the intruders.

MATTHEW
Get off of this boat you whale killing
pigs.

J.C.
Matthew.

The Japanese men take out their weapons.

                    J.C.
          There's no need for violence.

One of the Japanese men approaches J.C. and back hands him on the cheek.

                    J.C.
          Domo Arigato.

J.C. turns the other cheek. This confuses the Japanese. They exit the boat.

                    MATTHEW
          Cool.

ONE YEAR LATER

EARLY MORNING on an OIL COVERED SHORELINE

About FIFTY MEN and WOMEN make an attempt to clean up an oil spill that has made it's way to the shore. From a boom box near the beach, Jimi Hendrix's, *CASTLES MADE OF SAND* can be heard. In the distance, a man heads towards the shoreline. He is walking on the water. It's J.C.

                    J.C.
          Hey, turn that up.

Matthew, Mark, Jude, Stuke and Magdelin gather on shore to marvel at this miracle.

                    MATTHEW
          Wow!

                    MAGDELIN
          Oh, my Lord!

                    JUDE
          It's a trick.

J.C. approaches the shore. He stops.

                    J.C.
          Hey, Jude.

Jude steps back.

                    J.C.
          Come on.

8

Jude walks towards J.C. He, too walks on the surface of the water. Jude still can't believe his eyes.

                    J.C.
          It's no trick. This water is so thick
          with oil, anyone can walk on it. Try it.

Matthew and Stuke walk on the water. Stuke runs and slides on his butt towards J.C.

                    STUKE
          This is a blast!

                    MARK
          Oh great! Now we've got to wipe you
          off. Don't we have enough crud to clean.

                    J.C.
          Mark's right. Let's get busy.

It's a few hours later. Some of the men help J.C. load oil drenched rocks onto a wheel barrel while Magdelin tries to clean off a BABY SEAL with some Bounty paper towels.

                    MAGDELIN
          They never try and clean these on TV.
          Whew! J.C. I'm whopped. I'm gonna
          take a break, sugar.

Magdelin walks back to an alcove and sits. J.C. follows. He squats down next to her and wipes some oil from her cheek.

                    J.C.
          I want to thank you for all your help.
          You left a high paying job.

                    MAGDELIN
          High payin'? Turnin' tricks got me
          high, but it didn't *pay*. Thanks for
          showing me the way. You saved my
          butt, J.C.

                    J.C
          And a nice butt it is.

THUNDER

                              J.C.
          Just kidding. Magdelin, you've been
          very devoted and I want to thank you.

                           MAGDELIN
          You're an inspiration. J.C. What makes
          you so dedicated, so caring?

                              J.C.
          My parents were good. They taught me
          a lot.

Magdelin wipes off some oil that's on J.C.'s bicep. She smiles.

                              J.C.
          I also hear this voice. It kind of leads me.

Magdelin snuggles up to J.C.

                           MAGDELIN
          Voice?

J.C. is now caught up in Magdelin's affection. She leans forward to kiss him. He
stops her. He then rises and helps Magdelin up. She leans in to kiss him again. They
connect. J.C.'s knees buckle as he gently pushes her away.

                           GOD (O.S.)
          Atta boy. Watch it, son. Women make
          legs weak.

                              J.C.
          Did you hear that?

                       ONE YEAR LATER

It's a hot, humid DAY in a SOUTH AMERICAN RAIN FOREST. From a clearing,
J.C. and company exit a PIPER CUB. FILIPE BENLADA, the pilot, is a young local
Hispanic. He has become a new disciple. Not far from the plane a CONSTRUCTION
COMPANY is leveling a portion of the forest.

J.C. and company approach the sight. J.C. stands in front of a BULLDOZER that's
about to plow down an area of timber. The DRIVER tries to wave them out of his
path.

                    DRIVER
Vaminos, pendejos!

                    MARK
Quis cu se, pendejos?

                    FILIPE
It means, ah…shithead.

                    J.C.
We're not moving.

A JEEP pulls up with several MEN. A construction FOREMAN and a local DEPUTY get out.

                    FOREMAN
You people are trespassing. If you
don't leave here, you'll be placed
under arrest.

                    J.C.
Don't you realize what you're doing here?

                    FOREMAN
Yeah, yeah. We knock down the trees so
the local peasants can plant crops in this
useless soil. We exploit the land and the
peasant. Plus, we suck the oxygen from
the Western Hemisphere which adds to
the ozone depletion. Oh, yeah, and we
make a buck in the process. Now get out.

                    J.C.
Over my dead body.

He lies down right in front of the bulldozer. The foreman signals to the driver. The bulldozer heads towards J.C.

                    MARK
        J.C. get up!

The bulldozer is now some ten feet from J.C. Magdelin tries to pull him out of it's path.

                    J.C.
No. This insanity must end now!

11

As the bulldozer edges closer, Mark runs up to the foreman.

                    MARK
        Stop! Are you crazy? You'll kill him!

Mark falls to the ground, crying hysterically. The bulldozer has now reached J.C. and crushes his foot. J.C. screams out. Matthew picks up a rock and throws it at the DRIVER, hitting him in the head. The blow renders him unconscious. As he falls from his seat the bulldozer stops. The men scramble from the Jeep and seize Matthew while the deputy cuffs him.

                    DEPUTY
        Ju'r going to jail, vatto.

Magdelin and Stuke tend to J.C. Mark is still hysterical.

                    MARK
        You monsters! You tried to kill the
        chosen one. Somebody call 9 11!

                    FILIPE
        Down here it's 6 11.

Mark runs over to J.C. and sees his bloody foot and faints.

                    DEPUTY
        Puto.

                    FOREMAN
        I warned you people.

He goes to the Jeep, gets on the CB and radios in for help.

                SEVERAL YEARS LATER - IRAQ

An ICRC TRUCK pulls up to an IRAQI MAN, WOMAN and TWO YOUNG CHILDREN. They have just left their home which is burning in the background. The Iraqi man's clothes are on fire. J.C. is dressed in kakis with a Red Cross insignia arm band. He gets out of the vehicle, limps up to the man and tries to put the flames out with his hands. He, then, tackles the man down to the ground and as they roll in the dirt the flames are extinguished. J.C.'s hands are badly burned.

An ARMY CHOPPER lands. A SOLDIER gets out and carries J.C. to the craft. From the pilot's window, Jude frantically waves them in. J.C. smiles, glad to see his old friend.

JUDE

Just watchin' your back. I'm outta here
next month.

ONE WEEK LATER - OUTSIDE OF A HOSPITAL - USA

INSIDE of a HOSPITAL ROOM, J.C. lies in bed with his hands bandaged up and
watching TV. Magdelin, Matthew, Mark, Stuke and Filipe enter. Mark puts some
roses in a water jar. Magdelin kisses J.C. on the forehead.

FILIPE

Saving the world can be hazardous to
your health.

J.C.

I have to stop being so hands on.

LATER THAT NIGHT. J.C. is asleep. God appears to him in a DREAM.

God is in the hospital room. He picks up the roses and hands them to J.C. His hands
are not bandaged. J.C. pricks his finger on a thorn.

J.C.

Ouch!

GOD

For every rose, there's a prick.

J.C.

Is there a place where there's no pain?

GOD

Heaven.

J.C.

I've tried. I've really tried to make a
difference, but I keep getting whacked.

GOD

Welcome to the savior business.

J.C.

Is it a business?

GOD

Are you kidding? Look at the Catholic Church.

                    J.C.
Well, a miracle or two couldn't hurt.
I mean, Jesus had a few tricks.

                    GOD
He needed them. It's a high tech world
now. Miracles are a dime a dozen. To
save the world you must use your mind.

                    J.C.
How?

God's beeper goes off.

                    GOD
Oh, gotta run, son.

God disappears. J.C. WAKES UP.

On the TV above, a show called *AMBUSH* is in progress. The host is BOB SEIL.

                  BOB SEIL
Bob Seil here. The show, *Ambush*. If
you have dragons to slay, this is where
we slay 'em. Today's topic: gay Senators.
But first the news. Today, the sponsors of
this show, Axxin Oil and Specific Motors,
merged.

                    J.C.
Oh, great.

SERIES OF SHOTS - DAY - MUSIC - Jimi Hendrix's, *AXIS BOLD AS LOVE*

J.C. speaks at a rally to "Save the Environment." - Another rally to boycott Specific Motors. The PRESS is there. - J.C. and crew protest yet another oil spill by Axxin Oil.

WALL STREET - AFTERNOON - In front of the NYSE building, a Lincoln TOWN CAR is parked on the street. The windows are tinted. The back window is opened a crack. From inside we HEAR two men conversing.

                   MAN # 1
This J.C. character is giving us bad press.

MAN # 2
Maybe we can use it to our advantage.

MAN # 1
Infiltrate his group from within.

TV STUDIO - J.C. is a guest on *Ambush.* **SUMMER 2008**

BOB SEIL
Our guest tonight is probably the most
famous activist since Abbie Hoffman.
Jerry Collins. J.C. to his friends. Are
you the new Christ?

J.C. seems embarrassed by the comparison.

J.C.
The top polluter in this country is Axxin
Oil. And now they've merged with the pigs
at Specific Motors. They've stalled on their
alternative fuel cars. These giants may lower
their prices, but don't be fooled. You'll pay
in end with global warming people! Boycott
these corporations and get out and vote!
No more idiots. We need change!!

BOB SEIL
Easy, they're my sponsors.

J.C.
Take action now, people! There's no more
time for denial. Stop being sheep!

BOB SEIL
Well, so much for "The meek shall inherit
the Earth."

In his DRESSING ROOM, after the show, Bob Seil offers J.C. a seat.

BOB SEIL
Great show. J.C.

He opens up an attaché case filled with one hundred dollar bills.

                                BOB SEIL
                    Many people believe in you. Please take
                    this ah…
                            (removes a stack)
                    …nine hundred thousand dollars for the
                    cause. If you want to slay these dragons,
                    get 'em by the balls.

                                J.C.
                    What do you mean?

                                BOB SEIL
                    What do you think would be the most
                    important thing to a very powerful man?

J.C. thinks for a moment.

                                J.C.
                    His children?

                                BOB SEIL
                    Go get 'em tiger.

                                J.C.
                    Where did you get this money?

                                BOB SEIL
                    I passed the collection plate.

J.C. struggles for a moment. Bob Seil closes the attaché case and hands it to J.C.

MIDDAY - A VAN with "THINK GREEN" plates on a highway - J.C. and company are on the road. INSIDE of the van, J.C. is reading the paper.

CLOSE UP of two ads in the classifieds reads: **WANTED - CHOPPER PILOT FOR HIRE FOR SPECIFIC MOTORS EXEC. CALL 1-800-BIG-BUKS.**

WANTED - CARETAKER NEEDED FOR AXXIN OIL EXEC RESIDENCE. MUST SPEAK SPANGLISH. CALL 1-800-JOB-SPIC.

J.C. shows the ads to Jude and Filipe.

WASHINGTON D.C., OUTSIDE of the CAPITOL BUILDING, It's a RAINY DAY. J.C. and crew get into it with some LOBBYISTS - NEWSPEOPLE are there. As SECURITY whisks J.C. away, he begins to rant.

J.C.
These lobbyists are extorting your
future, people! Stop them! And
remember, boycott all Axxin Oil
and Specific Motors products.
They're killing you!!

As the CAMERA PULLS BACK, we SEE this is on "Prime Time News." The TV is being watched by a man INSIDE of his limousine. GRANT METHAMIN, smiles and turns off the TV as they pull up to his mansion.

STONY POINT, MICHIGAN

A huge wrought-iron gate stands guard in front of this old Victorian Mansion built during the golden age of the Motor City. A placard reads, "Grant Methamin - Specific Motors." The gate opens as the limousine pulls through and drives up to the mansion. A CHAUFFER gets out and opens the rear passenger door. Methamin is a debauched, but handsome man in his late fifties. He gets out and enters the mansion where he is met by a SERVANT who escorts him in.

SERVANT
Did you enjoy your take-over, sir?

METHAMIN
Same as usual.

INSIDE - The front room is adorned with Persian carpets, antique furniture and Ming Dynasty vases. Two children descend the ornate mahogany stairs to greet their grandfather.

CHELSEA, age eleven and JASON, age ten are dressed like little Lady and Lord Fauntleroy. Jason runs to his side. Methamin hugs Chelsea and gives Jason a "high five."

METHAMIN
Jason, get out of those clothes would
you? You look like a little wimp.

JASON
I promised Gramma I'd wear these 'til
puberty.

METHAMIN
Well, she's dead now.
(a beat)
Moment of silence.

17

About two seconds pass.

                    METHAMIN
          Okay, that's enough. Change and later
          I'll have a treat for you.

Descending the stairs is RUTH, Methamin's daughter, mid-thirties. She misses a step.

                    METHAMIN
          Ruth.

                    RUTH
          Hmm. Father, please. You'll spoil him.

                    CHELSEA
          Too late.

SUNDAY MORNING. From outside of the mansion, the CAMERA PUSHES THROUGH Methamin's office window. INSIDE, a MAID sets a tray of breakfast on a huge maple desk and leaves. Methamin is on his computer, going over stock quotes.

Ruth and Jason enter.

                    RUTH
          Will you be joining us for church?

                    METHAMIN
          No, Ruth, I've got a few empires to
          crumble, here.

Ruth frowns. Methamin cheerfully announces…

                    METHAMIN
          They're demolishing one of my apartment
          buildings today. I've hired a chopper to
          watch. I want you and the children to join
          me.

                    JASON
          Yeah!

METHAMIN
You'll have to skip church.

JASON
Yeah!

Ruth and Methamin exchange dirty looks. Methamin's are dirtier.

RUTH
Isn't it a bit unethical to blow buildings
up on Sunday?

METHAMIN
Unethical, unshmethical. Now chop-
chop!

He laughs. Jason joins in. Ruth takes Jason's hand and snaps out of the room.

INSIDE SOPOE HEADQUARTERS, on a dart board there's a picture of Methamin. In the background there's a BUZZ of a busy office. J.C.'s HAND comes into view. His UC at Berkeley College ring adorns his hand. He exposes a dart that he throws. The dart lands square between Methamin's eyes.

On an adjacent wall is a SOPOE POSTER with a picture of Bob Seil, SOPOE sponsor. The SOPOE acronym spells out Save Our Planet Or Else.

J.C.'s cell RINGS. He answers. There is definite change in his look and manner.

J.C.
Hey, Jude.

CUT TO a SMALL AIRFIELD. Jude is on his cell near a CHOPPER ready for flight. He has to speak loudly to compensate.

JUDE
I'm on my way. How's Filipe?

BACK TO J.C.

J.C.
Filipe's great. He's Hammer's new
caretaker.

PACIFIC PALISADES

EARLY AFTERNOON - High atop a cliff at the edge of a massive estate, an Art-Deco PALACE overlooks the Pacific Ocean. A HUMMER pulls up. INSIDE the Hummer, a man is on a headset, connected to his iPhone. He scrolls around, looking for porn. On his FINGER, is a UC at Berkeley ring that he still wears. Kirk Manwaring, J.C.'s old college alum, now thirty three, gets out of his vehicle and enters the palace.

INSIDE - A huge living room is surrounded by tinted windows that expose a breath taking view. Above the fireplace there's a portrait of a stately looking gentleman in his late sixties. An inscription below the portrait reads: JOHN HAMMER "I don't trust air I can't see." On the mantle, just below the portrait, are two golden oil drill statuettes with a logo on each that reads: AXXIN OIL "Thrills and spills." Kirk checks a message light that is blinking on a BIG MESSAGE SCREEN. From the screen, John Hammer appears.

>   HAMMER
>   Kirk and Diana. I'm in Washington. I'll
>   be home at eight p.m. your time. Have
>   my martini ready.

Kirk is Hammer's son-in-law. He makes a call.

>   KIRK
>   (on headset)
>   Dicky. I'm on my way downstairs. Just
>   got back from my "meeting." Thanks
>   for covering…of course I boned her.
>   Slow. Do it slow. They love it.

Kirk walks down some marble steps that lead to the tennis court. As Kirk walks through the TENNIS COURT, his step-daughter, COURTNEY, age twelve, is practicing her serve. She comments about Kirk's constant iPhone use.

>   COURTNEY
>   Why don't you just get that thing
>   surgically implanted, Kirk?

>   KIRK
>   Hello, l'il princess.
>   (on phone)
>   That's Courtney. Is her mother down
>   there?

As Kirk walks through the BATHHOUSE that leads to the POOL AREA, there's a crowd of PEOPLE enjoying a barb-b-que. On a platform just above the pool, DICKY, Kirk's valet, wears his headset talking with Kirk while toiling over the hot bar-b-que. Kirk's wife, DIANA Hammer Manwaring, ten years his senior enters the platform. She snaps.

                    DIANA
         Will you two grow up! Dicky, go get
         some ice. Kirk, I need some help.

                    KIRK
         Well, Diana, where's our new caretaker?

                    DIANA
         Feeding the scorpions.

On the other side of the estate there's a CORRAL where the Hammer's keep their horses. Inside, TWO GROUNDSKEEPERS are brushing a PALOMINO. Outside of the corral, in a small cage, some SCORPIONS feed on BUGS. There's a sign on the cage that reads: "Kirk's Petting Zoo." Filipe drops more bugs in the cage. He then gets on his cell.

                    FILIPE
         The ol' man's in Washington, lobbying.
         They're partying here. Now is a good
         time as any.

INSIDE SOPOE Headquarters, J.C. is on his cell and responds.

                    J.C.
         Good work Filipe. Now it's time to
         kick ass.

J.C. disconnects. He then picks up a dart and throws it at a dart board with a picture of HAMMER. Matthew, Mark, Stuke and Magdelin take darts from their desks and throw them at the dart boards of Methamin and Hammer.

                    J.C.
         I think they'll get the point.

The action is suspended as a heavenly ray of light spills down on J.C.

                    GOD (O.S.)
         I must admit Jesus was a kinder, gentler
         savior. But it's a tougher world today.

J.C. pensively, looks out of the office window. Outside, He sees LOS ANGELES covered in a blanket of smog. He speaks quietly to himself.

                         J.C.
              It's a sick world, with some sick
              people pullin' the strings. I wonder
              what sick bastard's pulling their
              strings.

                         GOD (O.S.)
              Is that suppose to be me? This boy's
              getting a bad attitude.

THUNDER

                         GOD (O.S.)
              Well, I didn't think things would get
              this far out of hand. That's what I get
              for giving Man a free will. You guys
              just can't handle the freedom.

Meanwhile in DOWNTOWN DETROIT. A chopper is in flight, circling high above the building that's about to be demolished.

INSIDE the helicopter, the pilot, Jude, lowers the aircraft and hovers. Methamin checks his watch. In the back seat, Jason, gleefully looks at the view below. A frightened Chelsea clutches onto Ruth who is quite put off. Methamin gets on his cell.

                         METHAMIN
              Okay, in about thirty seconds.

From the OLD TENAMENT on the second floor, a WINO sticks his head out of a window. Some MEN from the demolition crew scream at him to evacuate. The wino smiles and takes a swig from his bottle.

Inside the chopper, Methamin gets the news.

                         METHAMIN
              A wino? I've got a meeting at twelve
              thirty. Do it or you're fired! Ten
              seconds, pal.

Outside of the building, the crew is still waving and screaming. The demolition BOSS signals to go. The wino looks out and waves. Suddenly there's a huge IMPLOSION as the building topples to the ground in a cluster of smoke.

Inside the chopper, Jason unbuckles his seatbelt, gets up front and starts messing with the controls. Methamin pushes Jason back to his seat.

                    METHAMIN
          Ruth, give Jason his pill.

Jude suddenly lowers the chopper to a vacant lot nearby.

                    METHAMIN
          What are you doing?

They are about one foot from the ground when Jude takes out a pistol and points it at Methamin.

                    JUDE
          Get out.

                    METHAMIN
          What?!

Jude pulls back the hammer of the gun. Methamin jumps from the craft. Ruth hasn't quite grasped the situation. Chelsea starts to cry while Jason spits out his pill.

                    JASON
          Grampa!!

                    JUDE
          Sit back!

Jude brings the chopper up and speeds away high into the sky. Below, Methamin sits on the pavement nursing his twisted ankle. He then looks up and snickers.

Meanwhile at the Hammer palace, Diana comes out from the house to the pool. She's in a bit of a panic as she approaches her husband.

                    DIANA
          Kirk! I can't find Filipe anywhere.
          And where's Courtney?

On a SMALL AIRFIELD near the Hammer compound a PIPER CUB takes off from the air strip and becomes airborne. INSIDE the plane, Filipe is on his headset while Courtney blissfully checks out the view below.

                    COURTNEY
          This is so cool. I can see our pool.

23

An AERIAL VIEW the pool below.

                    FILIPE (O.S.)
          I promised you we'd go flying.

                    COURTNEY (O.S.)
          It's so great to get away from Kirk and
          my mom.

Inside the plane, Filipe checks the fuel gage.

                    FILIPE
          Ah, a nice, full tank.

                    COURTNEY
          How far are we going?

                    FILIPE
          Far enough.

AT THE POOL, Dicky points to the sky. Kirk spots the plane above.

                    KIRK
          That's my plane! The boys in the
          D.C. Hooker Club gave me that
          fuckin' plane!

Meanwhile, INSIDE of a boardroom a group of MEN in pin striped suits are
conferring at a round table. One of the men, JOHN HAMMER, is approached by a
MESSENGER.

                    MESSENGER
          There's a call for you, Mr. Hammer.
          She says she's your wife.

                    HAMMER
          My wife died years ago.

He excuses himself from the meeting and takes the call in a PRIVATE ROOM next
door.

                    HAMMER
          Who is this?!

INSIDE SOPOE HEADQUATERS, the office is being evacuated as Matthew, Mark and Stuke dismantle the office equipment. Magdelin hands J.C. the phone.

                              J.C.
                    Mr. Hammer.

INTERCUT - J.C. AND HAMMER

                              HAMMER
                    Who is this?

                              J.C.
                    Never mind. We have your granddaughter.
                    She's in nurturing hands for now. Very
                    soon you'll have to shut down all of your
                    poisonous operations or you may never see
                    Courtney again.

                              HAMMER
                    If you harm my granddaughter in any
                    way, I'll eat your pancreas with a with
                    a Fume Blanc.

                              J.C.
                    I think a Pinot Noir would be a better
                    pairing.

THE NEXT DAY - On a TV SCREEN, Anchor, MELANIE STILLBOURNE is presenting the news from CNM. Cable News Monopoly. Off to the side, there are PHOTOS of whom she is reporting.

                              MELANIE
                    Ruth Methamin, The daughter of Grant
                    Methamin, CEO of Specific Motors and
                    her two children have been kidnapped.
                    Also, billionaire oil man, John Hammer's
                    granddaughter has just been abducted.
                    An environmentalist group calling itself
                    SOPOE, Save Our Planet Or Else, is
                    claiming responsibility. Here's more on the
                    story from Fox Shitzer, live from Pacific
                    Palisades.

The SHOT SWITCHES to FOX who is standing outside of the Hammer Compound.

FOX
The last time anyone saw twelve year old
Courtney Hammer Manwaring, grand-
granddaughter of billionaire, John Hammer,
she was lobbing tennis balls inside of this
fortress.

Meanwhile, from an OASIS in the desert, J.C. checks his surroundings, opens a trap
door and descends into the ground.

INSIDE of the SOPOE HIDEOUT, J.C. enters a room with a big shoulder bag. On
a LAP TOP SCREEN, the same report is being viewed by the group. They all carry
walkie-talkies. They bond for a moment with high fives and hugs.

FOX (O.S.)
Also missing is Filipe Binladen, head
caretaker of the Hammer estate.

FILIPE
Binladen? It's Benlada! This guy's
trying to give me a bad name.

J.C.
Too late.

MELANIE
(on screen)
Thanks Fox. Hammer told authorities
that the terrorists wanted him to shut
down all of his operations if he ever
wanted to see his granddaughter again.

J.C.
Terrorists?

INSIDE of the Hammer Estate, some FEDERAL AGENTS have just examined what's
left of Filipe's belongings. One of the agents, Sean Young, looks like Quasimodo on
a bad day. His face has burn scars, he's missing an eye and has a hump. On his
finger is a UC at Berkeley RING. He spots a crumpled piece of stationery and subtly
slips it in his pocket. Another AGENT dusts for prints. Kirk enters.

KIRK
What in hell are you doing?

                    AGENT
Dusting for prints.

                    KIRK
For what? We know who he is.

                    AGENT
He may have an alias.

                    KIRK
No, no, no. The guy was an illegal.
Listen, Bub, I was doing this when
you were poppin' zits off your
mother's butt.

                    SEAN
Well, I see you haven't changed.

Kirk looks at Sean and winces at the sight of him.

                    KIRK
That voice, that eye.

Sean extends his hand for a hand shake. Kirk notices Sean's Berkeley ring.

                    KIRK
Berkeley. Sean. Sean Young. I
thought they hung you out to dry.
I'd like to say it's great to see ya'.

                    SEAN
Always the diplomat. I haven't been
in the field since Waco. When I heard
they abducted your step-daughter, I
had to make an appearance. It seems
you've married well, old friend.

                    KIRK
Oh, yeah. But how come the Bureau
isn't moving on these pieces of shit?

                    SEAN
We don't know where they are. And
because of the rich brats involved...

KIRK

Hey! Are you implying that my spoiled
rotten, step-daughter is a brat?

SEAN

Well...ah, we have to lay back. The Feds
have been under scrutiny since Waco.

KIRK

Hmm. So they put you behind a desk.

Kirk steps in closer to Sean.

KIRK

Do you want to see some action again?

SEAN

Did Hoover wear a dress?

KIRK

Let's get away from these amateurs.

POOL AREA - It's about a half an hour later. Kirk and Sean have just been served
brunch. As the MAID turns to leave, Kirk lifts up her dress for a little peek.

KIRK

Love your work, babe.

Sean takes out the piece of stationery that he concealed earlier. The stationery logo
reads: SOPOE. Save Our Planet Or Else. He gives it to Kirk.

SEAN

I found this in Filipe's quarters.
Remember back at Berkeley, a guy
named J.C.? He's the same guy
who's been ranting and raving
on the news about the environment.

KIRK

Oh, yeah. Back in school he was a
pussy cat. These guys are evil.

SEAN

People change. Look at you. From
FBI man to Washington pimp.

KIRK

And look at you. Well, on second
thought…Look, I'm gonna play a
hunch. Benlada, took my plane. He
was heading south. The plane was
very low on fuel.

SEAN

Couldn't he refuel?

KIRK

My fuel gage is tweaked. It reads
full. Get us a plane. I'll tell Diana
we're goin' hunting.

INSIDE of the SOPOE hideout. J.C. addresses Magdelin.

J.C.

How are the kids?

MAGDELIN

They're not very good.

J.C.

This must be very traumatic for them.

In the background we HEAR the kids raising hell. Magdelin signals to J.C. to follow
her. As they exit, the rest of the group is riveted to the laptop. A CNM news report is
in progress.

MELANIE

"…not to comply would be immoral."
So, CEO chairman Grant Methamin
will close down his plants in Detroit
until further notice.

The group CHEERS. On TV, the shot switches to Methamin being interviewed.

METHAMIN

…but, I'm warning you thugs. If you
harm one hair of my babies, I'll hunt
you down and chop you into such
small pieces, midget maggots won't
be able to find you.

JEERS, BOOS and CAT CALLS from the group. In the background we HEAR more uproar from the kids. Jude and Stuke voice their opinions.

                    JUDE
        Harm his babies, please. The abductees
        in Iraq only have to deal with Al Qaeda.
        We've got the brats from hell.

                    STUKE
        Let's go show those little shits who's boss.

They exit.

INSIDE the NEXT ROOM, J.C. and Magdelin are looking at maps from a laptop. Jude and Stuke enter and pass through the room to a corridor. Magdelin is seducing J.C.

                    MAGDELIN
        J.C. I really need you to jump me.

                    J.C.
        Oh, Zeus, the Siren sings. Earplugs,
        please. Come on, Magdelin, we've
        discussed this. No fraternization. If
        we're going to pull this off, we can't
        get locked in some binomial quagmire.

She hugs him.

                    MAGDELIN
        You mean love?

J.C. gently pushes her away. Magdelin pouts.

                    J.C.
        Let's take care of business first.

He touches her shoulder.

                    J.C.
        When our work is done here we'll
        have a little coitus or something.

MAGDELIN
(sarcastic)
Oh, goodie.

J.C.
Let's go see how the kids are doing.

The action is SUSPENDED. A heavenly LIGHT shines down as God speaks.

GOD (O.S.)
Alright so J.C.'s no Jesus. Well, Jesus
didn't have much of a sex drive. His
mother was a virgin, and I sent Gabriel
down with the seed. You see, I can't
fool around with anyone I've given life
to. That would be Creation Molestation.
This is a lonely job.

The light fades as the action continues.

Along the CORRIDOR, J.C. and Magdelin approach a door marked "Hostage Lounge." They enter. INSIDE, Jude and Stuke tend to the kids, Chelsea, Courtney and Jason. Jude is making a peanut butter and jelly sandwich. Stuke is blowing up and twisting animal balloons.

JUDE
Last call for peanut butter and jelly
sandwiches.

Jason comes up, takes the sandwich and inspects it. He opens it up and samples the contents with his pinky.

JASON
This is unacceptable.

STUKE
What are you a PB&J sommelier?

Stuke goes back to blowing the balloon. Jason pops it in his face.

COURTNEY
If you jerks think you'll get ransom
for me, guess again. My grandfather
doesn't even tip bell boys.

JASON
I want my Ritalin.

Jason takes a peanut butter and jelly sandwich and throws it in J.C.'s face. J.C. wipes some peanut butter and jelly from his face and samples it.

J.C.
Jude. Jason's right. This is unacceptable.
Okay, kids, I know this may be hard to
understand. We don't want any ransom.

Jason grabs another balloon and pops it in J.C.'s ear. J.C. holds his ear in pain.

J.C.
Okay, kids. Just try to behave for
a little while. Then you can go
home and torture your parents.

From J.C.'s TRANSMITTER.

MATTHEW (O.S.)
Lamb one, come in. Over.

J.C.
(into walkie-talkie)
Lamb one, copy.

MATTHEW (O.S.)
We have a problem with the mother.
You better get over here.

J.C.
Be there in a minute.

J.C. takes out a camcorder out of his shoulder bag.

J.C.
Okay, kids. We're going to make
some home videos.

COURTNEY
America's Funniest Hostages.

J.C.
Jason, would you like to speak?

32

JASON

No!

J.C.

I'll get you Ritalin.

JASON

Is over here okay?

POV - THROUGH CAMERA ON JASON. Jason slicks back his hair.

J.C. (O.S.)

Magdelin, the cards are in the bag.
Okay Jason, just read what's on the
cards. Ready?

INSIDE Methamin's office from a wall TV, Methamin watches his grandson reading the speech that's being aired on CNM.

JASON
(on video)
Alternative fuels are available. It is time
to ag-aggressively im-implement them.
And you'll have to comp-comply. Comply
with CFC standards. That means you'll
have to shut down all of your air conditioners
in all of your offices…I miss you Grampa.

The SHOT SWITCHES TO Melanie, live at CNM.

MELANIE
It's only been a few days since SOPOE
made their grand abductions. It's effects
can already be seen in the auto industry.
We take you now to Fox Shitzer, live
from the Motor City.

The SHOT SWITCHES to Fox.

FOX
This Specific Motors plant lies dormant.
A few days ago, thousands of blue collar
types would pour from these huge iron
gates and into nearby bars, get drunk and
pummel each other silly. Now, there are
no sirens. Instead of watching flat line,
paramedics watch *Nightline*. It's a ghost
town here, Melanie.

INSIDE of the SOPOE hideout - RUTH'S QUARTERS. It's a few days later. Ruth, in a nightgown, is sitting on her bed watching the news on a laptop. She takes a catheter, ties her arm off and gives herself an injection. There's a knock at the door.

                    J.C. (O.S.)
Hello, Ruth, may I come in?

                    RUTH
If you must.

J.C. enters

                    J.C.
How are you doing?

                    RUTH
Fine. Thanks for scoring for me.

                    J.C.
This is it. Heroin for you, Ritalin
for Jason. "Excuse me, would you
please close down your air polluting
factory while I cop some drugs for
your family?" How did a woman like
you get to be a junkie?

                    RUTH
Well, that's the kidnapper calling the
addict, black.

                    J.C.
Listen, I know this seems abhorrent to
you, but men like your father are sucking
the life from our planet. Change must
come now.

                    RUTH
My father is responsible for the well
being of thousands of people who are
now out of work because of you.

                    J.C.
                  (lightening up)
You're free to roam the premises.
We're completely self-contained and
have plenty of food and entertainment.

                              RUTH
Just like Waco.

                              J.C.
But, not as hot.

Ruth smiles. The drug has taken affect.

                              RUTH
How long will you keep us?

                              J.C.
Until there's change.

                              RUTH
You're not naïve enough to think that
the world will change…
…cuz you have…me and a few kids
held…captive.

From the LAPTOP SCREEN, Melanie Stillbourne gives an update on the ongoing
news saga.

                            MELANIE
Grant Methamin, head of Specific Motors,
closed down some subsidiary operations which
included some two hundred office buildings.
John Hammer, president of Axxin Oil, shut
down all oil drilling operations in California.

                              J.C.
You underestimate yourself.

Ruth nods out.

Some FOOTAGE of Methamin and Hammer being interviewed.

                           METHAMIN
Yes, this hurts Specific Motors. But
It's the shareholders who'll suffer the
most. Now, in the name of everything
that's decent, I want my family back.

                            HAMMER
This is extortion, pure and simple.

                         REPORTER (O.S.)
You mean the price of gas?

                         HAMMER
Well, people need gas.

Hammer holds his stomach and belches.

                         REPORTER (O.S.)
Gas?

                         HAMMER
Yeah.

THE NEXT DAY, Inside the SOPOE compound RECREATION ROOM, Magdelin, Jude, the kids and Ruth sit in the audience. Ruth is edgy. J.C. comes out on a make-shift stage.

                         J.C.
Hello. I want to thank everyone for being so co-operative. You're the best captives a guy could hope for.

Some laughter from the group.

                         J.C.
Does anyone need anything?

                         COURTNEY
I'm jonesing for tennis.

                         JASON
I'm jonesing for mischief.

                         RUTH
                       (to herself)
I'm just jonesing.

                         CHELSEA
Mommy, what's jonesing?

                         RUTH
Don't ask.

                    J.C.
Well, I see everyone's trying to
keep up with the Joneses.

                    RUTH
My father shut down his factories.
Hammer has followed suit. When
can we go.

                    J.C.
Soon. We just need for them to
comply with a few standards to
keep their acts clean.

                    RUTH
That could take years. What about
other industries. Are you going to
kidnap everyone? You'll need a
bigger gun.

                    J.C.
If your father and Mr. Hammer agree
to clean up, it will set a precedent, an
example; maybe other industries will
follow suit. Even Wall Street.

Ruth is starting to withdraw. J.C. notices.

                    J.C.
Okay, kids, we've got a special treat
for you. Mark.

Mark comes on stage as J.C. approaches Ruth. He and Ruth leave the rec room

                    MARK
Okay, kids, today's movie is *Mary
Poppins*. Ah, hem!

Magdelin, Filipe and Stuke come out with big bowls of popcorn and pitchers of
lemonade.

                    FILIPE
Popcorn and lemonade!

They distribute it to the kids.

                    JASON
I want root beer.

                    MARK
There's a lot of sugar in root beer.

From a battery operated projector, images beam onto a makeshift screen as the
credits for *MARY POPPINS* roll.

                  COURTNEY
Not as much as there is in this movie.

                    JASON
I want *Apocalypse Now*.

                  MAGDELIN
Apocalypse, later.

                    JASON
       Now!

                    FILIPE
Here, have some lemonade.

Jason takes a sip and spits it in Filipe's face.

                    JASON
You call this lemonade? I think not.

The kids start throwing popcorn around and spitting lemonade on Stuke.

                    STUKE
Hey, why don't you spit it on her?

Jason takes a sip and walks up to Magdelin.

                  MAGDELIN
       No you're not!

He defiantly spits in her face and runs. She chases him and soon the room is lousy
with riotous disruption. Matthew and Mark roll their eyes and commiserate.

                  MATTHEW
I could've been a pro wrestler.

MARK
I could've been a Catholic Priest.

Inside RUTH'S QUARTERS, she lies on her bed. She's in a cold sweat. J.C. brings in some hot, damp towels and applies one to Ruth's forehead.

J.C.
Here, hold this.

RUTH
Listen, I need something.

J.C.
I told you, that's it.

She begins to weep.

RUTH
You get Jason Ritalin.

J.C.
Not anymore.

RUTH
Then you may have a real mess
on your hands.

In the background J.C. hears the COMMOTION.

J.C.
Too late. Listen, Ruth, you come from
a wealthy family and you have two...
ah, relatively nice kids. What's the
matter, too much spare time?

RUTH
It's a long story.

J.C. gets another towel and gently wipes Ruth's forehead.

RUTH
I was moral once. I had everything.
And now look at me. Does God hate
me?

                            J.C.
          I think people have a tendency to credit
          God for their destinies. We're responsible
          for our own lives. God's highly over rated.

THUNDER - J.C., nervously looks around.

                            J.C.
          Although, recently, I needed to raise
          money to kidnap you lovely people.
          Abducting rich people ain't cheap.
          Anyway, I threw the ball upstairs
          and said, you know, a prayer. The
          next day a man gave me a huge
          some of money.

                          RUTH
          Do you think he has a methadone
          connection?

J.C. laughs.

                            J.C.
          What happened to your husband?

                          RUTH
          My father fired him.

                            J.C.
          From your marriage?

                          RUTH
          He's a very controlling man.

                            J.C.
          How did you get addicted?

                          RUTH
          My ex-husband abused everything,
          especially alcohol. He drove us off of a cliff
          one night. In the hospital I became addicted
          to Morphine. When I got out, my guilt-ridden
          husband thought he'd help my pain by
          getting me heroin. He smuggled it in when
          he visited the kids.

                         J.C.
You have heard of the Betty Ford
Clinic, haven't you?

                        RUTH
I was *there*. I met this man. We got
bored with the program and ran off
with some hippy-types. Well, the next
year was kind of a blur. I finally came
home. Now, one of my domestics scores
for me.
                   (sweating)
J.C. I'm burning up.

She rips open her blouse, exposing her bra. She then embraces J.C.

                        RUTH
Help me, J.C.

Suddenly Jason and Chelsea bolt into the room, followed by Magdelin who is chasing
them. Magdelin and the kids stand there in shock.

                         J.C.
So, how's the movie?

An AERIAL VIEW of the oasis near the Mexican Border. INSIDE of a small plane, Kirk
and Sean have launched their own manhunt. Kirk is looking through his binoculars.
He then gets on the radio.

                        KIRK
D.C. Pimpboy to Captain Culo. Come in.

From the SPEAKER.

                 CAPTAIN CULO (O.S.)
Copy. Hey, two men in a van with "Think
Green" plates bought some supplies here
yesterday.

                        KIRK
                   (to Sean)
Circle again. I think I saw something.
                   (on radio)
Captain, I'll get back at ya.

They circle the area again. Kirk makes a positive sighting.

> KIRK
>
> Bingo! There's a small plane under that
> brush. If we score, the ol' man will take
> good care of us.

Sean looks at his reflection on the chrome panel.

> SEAN
>
> I can get my face and hump fixed.

> KIRK
>
> And I'll be a hero *and* get my
> baby back.

> SEAN
>
> Courtney?

> KIRK
>
> Fuck, no. My plane.

Sean flies lower for a better look. On the side of Sean's plane, is the FBI logo.

> SEAN (V.O.)
>
> I've got to get this baby back tonight.
> Did the D.C. Hooker Club really give
> you that plane?

> KIRK
>
> Do you doubt my veracity?

> SEAN
>
> Not when it comes to pimping. How
> come you never hook up us Feds?

> KIRK
>
> Feds aren't allowed to get hard-ons.
> However, the boys in the Senate…

WASHINGTON D.C.- DAY - From a hotel window - POV of a man laying in bed.
He sees the Washington Monument and then looks down at a lump he has under
his covers. The man is Senator DAVID BITTER. Next to him a HOOKER makes a
comparison. She, too, looks at the monument and then the lump under the covers.

                              HOOKER
              You've got a lot to live up to, Senator.

                              BITTER
              I'm not the head of the Ways and Means
              Committee for nothing.

                              HOOKER
              Where to Senator?

                              BITTER
              Around the world would be nice.

As the Hooker goes under the covers, Bitter cryptically exclaims…

                              BITTER
              Kirk, you've done it again.

Meanwhile, back in Ruth's room. J.C. gets up and puts a blanket over Ruth. Magdelin,
Chelsea and Jason are still in shock.

                               J.C.
              Your mom's cold. Keeping her warm.

                              CHELSEA
              Then why is she sweating?

Ruth starts convulsing.

                               J.C.
              Magdelin.

Magdelin, realizing the situation, tries to lighten things up.

                             MAGDELIN
              A spoon full of sugar makes the
              medicine go down. Everybody.

J.C. joins in.

                        J.C. AND MAGDELIN
              The medicine go down.

The kids join in.

JASON AND CHELSEA
The medicine go down. A spoon full of
sugar makes the medicine go down.

Ruth throws up on J.C.

J.C.
In the most delightful way. Magdelin?

Magdelin takes the kids and leaves. J.C. gets a towel and wipes himself off. Ruth is
convulsing out of control. J.C. tries to hold Ruth still.

J.C.
Come on Ruth, hang in. You don't
want your kids to be Ruthless, do you?
Although I think Jason's half way there.

A faint smile from Ruth. She stops convulsing. She lies still. J.C. checks her vital
signs. She's stopped breathing. J.C. panics.

J.C.
Oh, no! Ruth. No, Ruth!

OUTSIDE of METHAMIN EDISON, it's a sweltering summer day. INSIDE one of
the offices, PEOPLE are hot and sweaty. At her desk, a supervisor named BETTY
makes a call.

BETTY
Betty over at collections. How long is he
going to keep the air off? What? How the
hell does SOPOE know if we have our air
on or not? Save his family? Methamin
wants to save money, period!

She slams down the phone and leaves. People sit at their desks, fanning themselves.
There are some electric fans on. A man named BIFF complains.

BIFF
All we're doing is moving hot air around.

He takes a bottle of soda water, shakes it up and shpritzes it into the fan to get a cool
spray. The water shorts out the fan. Sparks fly, igniting some papers on his desk.
Soon, the whole desk is in flames. The flames set off the sprinkler system. The office
is now a big shower. After a moment the system shuts down. Everyone is soaking
wet, but smiling with relief.

EVERYONE
Ahhh, thanks, Biff.

A sopping wet OFFICE MANAGER comes out from his office.

OFFICE MANAGER
Ahhh, you're fired, Biff.

On the SET of *AMBUSH,* Bob Seil is in the AUDIENCE getting responses to the topic of the day. RALPH NATEL is on stage.

BOB SEIL
Ralph Natel, consumer advocate and
undaunted spokesman for social injustice.
What are your views on what's happening,
concerning the SOPOE kidnappings.

RALPH NATEL
We're seeing some incredible things
occurring as a result of the shut-downs
proposed by SOPOE. For instance, in
Los Angeles…

As Ralph Natel explains, we SEE the action at DIFFERENT LOCATIONS.

AN AERIAL VIEW OF LOS ANGELES. Picture postcard, perfect,

RALPH NATEL (O.S.)
In Los Angeles, gas prices have gone up so
dramatically, hardly anyone's driving. The
smog has disappeared.

INSIDE AN APARTMENT, a cage with several HAMSTERS running inside of their little wheels. The wheels are connected to a small turbine that powers the apartment. One line goes to a stereo system. Two MEN are dancing to the music.

RALPH NATEL (O.S.)
People are breeding Hamsters to run
small turbines to power their utilities.

In the audience an OLD WOMAN takes Bob's microphone and speaks out.

OLD WOMAN
These changes don't justify a bunch of
punks kidnapping children.

Bob snatches the mic back.

> **BOB SEIL**
> These punks infiltrated the lives of some
> very powerful people. How do you
> suppose they got so resourceful?

> **RALPH NATEL**
> God only knows.

HEAVEN - White, puffy clouds. In the distance we HEAR electric guitars. Soon, two hazy figures with guitars appear. GOD and JIMI HENDRIX are jamming. God hits a lame note.

> **HENDRIX**
> Click, bang, what a hang. No, man,
> on the fret. You'll get more feedback.

Hendrix demonstrates. God gives it a whirl and does it better than Hendrix.

> **HENDRIX**
> You're good, God.

> **GOD**
> Aw, shucks. If my daddy could see
> me now.

> **HENDRIX**
> Who's your daddy?

> **GOD**
> Ah, well…*me*.

God's beeper goes off.

> **GOD**
> Excuse me while I answer this.

> **HENDRIX**
> Excuse me while I kiss the sky.

Hendrix starts kissing clouds while God shines his light on Earth and inside Ruth's room at the SOPOE compound.

J.C. is trying to revive Ruth. He tries mouth to mouth. Nothing. He bangs on her chest. No signs of breathing.

                              J.C.
                    Oh, please God. Don't let her die.

                          GOD (V.O.)
                    I love it when he throws the ball
                    upstairs. Okay, son.

Ruth starts breathing.

                              J.C.
                    Yes!

Ruth is completely revived and feeling better than ever. She gets up quickly and stretches.

                             RUTH
                    I'm famished.

J.C. looks at Ruth in amazement.

LATE AFTERNOON. We SEE a sign that reads: CULO VILLAGE "A Nice Place To Live, But You Wouldn't Want To Visit Here."

Next to a river in this one horse town near the Mexican border, there's a general store, a gas station and the police station. Across the street there's a bar, some old abandoned stores and an x-rated theater. In the front is a poster of a HUGE BUSTED WOMAN in a movie entitled, *TWO'S A CROWD*. Outside the POLICE STATION, Kirk, Sean, the town sheriff, CAPTAIN CULO and his deputy SCOTTY, introduce each other.

                             KIRK
                    Captain Culo, Sean Young.

                        CAPTAIN CULO
                    I must say, you were cuter in *Blade
                    Runner*.

                             SEAN
                    You're a caution, Captain.

                        CAPTAIN CULO
                    Scotty, beam me up.

                         SCOTTY
              Aye, Captain.

Scotty, a dim witted man, whips out a pint of JIM BEAM. Captain Culo takes a snort
and goes through his little ritual of smacking and other audible noises resembling
barnyard animals.

                      CAPTAIN CULO
              Ah, there's nothing like a stiff one in
              the afternoon.

Kirk looks over at the x-rated poster.

                         KIRK
              Yeah, I know what you mean.

He offers a pull to Sean. He passes but, Kirk takes a hit.

                      CAPTAIN CULO
              So, you think the SOPOE gang is hidin'
              out in these parts?

                         KIRK
              Yup.

                      CAPTAIN CULO
              Well, then why don't you get your FBI
              to storm their asses?

                         KIRK
              Look, we just want to keep this thing on
              the down-low. If we surprise them, the
              four of us could take 'em. C'mon, there'll
              be a nice reward.

                      CAPTAIN CULO
              What the hell. I ain't seen any action since
              Orville's cow took a dump on my petunias.

Scotty, stares at Sean for a moment.

                         SCOTTY
              Hey, what happened to you?

Sean is a bit taken back. Captain Culo elbows Scotty in the side. Scotty doubles over.

                    CAPTAIN CULO
        You'll have to forgive my deputy,
        gentlemen. He's a fuckin' idiot.
                    (to Scotty)
        Don't you know that excretion is the
        better part of valor, for Christ sakes?
                    (to Sean)
        What did happen?

                    KIRK
        There's your excretion.

Down the hill on the river, in a boat, FOUR MEXICANS try to sneak across the border. Captain Culo takes out his six shooter and peppers the boat with holes, causing it to sink. Apparently the Mexicans can't swim.

                    CAPTAIN CULO
        You know what you call four Mexicans
        drowning?...Quatro sinko.

As the last one goes under for his river nap, Kirk comments.

                    KIRK
        Shit, Culo, I could've used those Mexicans.

                    CAPTAIN CULO
        You're right. There goes four hundred
        bucks.

INSIDE of the SOPOE CAFETERIA, J.C. and crew, Ruth and the kids are about to eat when Magdelin speaks up.

                    MAGDELIN
        Ah, hem. Aren't we forgettin' somethin'?
        Courtney, would you like to say grace?

                    COURTNEY
        Grace.

                    MAGDELIN
        Thank you, child.

They begin eating when J.C. notices an empty chair.

> J.C.
> Where's Jason?

> MAGDELIN
> He won't come out of his room.

> J.C.
> Excuse me.

J.C. gets up and leaves the cafeteria.

INSIDE JASON'S ROOM, he is lying face down crying in his pillow when he hears a knock.

> J.C.(O.S.)
> Jason, are you alright?

J.C. enters the room.

> JASON
> (sobbing)
> Go away.

J.C. sits on the bed and pats Jason on the head.

> J.C.
> What's the matter?

> JASON
> I wanna go home.

> J.C.
> I know. You will soon.

> JASON
> You said that last week.

> J.C.
> Well, your grandfather is now doing
> his part to clean up the air so we can
> all breath healthier. Now, all we need
> for him to do is keep it that way. And
> that'll take a little more time.

                    JASON
I want my grampa. I miss my mansion.
I want to go outside.

He begins to cry uncontrollably. J.C. tries to console him to no avail. Jason is now in
tantrum mode.

                    J.C.
We've got veggie burgers out there
for ya'. With cheese.

                    JASON
Cheese this.

J.C. is now riddled with sadness and guilt. He leaves.

J.C.'s ROOM. J.C. sits on his bed, depressed. There's a knock.

                    J.C.
Yes?

                    RUTH (O.S.)
May I come in?

J.C. gets up and lets her in.

                    J.C.
Is there anything wrong?

                    RUTH
No.

                    J.C.
Have a seat.

They sit. There's a lull.

                    J.C.
So, how 'bout those Dodgers?

                    RUTH
Do you think they'll go to the World
Series?

                    J.C.
Yeah, if they get tickets. Hey, are you…

                    RUTH
Jonesing? It's strange, but I'm not.
Do you think it would be possible to
go outside? We haven't seen daylight
in so long.

J.C. ponders this notion for a moment.

                    J.C.
Moral has been pretty bad. Why not.

OUTSIDE of the COMPOUND, it's a hot sunny day. The small oasis is surrounded with trees. As if from nowhere, a wooden door flies open from the surface of the ground. After some dust settles, J.C.'s head pops up. He does a 360 and pulls himself onto the ground that is surrounded with desert shrubbery.

                    J.C.
Okay, let's go.

Magdelin and Filipe eject themselves out. They pull Courtney and Chelsea out, followed by Stuke and Jude who lift up Jason. J.C. and Filipe help Ruth up. Mark passes up some blankets, some picnic baskets, a ball and other toys. Matthew passes J.C. his walkie-talkie. Matthew and Mark go back down.

J.C. maneuvers the door down, closing it. Chelsea playfully squirts Jason with a squirt gun. Jason exposes a toy grenade.

                    JASON
Do that again and I'll pull the pin
and stuff this down your pants.

                    J.C.
Okay troupes.
          (as Yogi Bear)
Fall in for "Operation Pic-in-nic
Basket."

The kids blissfully line up.

                    J.C.
Second flank.

The adults exuberantly line up behind the kids. Everyone is excited as they start marching to a clearing. Off to the right, Kirk's Piper cub is buried under a pile of brush. They all march to the perimeter of the oasis.

                    J.C.
          Company halt! Let's set up here.

Off in the distance are rows upon rows of sand dunes.

                    JASON
          Wow, look at the funny looking hills!

The kids all scramble from the oasis to play in the sand.

                    J.C.
          Hey, guys, stay back here.

The ignore him. J.C., Stuke and Filipe round up the kids.

POV BINOCULARS - J.C., Stuke and Filipe wrangling the kids.

In the desert, on the crest of a DUNE, Kirk lowers his field glasses. Behind him a tarp covers Captain Culo's Jeep.

                    KIRK
          Bingo! Sean, you and Scotty go to the
          left. Culo. You and I'll take the right.

                    SCOTTY
          Why don't I wait here?

                    KIRK
          Come on!

They check their weapons and traverse towards the oasis.

Back at the picnic, J.C. spreads out a big blanket while Magdelin passes around sandwiches. Jude pours lemonade while Stuke tries to open a pickle jar. He hands it to Magdelin who opens it with ease and passes it back.

                    JASON
          Hey, jerk, gimme some pickles.

                    RUTH
          Please.

JASON

Please, jerk?

MAGDELIN

Oh, dang. J.C. I need to go back in.

J.C.

For what?

MAGDELIN

I have to tinkle.

The kids start giggling.

J.C.

Come on Magdelin, go find a bush.

COURTNEY

I have to go too.

CHELSEA

Me too.

MAGDELIN

Alright, girlfrends, let's go.

STUKE

Have a nice pee.

Jason giggles as the girls exit.

J.C.

Hey, let's sing some tunes.

FILIPE

Like what, J.C.?

J.C.

How 'bout some Hendrix?

RUTH

Cool.

J.C.

Anybody have a fave?

JASON
My dad liked, *Hey Joe*.

J.C.
And a one and a two...

EVERYONE
Hey, Joe, where you goin' with that
gun in your hand?

JASON
Gonna shoot my ol' lady. Caught her
messin' around with another man.

RUTH
And that ain't too cool.

On the PERIMETER of the oasis, Kirk, Sean, Captain Culo and Scotty poise for action, weapons drawn. They hear the singing in the background. Scotty loading up his revolver absent-mindedly sings along.

SCOTTY
Hey, Joe, where you goin' with that...

KIRK
(quietly)
Shut the fuck up you idiot! Okay,
we've got to surprise them.

Kirk takes out a photo of Courtney.

KIRK
Don't shoot Courtney. She's our
meal ticket. Ready?

BACK AT PICNIC. Stuke gets a lip lock on a pickle as Kirk and his boys raid the picnic. Weapons pointed, they surround the group.

KIRK
I hate to break up your party, but
Courtney has a piano lesson...

J.C.
Kirk? Kirk Manwaring?

Sean stares at Ruth.

                                    KIRK
                    Hi, J.C. Long time no see. Filipe,
                    you shouldn't have taken my plane.

Kirk walks up to Filipe and hits him in the head with the butt of his automatic weapon.
The blow knocks him out. Ruth becomes hysterical.

                                    STUKE
                    Hey, knock it off!

They direct their weapons at Stuke.

                                    STUKE
                    I meant her.

Jude takes out his gun and aims it directly at Scotty. He pulls the hammer back.
Scotty sees yellow.

                                    SCOTTY
                    Screw this.

Scotty makes a dash from the oasis. Jude takes off after him. J.C. commandeers
Kirks rifle and puts the gun to his head.

                                    J.C.
                    Okay Kirk, tell them to drop their guns.

Sean and Captain Culo wait for Kirk's response. In the background TWO SHOTS
are fired.

                                    KIRK
                    Scotty? Scotty!

Scotty is heard whimpering in the background. Ruth begins to cry. Jason seems
annoyed.

                                    J.C.
                            (to Captain Culo)
                    Drop it or Kirk takes a sand nap.

Captain Culo has his weapon pointed at Ruth who is weeping like a willow.

CAPTAIN CULO
No, I don't think so. You shoot Kirk, I'll
shoot the cry baby. Drop the rifle.

Magdelin has been watching behind the shrubbery. She takes out her gun.

MAGDELIN
(quietly to the girls)
Stay here.

CAPTAIN CULO
I'll count to three. One. Two…

Suddenly the barrel of a 45 caliber appears at Captain Culo's head.

MAGDELIN
Don't say three. Now you have to
three to drop yours. One. Two…

Just then the barrel of a revolver appears at Magdelin's head.

SEAN
Now, don't you say three. Drop it.

Magdelin turns to Sean. His appearance startles her. Filipe has regained consciousness and is pointing his gun at Sean.

FILIPE
Okay handsome, now *you* drop it. I'm
gonna count to three. One. Two. Three.

Nothing. There seems to be a Mexican stand-off as each gun is pointed strategically.

KIRK
Has anybody ever seen *Reservoir Dogs*?

EVERYONE
Huh?

KIRK
Well, in that movie there's a scene
where everyone has a gun pointed
at each other. And they all shoot.
And of course, they all die. Will life
imitate art?

Jason slips out his toy grenade and rolls it towards Stuke.

                              STUKE
                    Grenade!!

Kirk, Sean and Captain Culo dive for cover. J.C., Magdelin and Filipe fix their weapons on them. Stuke picks up the toy grenade and tosses it to Jason. They play catch with it.

                              J.C.
                    Nice move boys. All right you guys,
                    grab some sky.

                              KIRK
                    Grab some sky?

                              FILIPE
                    No, grab some ground.

Filipe whacks Kirk in the head with his gun. Kirk hits the ground.

                              J.C.
                    Stuke, Magdelin, get these guys inside.
                    Ruth, get the girls. Jason, catch the door.
                    Picnic's over. Filipe, come with me.

Ruth comes back with a very bewildered Courtney and Chelsea as J.C. and Filipe exit.

About ten feet from the oasis on a dune, Jude lies holding his chest. Scotty is face down in the sand. J.C. approaches Jude and kneels. Jude tries to speak.

                              JUDE
                    J.C. I, I need to tell you something. I, I...

Filipe approaches with anticipation. Jude expels his last breath.

                              J.C.
                    Jude!

J.C. shakes Jude's body hoping to revive him while Filipe approaches Scotty. He turns him over and checks for vital signs. There are none. J.C. looks at both corpses.

                              J.C.
                    I never dreamed it would come to this. Two dead.

Shortly after, J.C. clears their tracks as Filipe descends into the hideout.

LATER - INSIDE of the compound, J.C. and crew are viewing the news on a laptop.
J.C. Kirk, Sean and Captain Culo are cuffed to their chairs. J.C. addresses Sean.

> J.C.
> You can take off your mask now.

> SEAN
> It's not a mask. We went to Berkeley
> together. I'm Sean Young.

> MARK
> You were a lot cuter in *The Boost.*

J.C. looks at him in shock. Stuke enters. He is very upset.

> STUKE
> Jude and that asshole are buried now.

Stuke sinks to the floor and weeps. Something on the news gets everyone's attention.
ON SCREEN, Melanie Stillbourne reports a news bulletin.

> MELANIE
> John Hammer, president of Axxin Oil,
> is holding a press conference.

The SHOT SWITCHES to Hammer who is at a podium inside of his office. Some
REPORTERS stand in back.

> HAMMER
> Good afternoon, ladies and gentlemen. The
> Board of Trustees and I have indefatigably
> pondered our responsibilities concerning this
> hostage situation. We feel we owe it to our
> shareholders to continue full-scale production
> which will begin tomorrow.

> REPORTER
> Mr. Hammer. What about the hostages, one
> of which is your granddaughter?

> HAMMER
> I'm deeply concerned.

59

                    HAMMER (Cont'd)
But the lives of millions of people are being
effected. We won't let these thugs continue
this extortion.

                    REPORTER
Will prices at the pump go back down?

                    HAMMER
Eventually.

                    REPORTER
Now, *that's* extortion.

                    HAMMER
This press conference is over.

As he leaves, the reporters AD LIB a bevy of questions.

Sean speaks up.

                    SEAN
That's just great.

                    KIRK
Why that son-of-a-bitch!

Filipe checks his watch as another news blurb catches everyone's attention.

                    MELONY
                  (on screen)
We take you now to FBI headquarters
in Washington.

The SHOT SWITCHES to an interview already in progress with the FBI chief.

                    FBI CHIEF
                  (holding photo)
We think the leader of this SOPOE group
is activist Jerry Collins. No one's seen or
heard from him since the kidnappings. If it
is in fact, *not* Mr. Collins, let him step forth.

The screen goes blank as J.C. shuts off the laptop and flops onto a chair.

                    KIRK
Well, buddy. Looks like you're in deep
do-do.

                    FILIPE
I'm going to check on the kids.

Filipe exits.

OUTSIDE, Filipe pulls himself out and takes out his cell phone.

A LEAR JET looms down from the clouds. INSIDE the coach, Hammer's VALET has just handed him a drink. He is on his cell.

                    HAMMER
Keep me posted. Got another call.
            (clicks other call)
Grant, I should be in New York by ten.

INSIDE of Methamin's limo.

                    METHAMIN
I'm on my way to my plane now.

INTERCUT- HAMMER AND METHAMIN

                    HAMMER
I got us a table at Frou Frous. The
market's soaring; our commodities
are sky-high

                    METHAMIN
This is going better than I thought.

                    HAMMER
I feel like a rotten teenager again.

                    METHAMIN
How are the kids?

                    HAMMER
There was a ruckus. My vermin
son-in-law, Kirk stepped in. Filipe
has assured me that everything's
under control, now.

                    METHAMIN
I miss my grandson. Is he okay?

                    HAMMER
Yes. Well, we've got them over a
barrel, now. They've got no reason
to hold them. Did you order the Opus?

                    METHAMIN
And some Beluga. I wonder what the
poor people are eating?

                    HAMMER
Let them eat shit.

They both have a good laugh.

WASHINGTON DC - NIGHTIME - BANQUET HALL

A charity fund raiser has a slew of Washington BIG-WIGS gathered for this festive
occasion. Senator Bitter and the FBI Chief are conferring near the punch bowl.

                    FBI CHIEF
Some more punch, Senator?

He pours himself and the Senator a heaping cup.

                    BITTER
Did you know that all our great leaders
were horn dogs? Jefferson, Roosevelt,
Kennedy and Clinton?

                    FBI CHIEF
Maybe, someday *you'll* be President.

                    BITTER
                  (he toasts)
To illicit sex. Where the hell has Kirk
been? My prostates swelling up like a
truck inner tube.

                    FBI CHIEF
He hasn't checked in. We have a
device aboard the plane you gave him.

                          BITTER
            The man has talent. He could get the
            best women the tax payers money
            could buy.

They toast. The senator is getting tipsy.

                          BITTER
            I haven't had a woman in days. If this
            keeps up, I'll have to sleep with my
            wife. Find him.
                       (a beat)
            Now would be good. I have a TV
            interview tomorrow. I'm out of here.

Bitter exits. The FBI Chief signals to his head lieutenant, COMMANDER KELLY, who
is serving as head of security for this event. He approaches the chief.

                       FBI CHIEF
            Commander Kelly, our country needs Kirk.

                    COMMANDER KELLY
            We tried to contact him. His wife said he
            went hunting. Hunting for his plane, no
            doubt.

                       FBI CHIEF
            My guess. Wherever his plane is, he is.
            There's a homing device on his plane.
            Activate the signal and find it.

At the OASIS from beneath a blanket of branches, Kirk's plane can barely be seen.
From inside the plane there's a succession of BEEP SOUNDS. The homing device
has been activated.

On THE SET OF *AMBUSH*, Bob Seil, Senator Bitter and a NEWSMAN are
debating.

                          BITTER
            Industries are being shut down left
            and right. In some regions the economy
            is near the brink of depression. Shoddy
            journalism has this country believing
            quite the opposite.

                           NEWSMAN
                Well, Senator, is that why the market
                jumped five hundred points last week?

                           BOB SEIL
                You're both right *and* wrong. Prices
                have become grotesquely inflated.
                Manufacturers and retailers are having
                a field day while half of the population
                suffers. Gentlemen, let's look on the
                bright side. There are some positive
                ramifications to all of this adversity.

As Bob expounds, his scenarios come to life in DIFFERENT SHOTS.

INSIDE OF A BATHRROOM, a family of four take turns looking in the mirror,
demonstrating their weight loss. DAD pulls his belt back three notches. MOM
proudly models an old swim suit. The KIDS look at old snapshots of when they were
obese.

                         BOB SEIL (O.S.)
                Because food is so expensive, people
                are eating less. Weight challenged folks
                aren't fat pigs anymore.

ON A CITY STREET, a large group of PEOPLE are biking.

                         BOB SEIL (O.S.)
                The unemployed are now riding bikes.
                They clean up their cholesterol while
                cleaning up the air.

Just then, a TRACTOR TRAILER veers off the road and wipes out the group.
ANOTHER SHOT shows them all in body bags lying on a curb and being loaded
into a meat wagon.

                         BOB SEIL (O.S.)
                This is also good to curb the population.

BACK ON SET

                           BITTER
                Absurd. Isn't it true, Bob, that you were
                fired from Bank of America for extortion?

BOB SEIL
No, it was Wells Fargo. Oooopsie.

BITTER
Punked on your own show.

REPORTER
Isn't it true that during the George -
One Administration, you sold Dan
Quayle, quaaludes?

BITTER
No, it was darvon.

BOB SEIL
Ambush! Okay, we're out of time. Thanks
for joining us. Next week on *Ambush,* the
Pope, live from the Vatican.

At the SOPOE DINING ROOM TABLE, Mark and Magdelin serve breakfast. J.C.
is at the head of the table. The kids, Courtney Chelsea and Jason sit on one side.
Ruth, Kirk, Sean and Captain Culo sit on the other. Matthew and Stuke stand at the
doorway. The mood is somber. Filipe makes an entrance.

FILIPE
Morning.

J.C.
Good morning everyone.

Ruth and J.C. share an amorous glance. Magdelin takes notice and flashes them a
filthy look. Sean addresses Ruth.

SEAN
Ruth, could you pass the salt?

As she passes the salt, she has a revelation.

RUTH
That voice, that eye.

Stuke takes a seat while Magdelin pours everyone milk.

KIRK
You got any espresso?

She ignores him. Kirk digs in voraciously.

                    MAGDELIN
          Hey, drop that fork and clasp your
          palm. We say grace at this hide-out.

                    JASON
          I got this one. Ah, hem. Give us this
          day our daily bread. Lead us not into
          indigestion and deliver us a pizza...

Courtney and Chelsea join in.

                    KIDS
          Amen.

                    KIRK
          I've got a whale of an appetite.

                    J.C.
          Speaking of whales. Didn't your father-
          in-law, John Hammer, wipe out a whole
          colony during an oil drilling off the coast
          of Santa Barbara?

                    KIRK
          Save the whale. Save the owl. You'll
          eat a cow or a chicken, but don't touch
          that tiger, an animal that would just as
          soon eat you.

                    RUTH
          You're despicable.

                    J.C.
          Ruth's right. Try and keep your
          opinion to yourself.

J.C. and Ruth gloat at each other. Jealous, Magdelin takes an opportunity.

                    MAGDELIN
          Kirk's right. He may be a lot of things,
          but at least he's not a hypocrite.

                         J.C.
Oh, and I am?

                      MAGDELIN
Well, J.C. in your quest to save the
world, you're messing things up
pretty badly.

                         KIRK
People out of work, food shortages,
inflated prices. For what? All the fat
cats are back to business as usual.
Not to mention the two stiffs buried
outside. You made a big kaka, dude.

                     COURTNEY
And I want out of here.

                         KIRK
That's my little princess.

                     COURTNEY
But not with you, creep.

                        SEAN
Hey, come on, this is getting ugly.

Everyone looks at Sean. His ugly comment is quite ironic and everyone starts
laughing.

                         J.C.
Ice breakin' Sean. So, Sean, what have
you been doing all of these years?

                        JASON
Yeah, what happened to your face? Do
mirrors break when you look at them?

                        RUTH
No breakfast for you, young man.

Ruth gets up and takes Jason by the collar and whisks him out of the room.

                    CAPTAIN CULO
I want to know, too. What happened?

SEAN
Well, I was on this FBI case years ago.

J.C.
Oh, great. FBI.

SEAN
Yeah, well, back then, I was in the field.
I was undercover and well, as you can
see, things backfired.

CAPTAIN CULO
What about plastic surgery?

SEAN
It's an extremely expensive operation.
The department won't pay for it. And to
be quite honest with you, that's why I
made this trek. I thought if we got the kids
back home, Kirk and I would possibly…

KIRK
Get a reward. Well, that's fucking dead.

STUKE
Hey! Don't say, "fuck" in front of the
k-i-d-s.

OUTSIDE OF THE COMPOUND, from Kirk's plane, the beep sounds can be heard.
It's a WINDY DAY. The wind is brisk. From the dune nearby, the blowing sand covers
Captain Culo's Jeep.

High above the compound INSIDE of a CHOPPER, a PILOT and TWO FBI MEN
observe the ground below.

FBI MAN # 2
Wait! I see something.

From below something glimmers in the brush.

FBI MAN # 1
Bring 'er down.

Back at the hideout, Kirk addresses J.C.

                         KIRK
         Well, sport, what are you going to do
         now? There's no point in keeping us
         here anymore.

Matthew's VOICE scratches out from Mark's walkie-talkie. Mark acknowledges.

                         MARK
         Copy.
                  (to J.C.)
         J.C. We've got activity above. It's
         the Federalies.

Everyone reacts.

                         STUKE
         Do we have a drill for this?

                         J.C.
         The Feds. Huh. Okay, everybody…

                         KIRK
         Punt?

                         J.C.
         No.

                         STUKE
         Panic?

                         J.C.
         Getting warmer.

                         SEAN
         Hide.

                         J.C.
         We're already doing that.

                         CAPTAIN CULO
         Down here! We're down here, help!

                         SEAN
         Shut up! If they find me down here. I'm screwed.
                  (to Kirk)
         They'll know we went behind their backs.

KIRK
Is there another way out?

J.C.
There's another exit. Everyone grab
their bare essentials and meet me here
in two minutes. Move!

OUTSIDE, three choppers are now hovering over the oasis. They land on the
perimeter. TWELVE FBI MEN spill out from the choppers and snake their way to
Kirk's plane. Methodically, they peel the camouflage from the aircraft. One of the
men gets in the plane and looks about. He then addresses Commander Kelly.

FBI MAN
What the hell's his plane doing here?

Commander Kelly scratches his head and looks around. He then walks up to the
plane and opens the fuel hatch. He sniffs. He then takes a coin from his pocket and
drops it in the tank. The coin hits metal.

COMMANDER KELLY
This plane has no fuel. My guess is that it
ran out of fuel. The caretaker stashed the
plane here. Knowing Kirk, he was in pursuit.
Couldn't find it and went back home. Let's
head out.

The men file back into their choppers.

INSIDE of the compound, J.C. and company have regrouped. J.C. counts heads.

J.C.
Where's Filipe? Where are the kids?

OUTSIDE from the other end of the oasis, Filipe pops his head from a trap door.
He sees the choppers fly off in the distance. He spots the plane, cleared from the
camouflage.

FILIPE
(delighted)
Thanks fellas.

He springs from the ground and pulls Courtney up from the tunnel. He reaches down
and pulls Chelsea up. Jason climbs up on his own.

JASON

Yeah, I'm going home!

CHELSEA

Why can't we bring my mother?

FILIPE

I'll radio in for help.

JASON

Can we stop at McDonald's?

FILIPE

Sure. Come on, let's go!

INSIDE of the TUNNEL, flickering lights create an eerie glow as the crew make their way through the tunnel. Kirk takes Matthew's flashlight and shines it on Magdelin's derriere. She takes notice.

MAGDELIN

What are you doing?

KIRK

Checking for cracks.

MATTHEW

Give me that.

RUTH

J.C., what about Filipe and the kids?

J.C. gets on his walkie-talkie.

J.C.

Lamb one to Filipe. Come in.

OUTSIDE, Filipe tries to start the plane while the kids load themselves in. The engine stalls. He tries again. Nothing.

BACK INSIDE, J.C. reaches the end of the tunnel. As he climbs up the ladder, he hands Magdelin his flashlight.

J.C.

Everyone, quiet. I'm going to see
what's going on.

71

J.C. pushes up the trap door and pops his head OUTSIDE. He does a 180 and spots the choppers off in the distance. He hears something. J.C. pushes himself out and spots Kirk's plane. A billow of smoke emits from the exhaust.

INSIDE of the plane, Filipe tries the engine again. It stalls again.

> JASON
>
> How come it won't start?

> FILIPE
>
> Shut up.

Outside, J.C. approaches the plane, followed by Stuke. Filipe feverishly gives the engine another start. J.C. waves to Filipe. Filipe ignores him and tries the engine again. CONTACT. As Filipe revs the engine, J.C. climbs on the wing and bangs on the window. Filipe puts the plane in gear and rolls forward. J.C. bangs on the window again.

> J.C.
>
> Filipe, what the heck are you doing?

Filipe opens his window, takes out his pistol and whacks J.C. in the face. J.C. falls from the wing.

> COURTNEY
>
> What are you doing?

From the back seat, Jason attempts to put Filipe in a choke hold causing the plane to veer off course. Filipe points the gun at Jason.

> FILIPE
>
> Try that again and you're catsup.

> JASON
>
> Bite me.

Filipe takes Jason's hand and bites it. Jason yells out in pain. Chelsea starts crying.

OUTSIDE, as the plane heads out of the oasis, Sean, Matthew and Mark approach J.C. who is recovering from the blow. Stuke pulls out his weapon.

> J.C.
>
> Don't shoot!

J.C. dashes towards the plane, catches up and is about to jump on the wing when it speeds up. J.C. loses ground and falls. Kirk jumps over J.C. and catches up and yells to Filipe.

                    KIRK
          Did you refuel?

Filipe shakes his head, "no."

                    KIRK
          The fuel gage doesn't work. You're
          running on fumes!

                    FILIPE
          Bullshit!

The plane takes off. Ruth catches up as they all watch the plane shrink into the sky. Stuke helps J.C. up.

                    STUKE
          Should we dig up the vans?

                    J.C.
          Why did he take the kids?

                    KIRK
          Well, sport. It doesn't take a genius
          to figure it out. He's probably going
          to hold them for ransom. But they're
          not going to make it. The plane has
          no fuel. That dumb pendejo.

INSIDE of the plane we SEE the desert below. The plane starts to sputter. Filipe checks the gage which still reads full.

                    FILIPE
          Ooopsie.

The plane stalls and starts to plummet towards the ground.

Back at the OASIS Matthew, Mark and Stuke unearth their VANS. Kirk signals to Sean and Captain Culo.

                    KIRK
          Let's blow this pop stand.

                          RUTH
           Oh, no, my babies. J.C. you bastard!

She drops to the ground, crying in anguish. J.C.'s devastated.

                          J.C.
           What have I done? Oh, God, help me!

HEAVEN - God's beeper goes off. He checks his screen.

                          GOD
           Hmm. The Vatican.

INSIDE of the VATICAN PRESS ROOM, Bob Seil is grilling the POPE.

                        BOB SEIL
           How about celibacy? It's the reason
           priests are dating their altar boys. Your
           Holiness, your cap. It looks like a
           yarmulke. Are you a closet Jew?

                          POPE
                      (to heaven)
           Help!

                       GOD (O.S.)
           Get back to you later. Got another call.

From God's SCREEN we SEE Kirk's plane falling towards Earth. INSIDE the plane,
Chelsea prays.

                        CHELSEA
           Now I lay me down to sleep. I pray
           the Lord my soul will keep…

                       GOD (O.S.)
           Oh, my me. Where's J.C.?

At the OASIS, J.C. is on his knees praying.

                          J.C.
           It's nuts to believe in you. But it's also
           nuts not to. This is one of those
           not-to's. Please don't let anything
           happen to those kids.

Matthew, Mark, Stuke and Magdelin are digging up the vans. Ruth, sits on a stump in shock. Magdelin approaches J.C.

                    MAGDELIN
            We'd better go.

On the OUTSKIRTS of Culo Village, the plane plummets to the ground, crashes and explodes. Soon, a figure in a parachute floats down near the crash. It's Filipe. He lands and gathers his chute. He then wipes his brow.

                    FILIPE
            Shit.

Nearby, from a humble hacienda, a young woman comes running out in her underwear, responding to the commotion. She is CHIQUITA. She slips and falls on a banana peel that is on her porch. The fall renders her unconscious. Curious, Filipe wanders over to her. She is a voluptuous young woman. Filipe is aroused.

                    FILIPE
            Holy penocha.

From the burning plane, the kids climb out without so much as a scratch. A HEAVENLY LIGHT follows them. Filipe spots the kids. He rubs his eyes for a better take.

In HEAVEN, God smiles down. Suddenly, God's beeper goes haywire. He looks down at the Earth which is lit up like a Christmas tree. Each light representing someone in prayer.

                    GOD
            I haven't seen this much praying
            since the Cuban Missile Crisis.

THE EARTH. The ozone layer at the north pole is depleting rapidly. The snow caps at the Earth's highest summits are practically gone.

                    GOD (O.S.)
                (as Rod Serling)
            The world has reached another dimension
            of shadow and substance. There's a signpost
            ahead. You've just reached "The Twilight
            Ozone."

Big U.S. cities are brightly lit with prayer.

                    GOD (O.S.)
          L.A., Chicago and New York are really
          lit up. Ultra Violet Rays are burning
          everyone.

INSIDE - CITY OF ANGELES HOSPITAL - LOS ANGELES. The Emergency Ward is
maxed-out with PEOPLE of all different ages. Most appear to have some sort of skin
disorder. They are all praying. TWO DOCTORS examine a young BOY.

                    DOCTOR # 1
          Later stages of melanoma.

                    DOCTOR # 2
          At his age?

THE STREETS OF CHICAGO. The city has minimal traffic and a smattering of
people on the streets. A radio ANNOUNCER is giving a traffic and weather report.

                    ANNOUNCER (O.S.)
          Downtown traffic. There *is* none and it's
          rush hour. The weather today. Record
          temperatures and sunny. Let's pray for
          some clouds.

NEW YORK - CENTRAL PARK at the AMPHITHEATER, thousands of PEOPLE
have gathered for a mass prayer. They all have umbrellas to protect them from the
sun which is blazing. On STAGE, a MINISTER, a PRIEST and a RABBI lead the
prayer.

                    MINISTER
          Stand and pray.

                    PRIEST
          Let's get on our knees.

                    RABBI
          Can't we just sit?

From high atop an adjacent BUILDING on Fifth Avenue, the sea of umbrellas can be
seen by Grant Methamin who is sitting on his terrace. He wears a wide brimmed hat
to protect him from the sun. He steps into his PENTHOUSE. On the RADIO there's
a news report.

                    ANNOUNCER (O.S.)
          ...and if you're going outside, bring an
          umbrella or apply a fifty plus sun block.

He gets on his cell and steps into his OFFICE.

                    METHAMIN
          Buy up all the sun care products shares
          you can get your hands on. And that
          children's hospital we have in the Bronx.
          Revamp and set it up for an umbrella
          factory. Got another call.
                    (another line)
          Hello, John, old man. I'm still in New
          York finishing up a merger.

INSIDE the Hammer palace.

                    HAMMER
                    (on phone)
          Grant. Hold on a second.

Something on the TELEVISION catches his attention.

OUTSIDE of a DETENTION CENTER in SAN DIEGO, NEWS FOOTAGE of J.C.,
Magdelin, Matthew, Mark and Stuke being escorted into the building by U.S.
MARSHALS.

                    ANNOUNCER (O.S.)
          The members of the SOPOE gang have
          turned themselves in, in San Diego. Still
          missing are the children of the most
          infamous kidnapping since they put the
          snatch on the Lindbergh baby.

                    HAMMER
          Jerry Collins just turned himself in.

INTERCUT- HAMMER AND METHAMIN

                    METHAMIN
          That's good news old man. I miss Jason,
          a chip off the old block. Someone I can
          corrupt.

                    HAMMER
          That's lovely. Unfortunately, the kids
          are still missing.

METHAMIN
What?!!

HAMMER
Hold on.

Hammer sees something from outside of his window. Three FBI choppers are now hovering over his tennis court.

Meanwhile, INSIDE of a sleazy, little MEXICAN BAR, Filipe is doing shots of tequila with Chiquita. He puts a five dollar bill inside of her blouse and kisses her.

On the bar, a TV is on. The BARTENDER adjusts the rabbit ears for better reception. The news report of the SOPOE surrender continues.

ANNOUNCER
Also missing is Filipe Binladen.

FILIPE
Benlada, you pendejo. Chiquita, you
are looking at a very rich man, to be.
Soon, I'll have enough money to start
my own chain of restaurants. "Filipe's
Frijole Freeway." (Hic!)

He then takes out his cell and speed dials.

INSIDE the Hammer Palace, Hammer is still on the phone with Methamin.

HAMMER
This is bizarre. I've got three FBI choppers
hovering over my tennis court.
(a beat)
I've got another call. I'll call you back
later…Hello.

FILIPE (O.S.)
Mr. Hammer. I've got the kids. If you and
that other honcho want them back, it'll cost
you one million dollars per kid. That's
chump change for you.

Meanwhile, INSIDE of an OLD ABANDONED SHACK, Courtney, Jason and Chelsea are bound and gagged. It's 100 plus degrees inside and the kids are sweating profusely. From outside, the SOUND of a vehicle passes by.

OUTSIDE, Kirk, Sean and Captain Culo drive by. They drive up to the spot where they first met. They get out of the Jeep. Kirk has developed a sore on his forehead. Captain Culo takes notice.

CAPTAIN CULO
What the hell's that on your face?

Kirk caresses the spot. It's melanoma. Smugly, he dismisses it.

KIRK
Probably syphilis.

Kirk takes out his wallet and hands Captain Culo some cash.

KIRK
Here's a few hundred for your trouble.

Just then, from the bar across the street, Filipe and Chiquita come stumbling out. Kirk grabs a rifle from the back seat.

KIRK
Okay, scumbag, where's my fuckin' plane?

Filipe takes out his gun and uses Chiquita as a shield.

FILIPE
If it were up your ass you'd know.

SEAN
Where are the kids?

FILIPE
They fried along with that stupid plane.

Filipe shoots at Kirk and misses. Kirk fires back. The bullet grazes Chiquita's arm. She passes out and drops to the ground. Kirk shoots again, hitting Filipe square in the chest. He drops to the ground. Sean runs over to Filipe.

SEAN
He's dead.

CAPTAIN CULO
I'm not burying him…

Kirk pulls out another hundred.

                    CAPTAIN CULO
              …right this minute.

Chiquita comes around.

                         SEAN
              Senorita. Per favore. Havo you
              seeno a plane?

Sean's face has scared her. Captain Culo intervenes. He picks her up and SPEAKS
quietly to her in Spanish. She shakes her head "yes", and points. Off towards the
horizon, a wisp of smoke emits from the still smoldering crash.

                         KIRK
              Tsk. C'est la vie, dudes. Well, I've had
              enough of this friggin' desert.

                         SEAN
              What about the kids?

                         KIRK
              What about 'em?

                         SEAN
              We need to bring back their remains.

                         KIRK
              Yeah. We did try to rescue them. We'll
              be heroes yet.

LATER, AT THE CRASH SIGHT, Kirk, Sean and Captain Culo examine what's left of
the plane. There's a pile of ash surrounded by a burned out frame. Kirk squats down
and grabs a pile of ash.

                         SEAN
              Those poor kids.

                         KIRK
              Hey, Culo do you have a jar we could
              put them in?

Sean picks up some pieces of wood nearby and concocts three headstones.

                         SEAN
              We need to mark their graves. Culo,
              give me your pen.

KIRK
I'll make a news statement.

Meanwhile, back at the HAMMER PALACE, one of the FBI choppers sits on the tennis court while the other two hover from above. INSIDE, Commander Kelly introduces himself.

COMMANDER KELLY
Commander Kelly, FBI. Is Mr. Manwaring in?

HAMMER
No, but you could have gotten the same answer
by calling or faxing. Why are you parked on my
tennis court?

COMMANDER KELLY
Beggin' your pardon Mr. Hammer. Love your
work, but this is urgent government business.

HAMMER
Hmm.

A very distressed Diana enters.

DIANA
Have they found Courtney?

Just then from a FAX MACHINE on the bar, a memo cranks itself into view. The fax reads:

Dad - I raided the SOPOE hideout - Tried to save the kids - Filipe took the kids in my plane - The plane crashed - All dead - Will be home soon - Kirk

Hammer takes the memo and crumbles it.

DIANA
What is it?

HAMMER
(shaken)
Don't ask. Diana, I need to talk with the
commander.

Diana exits.

HAMMER
There's been a death in the family. I'll
contact Kirk. In all decency, could your
urgent government business wait until
after the funeral?

It's NIGHT FALL at Culo Village. Captain Culo and Chiquita are at the edge of town pulling a big burlap sack. They drag the sack by the shack. Captain Culo spots a shovel that's wedged into the door. He gets it. He then takes a few steps and begins digging a grave.

Chiquita pulls on the sack, exposing it's contents, Filipe's body. She begins to cry. Captain Culo stuffs some cash down her blouse. She takes a five and wipes her tears. He then takes out a bottle and hands her the shovel. Chiquita is now digging while Captain Culo finishes off the tequila. The grave's about half done. Chiquita drops the shovel.

CHIQUITA
No mas.

Captain Culo agrees and kicks Filipe's body into the shallow grave. He then begins covering the corpse with dirt. Chiquita bends over to pick up a bill that has dropped from her blouse. Gravity takes it's course, causing one of her ample breasts to flop out. Captain Culo becomes aroused. This arouses Chiquita.

Soon, in the throes of lust, they peel off their clothes as they drop to the ground, pumping, grunting and wheezing. They roll over into the hole and onto the stiff. Not missing a stroke, they continue copulating, humping and sounding like two jackasses getting their teeth pulled.

INSIDE of the shack - The racket from outside causes the kids to stir from their coma-like sleep. Courtney wiggles her gag off.

COURTNEY
Jason, Chelsea. Are you awake?

JASON CHELSEA
Hmmm, hmmm.

COURTNEY
Hear that?
(shouts)
Help us! We're in here! Help!

OUTSIDE, from the love pit, Captain Culo sticks his head up. Soon to be followed by Chiquita.

82

CHIQUITA

Que pasa?

From inside, they hear the kids screaming for help.

CAPTAIN CULO

It's the kids. El Ninos. Ondale!

They scramble out, buttoning up their clothes. Captain Culo feverishly shovels dirt on the grave.

CAPTAIN CULO

Hey, kids! Is that you, Courtney?

COURTNEY (O.S.)

Yes, we're in here. Get us out!

CAPTAIN CULO

What are you doing in there? I thought you'd be desert fries by now.

COURTNEY (O.S.)

We didn't get hurt, but Filipe took us here. Where is that turd?

CAPTAIN CULO

Resting in peace.

COURTNEY

Where's Kirk? Doesn't he know where I am?

CAPTAIN CULO

Oh, he will.

TELEVISION. A logo of half of a clock, ticking.

ANNOUNCER (O.S.)

Tonight, live on *Thirty Minutes*.

INSIDE OF JAIL. J.C. is mopping up a cat-walk corridor.

83

ANNOUNCER (O.S.)
Jerry Collins. Leader of the infamous,
radical, environmentalist group SOPOE.
Hero or villain? An exclusive interview
with Morty Hasereye.

INSIDE of a jail cell, J.C. is being interviewed by MORTY.

MORTY
You caused quite a ruckus, to say the
least. And the kids. Still missing. You
told the authorities that they were taken
by one of your cohorts.

J.C. begins ranting.

J.C.
We could all be on the brink of distinction.
Our sun is killing us. We're losing our
ozone. As we speak, they're still burning
the rain forests in South America. We
know we're in danger, but yet we let it
happen. It's mass denial. The kids. Let me
out! I've got to find them. I've got to save
them!

THREE GUARDS enter the cell. Two of them contain J.C. while the other whisks
Morty and his CAMERAMAN out of the cell.

Meanwhile, INSIDE of the Methamin mansion, Ruth and Methamin are watching this
broadcast on TV. As the guards subdue a raving J.C., a tear wells up in Ruth's eye.

METHAMIN
This man's a lunatic. Those bastards still
have my babies.

The NEXT MORNING on the PACIFIC COAST HIGHWAY, Kirk's Hummer heads up
from PCH to the road that leads to the Hammer palace. INSIDE the Hummer, Kirk
and Sean go over their story.

KIRK
Pretty much tell it like it is. Except
for the part where I killed Filipe.

                    SEAN
What about Captain Culo? Can you
trust him?

                    KIRK
Ah, he's too fuckin' stupid to be
devious. We'll be heroes. I can stop
pimpin' for the boys on the hill. Be
respectable. Open up a chain of drive-
through whore houses. "Snatch To Go"
featuring the "blowme sandwich."

                    SEAN
That's lovely, but what about me?
We didn't produce the kids. I'm
going back to Washington.

                    KIRK
I always wanted to ask you. Why
did you take that assignment in
Waco? You're no trouble shooter.

                    SEAN
I read a profile on one of Koresh's
followers. I had a compelling urge
to save her.

                    KIRK
Who was it?

                    SEAN
Hang on to your hat. It was…look out!

Kirk veers off of the road to avoid his father-in-law's Jaguar, coming the other way.

                    KIRK
Shit!

THE ROAD - Kirk gets out of his vehicle and approaches the Jaguar. From the
drivers side, the tinted glass slides down a few inches exposing Hammer's face.

                    HAMMER
What the hell's wrong with you?

                            KIRK
                What do you mean?

                           HAMMER
                That's a general statement.

He notices the sore on Kirk's face.

                           HAMMER
                If I were you, I'd get out of the Sun.

Kirk goes around to the other side of the Jag and gets INSIDE.

                           HAMMER
                I talked with Filipe on the phone. He said
                that the kids were still alive.

                            KIRK
                No! The kids died in the crash. Filipe
                must've parachuted. To be honest, I
                caught up with him. He shot at me so
                I killed him.

                           HAMMER
                Where is my granddaughter's body?

                            KIRK
                She was burnt to a crisp in the crash.

Hammer drops his head on the steering wheel.

AFTERNOON - INSIDE of the Detention Center's CATWALK, J.C. is mopping the
floor. Some other INMATES are pacing about. J.C. excuses himself as he tries to
mop up a section.

                            J.C.
                Excuse me, brother.

                         INMATE # 1
                I ain't yo mutha fukkin' brother.

J.C. mops around him. Through the bars in the guards area, a TV has been left on.

On the TELEVISION a news report about the kidnappings is on. A REPORTER
stands near the wreckage outside of Culo Village.

REPORTER
All that's left. A pile of ash.

The SHOT SWITCHES INSIDE a newsroom where Kirk is being interviewed.

KIRK
(on video)
That's when agent Young and I
moved in to rescue the kids. Benlada
commandeered my plane with the kids.
Low on fuel, I knew the plane had to be
close by. I was right. The plane crashed
and everyone inside was ashed. Those
poor kids. My little girl.

Kirk strains a bit to well-up a nice big crocodile tear.

Back at the catwalk, another inmate chides J.C.

INMATE # 2
Hey, Mr. Kidnapper, looks like you
got some blood on your hands.
(to another inmate)
Hey, Punchus. What do you say we
toughen this punk up for his stay in
San Quentin?

Punchus, reluctantly nods as the other inmates punch J.C. unconscious. They, then pick J.C. up and tie him to the bars, arms extended and feet tied together. Punchus waxes guilty.

PUNCHUS
I believe this is an innocent man, man.

He enters his cell as the other inmates tear off J.C.'s fatigue shirt. Inmate # 1 takes a broom and breaks it in half with his knee. The handle now has a sharp jagged edge. From a shadow on the floor we SEE the image of the spear-like object being plunged into J.C.'s chest. He CRIES OUT, in pain. J.C. struggles to take his last breath. A HEAVENLY LIGHT from above shines down as J.C.'s spirit rises. His mortal body lies hanging from the bars. The inmates scramble into their cells.

NOONISH, INSIDE of Methamin's office, Methamin is on his speaker phone with Hammer.

                    METHAMIN
John. Grant. How did this get so out of
control? I thought Filipe was suppose to
foil the coup. We should have given him
more than five grand. Well, at least we
saved some money on Jude. I only gave
him a down payment. Thirty pieces of silver.

HAMMER'S OFFICE

                    HAMMER
What about the million we gave to Bob
Seil to give to Collins? Sometimes you
have to count your loses. I lost a
granddaughter.

INTERCUT - METHAMIN AND HAMMER

                    METHAMIN
I see that and raise you two grandkids.
Well, John, we jacked up our commodities,
but we lost our most important resource,
the children.

                    HAMMER
Let's not get too sappy. Life goes on.
Your daughter can have more children.

                    METHAMIN
John, you are one cold son-of-a-bitch.

                    HAMMER
There's the pot calling the roach clip
illegal. What's done is done. I'm going
to have a eulogy dinner, a funeral of
sorts, here at the palace. I want you and
Ruth here. It'll be a media event. It'll
be the sympathy we need to keep our
prices up.

                    METHAMIN
I suppose you're right. Life goes on.

As they continue, the CAMERA PANS TO the OUTER CORRIDOR. Ruth stands
outside of the office in shock, having heard the whole conversation.

OUTSIDE, at the Hammer pool, it's LATE MORNING. Kirk sits poolside reading Hustler. His phone rings.

                    KIRK
          Culo. What's up?

INSIDE, Captain Culo's OFFICE, he looks through a travel brochure while talking on his cell.

                    CAPTAIN CULO
          Well, Kirkie. I got bad news *and* I got
          good news. The kids are still alive.

INTERCUT - KIRK AND CAPTAIN CULO

                    KIRK
          Okay, what's the good news? Wait!
          What do you mean they're still alive?
          I saw the twisted wreck that used to
          be my plane.

                    CAPTAIN CULO
          The plane went down, Filipe parachuted
          and the kids walked.

                    KIRK
          How's that possible?

                    CAPTAIN CULO
          It's a fuckin' miracle, but they're very
          much alive. I have them hidden away. If
          you want to talk to them, I can set it up.

                    KIRK
          Wait. I just told the whole world that
          they're dead.

                    CAPTAIN CULO
          The good news is, they'll keep thinking
          that if you *pay* your cards right.

                    KIRK
          I thought that was *play*. Culo, are you
          blackmailing me?

89

                    CAPTAIN CULO
Blackmail is such a dark word.

                    KIRK
Alright, how much?

                    CAPTAIN CULO
One million.

                    KIRK
What? Where the fuck am I gonna
that kind of money?

                    CAPTAIN CULO
Please, your father-in-law is filthy rich.

                    KIRK
Yeah, he is, but I'm not. Ah, okay. I'll
get the money somehow. I'll meet you
at your office tomorrow.

A PARK on the outskirts of Washington D.C. - AFTERNOON. David Bitter is jogging
with his FBI ENTOURAGE, one of which is Sean. Sean catches up with Bitter.

                    SEAN
                (breathing hard)
Senator Bitter. Sean Young.

                    BITTER
You looked better in *Wall Street.*
Sorry. What can I do for you?

                    SEAN
I was one of the agents at Waco.
It's about my face. The Bureau
won't pay for an operation.

                    BITTER
                (getting winded)
If I remember correctly, you
infiltrated without authorization.

                              SEAN
          And I was suspended for a year without pay.
          I understand you've been looking for Kirk
          Manwaring. And I know why. I could
          blab to the press, or get some nip/tuck.

                              BITTER
          Blackmailing a U.S. Senator. I like
          your style.

Back at the Detention Center, FOUR GUARDS discover J.C.'s body hanging from
the bars. One of the guards yells out at the prisoners.

                              GUARD # 1
          I can't leave you guys alone for five
          minutes!

Meanwhile, in HEAVEN, J.C. takes a seat next to God while Hendrix plays *Have
You Ever Been (To Electric Ladyland)*. J.C. can hardly believe his eyes as he looks
around.

                              J.C.
          Wow, this is a heaven. God, it's
          you.

                              GOD
          It took death to get your faith back?

                              J.C.
          The way things are on Earth. Yes, I
          did lose faith…Where is everyone?

                              GOD
          It's a tough place to get into.

J.C. spots Hendrix.

                              J.C.
          Wow, Hendrix. How'd he get in?

                              GOD
          I dig his chops.

                              91

Just then, JESUS appears. He is sweating. J.C. looks at him in awe. His resemblance to the Christ is uncanny. J.C. approaches Jesus. They embrace. J.C. takes a remnant of what's left of his jail fatigues and wipes Jesus' brow.

                    JESUS
          Thanks little brother. I just got back
          from Purgatory. (Whew!) You'll have
          about a billion people passing through
          those pearly gates anytime now.

AT THE GATES, SAINT PETER, LADY MADONNA, and THE SAINTS wave.

J.C. has a sudden realization. He addresses God.

                    J.C.
          Where are the kids? Why aren't they here?

                    GOD
          They're still alive. You must go back
          and save them.

                    J.C.
          Me? Jesus, can't you do it?

                    JESUS
          My work is done. You're the new Savior. I must
          say though, little brother, you have a very
          unorthodox style. Taking money from Bob Seil.
          You know that Bob Seil backwards is Bob Lies.
          Tsk, tsk, tsk.

                    J.C.
          Well, if you had done your job right,
          you wouldn't need me.

                    GOD
          Boys. The being who is without sin,
          cast the first stone.

From the PEARLY GATES, Lady Madonna throws a stone that whizzes by Jesus and J.C.

                    JESUS
          Mom!

92

GOD

J.C. You'd better go. You'll be re-
incarnated as the new Christ. You'll
have special powers. However, they'll
only last one day and then you'll be
mortal again. Spread some good, son.

J.C. looks at what's left of his jail fatigues.

J.C.

Alright. Jesus, may I borrow your
robe and your halo?

JESUS

Sure, but bring it back in one piece.

Jesus gives J.C. his halo. God hands J.C. an AMERICAN EXPRESS CARD.

GOD

Take this. I never leave heaven without it.

J.C. takes the card and his brothers' robe and vanishes.

At the Detention Center CATWALK, the four guards take J.C.'s body down from the
bars. J.C.'s SPIRIT enters his body which comes to life. His new image of the Savior
with robe and halo amazes the guards as they stand back. The inmates comment.

INMATE # 1

Cool. Now at least I won't get nailed
with a murder charge.

INMATE # 2

Yeah, you'll be too busy with your
other murder charges.

J.C. blesses the inmates, walks through the bars and out into the precinct's FRONT
OFFICE. J.C., then blesses the DESK SERGEANT and exits. The desk sergeant, in
awe, makes the sign-of-the-cross.

OUTSIDE, J.C. Looks around, getting his bearings.

J.C.

Let's see. The kids must be near the
crash sight.

J.C. tests his powers and does a running leap. He is now flying high, over the city. A crowd of onlookers view this with amazement.

                    ONLOOKER #1
          Look, up in the sky. It's a bird!

                    ONLOOKER # 2
          It's a plane!

                    ONLOOKER # 3
          No, it's Super Christ !

Meanwhile, Just outside of CULO VILLAGE, Kirk's Hummer ambles about on some rough terrain that leads to Chiquita's hacienda. Kirk's vehicle comes to a halt. As Kirk and Captain Culo get out, Chiquita comes out to greet them. Chiquita looks particularly succulent this morning. Kirk can't takes his eyes off of her as he removes his sunglasses.

                    CHIQUITA
          Buenos dias, Captain Culo. Ola, Kirk.

                    KIRK
          Boooiiinnnggg.

                    CHIQUITA
          Boooiiinnnggg???

                    CAPTAIN CULO
                    (interpreting)
          Bueno.

                    KIRK
          Tell you what Captain. I'll throw in an
          extra twenty five grand for the seniorita.
          Hey, listen, Chiquita, sorry about shootin'
          you in the arm.

Her arm has but a mere band aid on it. Kirk pulls out some cash from his pocket and stuffs it down her blouse. She smiles.

                    CAPTAIN CULO
          El nino.

Chiquita goes inside and brings out Courtney.

COURTNEY
Well, I never thought I'd see the day when
I'd be glad to see you.

She notices the sore on Kirk's forehead.

COURTNEY
What happened to your forehead?

KIRK
Racket ball. Hello little princess. Where
are the other kids?

CAPTAIN CULO
First the money.

Kirk and the Captain go over to the Hummer. Kirk opens the back latch. From under a compartment he takes out a briefcase and opens it. He shows the contents to Culo. He fondles the money feverishly.

CAPTAIN CULO
This is a million?

KIRK
You get the rest when I get all the kids
and Chiquita, too.

CAPTAIN CULO
Chiquita? You're a married man, man.

KIRK
She's not for me, she's for my boss.

Meanwhile in WASHINGTON - SENATOR BITTER'S OFFICE. From outside of the window, the Capitol Building is in full view. Senator Bitter is conferring with Commander Kelly.

BITTER
I received an invitation to the funeral
from John Hammer. I never got an
invitation to a funeral before. I trust
that Kirk will be there. I'll deal with
him personally, tomorrow.

A SHOT of J.C. flying over the oasis.

INSIDE of Chiquita's humble hacienda, Kirk, Captain Culo, Courtney and Chiquita make their way down to the cellar.

                    KIRK
          Where are they?

                    CAPTAIN CULO
          They're down here. Where's the rest
          of the money?

                    KIRK
          Show me the kids.

                    CAPTAIN CULO
          Show me the money.

From behind a storage door.

                    JASON (O.S.)
          We're in here!

Captain Culo reluctantly goes to the door. He takes out a key and unlocks the pad lock. Kirk looks in.

                    CAPTAIN CULO
          Okay, you can see the kids are okay. Now,
          get the money.

Kirk takes out his keys.

                    KIRK
          In the back of my Hummer, underneath
          the tire. It's in a garbage bag.

He throws the keys to Culo.

                    KIRK
          I'll wait here.

The Captain goes upstairs. The screen door is HEARD, slamming shut. Kirk pushes Courtney inside of the storage area and locks the door.

                    COURTNEY (O.S.)
          Kirk, what are you pulling now?

Chiquita begins crying. Kirk takes out a wad of bills and stuff it down her blouse.

                              KIRK
                    Shhh. Wait here. Comprendo?

                            CHIQUITA
                    Si.

Kirk runs upstairs.

OUTSIDE, Captain Culo is rummaging around in the back of the Hummer. He hears the screen door SLAM. Kirk is carrying the briefcase.

                         CAPTAIN CULO
                    Where's the bag?

Captain Culo pulls out a pistol and aims it at Kirk.

                              KIRK
                    It's all in here, man. The rest of the
                    money is in a compartment underneath.
                    I just wanted to be sure you had all the
                    brats. Here, take a look.

Kirk tosses the briefcase towards the captain. Culo cautiously steps over and opens the briefcase, keeping an eye on Kirk. He spreads the money on top, aside. He unsnaps the bottom compartment and opens it.

Inside, a SCORPION jumps up and strikes Culo in the neck. Horrified, he pulls the scorpion from his throat, throws it down and empties his gun, killing it. He goes to shoot Kirk, only to discover he's used up his amo.

                              KIRK
                    Boy, you are a dumb fuck.

Kirk empties his gun into Captain Culo. He drops to the ground, moaning. Kirk walks up to him.

                         CAPTAIN CULO
                         (gasping for air)
                    Shit, today is my birthday, too.

                              KIRK
                    Oh yeah. What's your sign?

CAPTAIN CULO
Scorpio.

He then gasps for his last breath and fades away. Kirk drags his body inside. He quickly comes back out, runs to the Hummer and gets a can of gasoline.

A moment later, INSIDE the hacienda, Kirk begins dumping gasoline on the floors and walls. He dumps the rest on a couch. He then runs to the cellar door.

KIRK
Chiquita. Come up here, andale!

Chiquita comes upstairs, sees Captain Culo's body and smells the gasoline. She grasps the situation and begins to freak out. Kirk lights a match. Chiquita is now SCREAMING.

KIRK
Don't worry, I'll give you mucho
dinero for the hacienda.

He tosses the match on the couch which throws up a huge flame. He grabs Chiquita by the hand and takes her outside.

OUTSIDE, Kirk gathers up some tossed stacks of money and puts them in the briefcase. He whisks Chiquita to the Hummer and they get in. As they spin off, smoke starts to pour out from the windows.

INSIDE the Hummer.

CHIQUITA
El ninos!

Kirk takes a stack of bills and stuffs them down her blouse.

KIRK
Fuck 'em.

CHIQUITA
Si.

J.C. lands at the CRASH SIGHT. He looks at the grave stones and ponders. He then makes the sign of the cross when something gets his attention. He sees billows of smoke in the distance. He jumps up and flies over to the burning hacienda.

At the hacienda, he hears SCREAMS from within. He inhales the billowing smoke and blows it out towards the desert.

He steps INSIDE and takes a deep breath. He exhales, blowing out the flames. From this, more smoke is created. He hears the screams from below becoming fainter. J.C. then tunnels through the smoke and smashes through the cellar door. In the cellar, he hears a faint CRY for help.

> J.C.
> It's Courtney!

He pulls the door from it's foundation. Inside the storage room, he sees the kids lying in a heap. The smoke has over come them. He quickly gathers the kids. Jason and Chelsea over one shoulder and Courtney over the other. He flies upstairs and out of the hacienda.

OUTSIDE, he lies the kids down. He then checks their breathing. Courtney has stopped breathing. J.C. administers mouth to mouth to her. She comes around. She sees a Jesus like figure with a halo, with his mouth on hers. She freaks out.

> COURTNEY
> Eeeeuuu! What are you doing?

She slaps his face.

> J.C.
> Saving your life.

> COURTNEY
> By kissing me?

She slaps him again.

> J.C.
> It's called resuscitation.

Another slap.

> COURTNEY
> Who are you?

> J.C.
> It's J.C.

Slap.

                    COURTNEY
What's with the halo?

                       J.C.
Okay, I'm the new Savior.

Slap. Slap.

                       J.C.
My sister. My daughter. Hey stop it.
This is J.C. I've made a bit of a
transformation.

He gets up, pulling Courtney to her feet. Jason and Chelsea come around.

                    CHELSEA
Is it Halloween?

                    JASON
That robe is totally gay.

                       J.C.
Jason, Chelsea, I'm J.C. And how 'bout
a little thanks for saving your lives.

The kids still have a hard time with this.

                       J.C.
Jason, if I'm not J.C., how would I know
your names? Remember we all stayed
underground? Your mom is Ruth. We
made you lemonade which you spit in
Stuke's face. You used to take Ritalin.

                    JASON
Now I need Thorazine.

                    CHELSEA
I want to go home.

                    COURTNEY
I'm starving.

J.C. thinks for a moment. DUSK is approaching.

J.C.

Okay, it's getting dark. There's a truck
stop not far from here. They have a diner
and a motel there. You can eat, rest up
and be fresh to go home in the morning.

He flies over to the porch, takes a small bench and puts it over his shoulders. He then squats down.

J.C.

Get on.

COURTNEY

I'm not getting on that thing.

J.C.

Would you rather walk?

JASON

You mean we're gonna fly?

J.C.

Yes.

Jason and Chelsea, gleefully get on. Courtney stands her ground.

COURTNEY

When you get there, send a cab.

As the Super Christ craft ascends upwards, Courtney jumps on.

COURTNEY

You would leave without me?

J.C. laughs as they all fly off into the sunset.

It's NIGHT TIME at a PRIVATE AIRFIELD. Methamin's CREW prepares his Lear jet for flight. INSIDE the plane, Ruth is asleep in her seat. Across the isle, Methamin is reading the paper. A headline reads:

BIG WIGS EULOGIZE KIDS AT HAMMER PALACE
WASHINGTON BRASS DUE TO ATTEND

INSIDE the Hammer Palace, Diana sits idle while a crew of DOMESTICS prepare for this gala funeral. Hammer is reading the same headline. Another headline reads:

101

SOPOE LEADER ESCASPES FROM JAIL
SUPERCHRIST SEEN FLYING OVER SAN DIEGO

POV of J.C. and the kids flying over a TRUCK STOP. They land and the kids dismount. J.C. hides the bench behind some bushes. They all enter the DINER.

INSIDE the diner, a CASHIER does a double-take as J.C. and the kids slide into a booth. A WAITRESS at another table is taking an order from TWO TRUCKERS. They give J.C. and the kids a stare. The cashier brings them menus.

CASHIER

Hi kids.

(to J.C.)

Is it Easter already?

J.C. smiles. The cashier chuckles as she goes back to the register.

J.C.

I thought you kids were killed in the
crash. It was in the news.

COURTNEY

I don't get it either. The plane exploded
and we just got up and walked.

CHELSEA

I said a prayer.

COURTNEY

And then Filipe took us to a shack and
tied us up.

JASON

His breath stinks.

J.C.

Kirk told reporters that Filipe died in
the crash.

JASON

He parachuted. Next day we heard shots.

CHELSEA

Captain Culo said that Filipe was
resting in peace.

102

                    COURTNEY
          Captain Culo took us to his girlfriends
          house and locked us up. And then Kirk
          showed up and set her house on fire.
          He's such a pain.

                    J.C.
          He set the house on fire? He must've
          killed Culo, too. The devil has a new
          name.

The waitress approaches the table with a smirk on her face.

                    WAITRESS
          Evenin'. Ready?

                    J.C.
          Yes. Four cheeseburgers, with French
          fries and four Cokes.

The waitress collects the menus.

                    WAITRESS
          Me and the boys was wonderin'. Your
          day job. Are you a fisherman?

                    J.C.
          Not anymore. The fish are too contaminated.

                    WAITRESS
          Not as much as the burgers you ordered.

NIGHTIME, INSIDE of a hotel room in Washington, Senator David Bitter and his
HOOKER DU JUR are getting dressed. She has huge breasts.

                    BITTER
          I'll be in L.A. for a few days. Try not
          to knock anything over with those things.
                    (pensive)
          Did I buy those?

                              HOOKER
            Yes, I got 'em at IN-N-OUT Knockers,
            remember?
                         (looks down and around)
            Where'd I put my shoes?

                              BITTER
            You're wearing them.

OUTSIDE of a MOTEL OFFICE, it's a star filled NIGHT. INSIDE, the PROPRIETOR
gives J.C. the keys while Courtney fills out the guest application.

                              PROPRIETOR
            You and the boy can take room 110.
            The girls can stay in 111. How will
            you be paying, Mr…

J.C. hands him his credit card.

                              PROPRIETOR
            Almighty?

                                J.C.
            No, that's Al Mighty.

He swipes and it's accepted. He looks at J.C.'s halo.

                              PROPRIETOR
            Lights and halos out at twelve.

He, then laughs insidiously. J.C. rolls his eyes.

                                J.C.
            Christ.

On the way out J.C. takes a newspaper. He reads the headline in amazement and
quickly scurries the kids out.

                              COURTNEY
            What is it?

                                J.C.
            I'll tell you in the morning. Let's get
            some sleep.

OUTSIDE, as J.C. and the kids head towards their rooms, the waitress and the two truckers peer out from the diner window.

INSIDE the hotel room, J.C. tucks Jason in. He then takes the newspaper over to the desk and reads.

BIG WIGS EULOGIZE KIDS AT HAMMER PALACE
WASHINGTON BRASS DUE TO ATTEND

SOPOE LEADER ESCAPES FROM JAIL
SUPERCHRIST SEEN FLYING OVER SAN DIEGO

Pacific Palisades - **Billionaire oil man, John Hammer will host a black tie eulogy dinner to commemorate the children who died as a result of the SOPOE kidnappings. The service will be held tomorrow morning at 11:00 AM. Washington leaders and Hollywood celebrities due to attend.**

San Diego - **A man looking like Jesus Christ was seen flying from a San Diego jail. SOPOE leader Jerry Collins was reported to have escaped around that time.**

J.C. nods off.

CRACK OF DAWN. J.C. is wakened by a knock at the door. He gets up and opens the door. Courtney's hair is wet and she's wrapped in a blanket.

> COURTNEY
> I'm up a little early. I haven't taken a shower
> in so long, I guess it was too invigorating.

J.C. comes OUTSIDE. They walk over to an old hitching post and sit.

> COURTNEY
> So many weird things have happened
> in the last couple of weeks. And now,
> you, with your super powers. How did
> you do that?

> J.C.
> I said a prayer.

> COURTNEY
> You said a prayer to become Super Jesus?

                            J.C.
                         (laughs)
Well, I'm not really super or Jesus. My
powers won't last much longer.
                         (a beat)
I'm so glad that you kids are okay.
Do you hate me for what I've done?

                         COURTNEY
At first I thought you were a jerk, but
when Kirk, my own step father showed
up, I realized that you were a prince.

                            J.C.
Me, a prince? I messed things up pretty
badly. Some men died because of me.

                         COURTNEY
You didn't cause their deaths. Kirk did.
You're a good man. I just hope they don't
crucify you, like they did the first Jesus.

                            J.C.
Jesus didn't have a lawyer. Maybe I can
get a good one. Look, we're all going to
your place later.

                         COURTNEY
Please, I don't want to go home.

                            J.C.
That's funny, you have everything. Maybe
I was right after all.

                         COURTNEY
It's a sick world, J.C. You were trying to
change it. I admire you.

                            J.C.
Coming from you, Courtney, that's an
honor. I think you and the kids are the
real heroes. You've seen and heard
some nasty stuff, came close to death
many times and you're all okay.

                    COURTNEY
Kids are tough. When we're adults we'll
probably need psychiatrists.

                    J.C.
What do you say we get ready. We should
all be fresh for your funeral.

                    COURTNEY
Huh?

                    J.C.
The world thinks you're dead. Your
grandfather is throwing a eulogy party.

J.C. walks Courtney to her room.

                    COURTNEY
Thanks, J.C.

They hug. Courtney goes in as J.C. heads towards his room. He stops and looks up.

                    J.C.
Well, Dad, things are looking...

Suddenly from above, a POLICE HELICOPTER appears and hovers over the motel.

                    J.C.
...yucky.

J.C. runs to the girls room and bangs on the door.

                    J.C.
Courtney! Chelsea! We've got to go
right now!

Courtney swings open the door.

                    J.C.
Get dressed now. We've got company.
I'll be right back. Go!

J.C. bursts into his room. INSIDE, he wakes Jason.

                    J.C.
          Jason, get dressed, now!

                  JASON
          Check-out time already? This is a
          cheap motel.

                    J.C.
          Hurry!

While Jason gets dressed, J.C. peers out the window. The chopper lands and TWO
ARMED SHERIFFS get out and head towards the motel.

                    J.C.
          Ready?

                  JASON
          Who's after us now?

J.C. opens the door.

                    J.C.
          Okay. Run over to the girls room.
          Now!

Jason bolts next door, followed by J.C.

OUTSIDE the sheriffs have their weapons drawn. They approach their room.

                SHERIFF # 1
          Come out with your hands up.

INSIDE, J.C. gives some last minute instructions.

                    J.C.
          I'm going to carry you out in front
          of me. Pretend you're my hostages.

                  JASON
          Again?

                  CHELSEA
          What if they shoot us.

                    J.C.
That'll never happen.

                 CHELSEA
Why, not?

                    J.C.
You're too rich. Now, hop on.

J.C. scoops up Jason and Chelsea with one arm and Courtney with the other.

                    J.C.
Hang on tight. Courtney, catch the
door.

                 COURTNEY
Why don't we just go with the police?

                    J.C.
And miss the party?

With her free hand she opens the door as they go OUTSIDE.

                SHERIFF # 2
Put your hands up.

                 COURTNEY
Who, me?

                SHERIFF # 2
No, him.

                  JASON
Me?

                SHERIFF # 1
No! You with the halo.

                    J.C.
If I raise my hands, I'll drop the kids.

With a single bound J.C. flies up and away. The two sheriffs can hardly believe their eyes. They jump back into the chopper and fly off after them.

INSIDE the Hammer Palace, Hammer barks out orders at Kirk's valet, Dicky, while the domestics finish up the BUFFET TABLE. Diana sits pensively.

109

                    HAMMER
          Dicky! Who put the pink vase on the
          buffet table?! Have you heard from
          Kirk?

Kirk and Chiquita enter. Diana perks up.

                    KIRK
          Hi, gang.

                    DIANA
          Where have you been? And who is she?

                    KIRK
          I thought you'd need more help.

                    DIANA
          An what's her specialty?

                    KIRK
          She gives good floor.

The domestic laugh.

                    HAMMER
          Shut up and get back to work! This
          palace has to be ready in one hour.
          Big shots from Washington and
          Hollywood are coming. Important
          people, you know?

                    KIRK
          Oh, yeah.

UP IN THE SKY, J.C. and the kids are now flying over San Diego. Soon, the police
helicopter catches up.

                    J.C.
          Hang on, kids.

He looms down to a lower level. The chopper follows.

INSIDE, the chopper, a PILOT confers with the two sheriffs.

PILOT
How is this guy flying?

They watch as J.C. does loops. They try and keep up. J.C. picks up speed and jets out of sight.

PILOT
I can't keep up. I'm going back.

He navigates the chopper around and heads the other way while Sheriff # 1 radios in.

OUTSIDE of the Hammer Palace, LIMOS pull up to the entrance. VALETS catch their doors and as CELEBRITIES and DIGNITARIES get out, the PRESS is soon upon them. SECURITY and FBI MEN surround the area. Methamin and Ruth are escorted from their limo. News woman, LORNA DIAZ, gets a quick interview.

LORNA DIAZ
Mr. Methamin. Lorna Diaz, CBF News.
Do you find all of this hoopla appropriate
for what should be a solemn occasion?

METHAMIN
If I may quote one of the greats. "Life is
for the living and may death come to
those who die."

LORNA DIAZ
Which great was that, pray tell?

METHAMIN
Hitler.

Methamin and Ruth enter the palace as another limo pulls up. Senator David Bitter, the FBI Chief and their WIVES are helped out. Lorna Diaz announces their arrival.

LORNA DIAZ
Senator Bitter, our FBI Chief and their
wives are also among the prestigious
guests here. This, the most publicized
eulogy party in recent memory.

INTERCUT - J.C. and KIDS - HAMMER PALACE

J.C. and the kids are now flying over the SAN ONOFRE NUCLEAR POWER PLANT. The two huge domes protrude from the Earth like the Grand Titons.

Two breasts are the focus as movie starlet, LINDA LONEHAND, stoops to conquer from her limo seat. She is accompanied by movie star, OWEN WILCOTT.

> LORNA DIAZ (O.S.)
> Ladies and gentlemen, Linda Lonehand
> and Owen Wilcott.

Lorna approaches them.

> LORNA DIAZ
> Linda, Owen. Will you stay for an interview,
> later?

Linda shakes her head, "no." Owen speaks into Lorna's mic.

> OWEN WILCOTT
> Sorry, but right after the buffet we have to
> get back to rehab.

J.C. and the kids fly over EL TORRO AIR FORCE BASE and are soon followed by TWO FIGHTER JETS. A jet zooms passed them. INSIDE the jet, a PILOT radios in his findings.

> PILOT
> I've got a Superman/Jesus prototype
> with three kids flying north. Affirmative.
> No, I have not been shrooming. Over.

Another limo pulls up. Bob Seil and his HAREM exit to vehicle to the red carpet.

J.C. and the kids are now flying over VENICE BEACH where a host of SIDE SHOW ACTS and WEIRDOS entertain. Two TOURISTS are watching as a MAN juggles four DEAD RATS. The tourists look up and see J.C. and the kids flying above.

> TOURIST # 1
> That's weird.

> TOURIST # 2
> (referring to juggler)
> No, *that's* weird.

INSIDE the Hammer palace, everyone is settling as they take their seats. Kirk takes a BURRITO from the buffet table and gives it to Chiquita. The sore on Kirk's face has gotten worse. Lorna Diaz and crew are taping in the back. John Hammer walks up to the podium and checks the microphone. In the audience, Ruth looks upon Hammer with disdain.

HAMMER
Good morning distinguished guests.
Grieving is not a pleasant experience. If I
may bring up to the podium, a woman who
paid the ultimate price. She lost two of her
babies. Grant Methamin's daughter, Ruth.
Let's hear it for her.

There's an exuberant applause as Ruth takes the podium.

RUTH
Thank you distinguished guests I'd
like to start out by saying that before
my ordeal at the SOPOE compound, I
was a heroin addict.

A gasp from the audience. Mortified, Methamin sinks in his chair.

RUTH
The terrorist, Jerry Collins helped cure
me from that addiction. The criminal,
Jerry Collins also helped cure my son,
Jason from his dependence to Ritalin.
When we were at the compound, I
wondered why the rescue effort was
so slow.

The FBI Chief sinks in his chair.

RUTH
It wasn't Jerry Collins who killed
those children. He did more to help
them than anybody in this room,
including me. My father and John
Hammer conspired to have me and
their grand children kidnapped so
that they could raise the prices of their
commodities. Through Bob Seil, they
duped Jerry Collins into kidnapping
us. Jerry abducted us, that's true, but...

Hammer will hear no more. He approaches the podium.

                    HAMMER
This woman suffers from delusions.
She obviously has not kicked her habit.

Linda and Owen sink in their chairs.

                    HAMMER
Security. Remove this woman.

TWO SECURITY GUARDS who are snaking canapés from the buffet, quickly munch down and head towards the podium.

                    RUTH
J.C.'s cause was noble. He didn't
kill those kids or anyone else.

                    HAMMER
That's rubbish and you know it.

The security men take Ruth from the podium. The audience sits in shock.

                    HAMMER
Jerry Collins killed those kids just
as sure as I'm standing here. To say
I took part in my own granddaughter's
demise is preposterous and insane.
Take that woman away!

Security takes Ruth to the palace entrance. From outside CHEERS can be heard. The limo drivers and valets seem to be hailing something. As security opens the door we now SEE the commotion.

OUTSIDE, J.C. and the kids make a soft landing on the red carpet. J.C. sets the kids down as some FBI men try to detain him. J.C. effortlessly picks them up and puts the men inside one of the limos.

                    J.C.
Stay.

INSIDE, J.C. enters and smiles at Ruth. Ruth and the security men look in awe.

                    HAMMER
Who is this person?

                    J.C.
Super Savior, at your service.

HAMMER
Well, you're not on the guest list. Get out!

Just then Courtney, Jason and Chelsea enter.

JASON
Mommy!

Ruth, Jason and Chelsea have an emotional reunion. Courtney runs to Diana's side. CHAOS. J.C. takes charge. He goes to the podium. His presence captivates the audience. The security men try to tackle J.C. and bounce off of him like rubber balls.

J.C.
Sorry to have interrupted your little
party, but I thought you might like
to see that the kids are okay.

J.C.'s tenure as the super Christ has met it's end. He slowly changes back to himself. The halo fades away.

J.C.
The public thought that the kids
were killed in the plane crash.

His glow is now reduced to his normal pallor. His robe fades into his jail fatigues.

J.C.
(as Nutty professor)
Sometimes you have to accept yourself
the way you are.

J.C. looks around. He has totally changed back to himself. The audience is mesmerized.

J.C.
The truth is, there's a conspiracy. Worse
than the Kennedy assassination, Watergate,
Iran/contra and the Iraq War. Complacency
is the conspirator. Money and power, the co
conspirators. And now here's a man who is
not only responsible for the death of two men,
but he also tried to burn these kids alive. Oh,
Kirk, you wanna stand up and do some time?

Kirk has disappeared. Chiquita unwraps a burrito.

115

COURTNEY
It's true, Kirk tried to kill us.

There is now total pandemonium. The FBI men and security try to locate Kirk. Lorna Diaz tries to interview anyone who will stop and speak. No one does. Linda Lonehand and Owen Wilcott leave. Senator and Mrs. Bitter are about to exit. Bitter spots Chiquita and signals to his wife to go on ahead.

Chiquita goes down on her burrito and it's love at first swallow. He approaches her and whispers in her ear. She waxes coy. He then sticks some cash down her blouse. She smiles. Hammer tries to regain control.

HAMMER
Please, everyone, take your seats.
This charlatan is filling your head
with lies. I can explain.

People grab goodies from the buffet table as they leave. Soon the palace is practically empty. Methamin approaches Jason.

METHAMIN
Let's go home, Jason.

Jason spits on him.

METHAMIN
That's my boy.

He then takes Jason by the arm. Jason pulls away.

JASON
No! I want to stay with J.C.

Methamin signals to security to escort Jason and Chelsea to the limo. Methamin takes Ruth by the arm.

METHAMIN
Let's go.
(to J.C.)
See you in court, pal.

TWO MONTHS LATER

INSIDE OF A COURTROOM IN LOS ANGELES

116

MUSIC – Jimi Hendrix's, *SPANISH CASTLE MAGIC*

Methamin is on the witness stand. He is being questioned by the PROSECUTING ATTORNEY. The JUDGE looks on contemplatively.

> PROSECUTING ATTORNEY
> Is the man responsible for your daughter and
> grandchildren's abduction in the courtroom?

> METHAMIN
> That's him, there.

He points to J.C. who sits at the defense table with Magdelin, Matthew, Mark, Stuke and their DEFENSE LAWYER. The JURY looks on attentively. The defense cross examines.

> DEFENSE LAWYER
> Your own daughter testified that you
> conspired to have your grandchildren
> kidnapped.

In the congregation, Ruth sits with Chelsea and Jason. Behind them, Courtney sits with Hammer, Kirk and Diana. Kirk has several band aids on his face.

John Hammer is now being cross examined by the Defense.

> DEFENSE LAWYER
> The prosecution claims that your caretaker,
> Filipe Binladen, was coerced by Jerry Collins
> to kidnap Courtney Manwaring.

> PROSECUTING ATTORNEY
> (objects)
> It's Benlada, your honor. Benlada!

> JUDGE
> Sustained.

Chelsea is now on the stand.

> CHELSEA
> J.C. read me bedtime stories.

Jason is now on the stand.

                            JASON
              J.C. got me off Ritalin. Now by my own
              will, I can chill.

Courtney is on the stand.

                            COURTNEY
              Kirk threw me back into the storage
              room. Then he and Chiquita went
              upstairs and Kirk set the house on fire.

OUTSIDE of the courthouse, TWO MARSHALS escort a MAN up the courthouse
steps. The man is quite handsome.

INSIDE the courtroom, the Prosecution questions Kirk as he reads from his notes.

                      PROSECUTING ATTORNEY
              Did anyone actually see you shoot and kill
              this ah, Captain Culo?

                            KIRK
              Nope.

                      PROSECUTING ATTORNEY
              The Prosecution rests.

The two marshals and the man enter the courtroom. The defense attorney makes a
motion.

                      DEFENSE ATTORNEY
              Your Honor, I'd like to bring to the stand,
              Sean Young.

There's a BUZZ in the courtroom. The marshals walk Sean to the gate. Sean takes
the stand. Everyone looks confused. Ruth has a sudden realization.

                            RUTH
              Oh, my God!

                            JUDGE
              Sean Young. I must say you looked
              shapelier in *No Way Out*.

                      DEFENSE ATTORNEY
              The witness recently had plastic surgery.

The BAILIFF swears Sean in.

                    BAILIFF
Do you swear to tell the truth, the whole
truth and nothing, but the truth, so help
you God?

                    SEAN
So help me, God.

This strikes a HEAVENLY CHORD which everyone responds to.

                    DEFENSE ATTORNEY
Mr. Young, were you at the SOPOE
compound?

                    SEAN
Yes, I was with Kirk when we raided
the SOPOE hideout. That assault left
two men dead. However, those men
shot each other in self defense.

                    DEFENSE ATTORNEY
Did Kirk Manwaring shoot and kill
Filipe Benlada?

                    SEAN
Yes.

                    KIRK
                (yells out)
That spic bastard stole my plane and
crashed it.

                    JUDGE
You are way, way out of order. Another
outburst and you're histo, mister. Continue
Mr. Young.

                    SEAN
Kirk and I went to the compound to rescue
the kids. However, we had an ulterior motive:
a possible reward. As it turned out, the kids
were in good hands.

SEAN (Cont'd)
Jerry Collins may have abducted the kids,
but I feel that the experience changed their
lives for the better. Especially Ruth. She
was a lost soul. I first met her at the Waco
compound. I was undercover and just before
the fire, I helped her escape. I was burned
very badly.

There's a BUZZ in the courtroom. Ruth takes the stand.

RUTH
My life was a blur during that period. I
barely remember those days with the
Branch Davidians. When I saw Sean walk
in with his new or shall I say old face, it all
came back.Thank you Sean.

They connect. It's love at second sight. Kirk yells out.

KIRK
This is bullshit! I tried to save those kids
and what did I get out of it? Jerry Collins
is no hero. I'm the fuckin' hero!

JUDGE
You are so in contempt that it's not even
funny. Guard!

Kirk has completely lost it as the guard drags him from the courtroom.

KIRK
I have rights. Attica! Attica! Soylent
Green is people!

Chaos has now ensued. The judge tries to get order as he HAMMERS his gavel.
The kids run up to J.C. and hug him.

JUDGE
Order in the court. Order!! Hey, don't
make me get up, damn it! Oh hell, this
court will be adjourn until tomorrow
at eleven AM.

Sean gets off of the stand and approaches J.C. They shake hands.

> J.C.
> You look better. Where'd you get the cash?

> SEAN
> A little dark mail.

Two guards escort Matthew, Mark, Stuke and Magdelin from the courtroom. One of the guards approaches J.C.

> GUARD
> It's time.

Magdelin smiles at J.C.

> J.C.
> Magdelin, this celibacy thing sucks.

They kiss.

DECEMBER 2008

In HEAVEN, God and Hendrix are shooting pool with a host of SOULS watching.

> GOD
> Eight ball, corner pocket.

God makes the shot. The souls CHEER. He turns to the CAMERA.

> GOD
> J.C. was acquitted. Methamin and
> Hammer paid major fines and are
> doing community service in Compton.

In COMPTON, Methamin and Hammer, dressed in fatigues, load big bags of debris from an old abandoned warehouse onto a dump truck.

> GOS (O.S.)
> And Kirk's doing a little time.

INSIDE of a PRISON SHOWER, Kirk is being cornered by SEVERAL INMATES.

> KIRK
> Hey, fellas, at least use some Vaseline
> this time, huh?

121

OUTSIDE of a HOUSE in the COUNTRY, it's a beautiful, sunny day. J.C., Magdelin, Sean and Jason are enjoying a picnic. They sing an old favorite.

> ALL
> Hey, Joe where you goin' with that
> gun in your hand?

Chelsea, gleefully runs out from the house.

> CHELSEA
> Diana called and said that Courtney
> can come visit us this weekend.

J.C. looks at a news headline that reads:

SPECIFIC MOTORS CHANGES WAYS – CONSUMERS CAN EXPECT CHANGES, CLEANER FUEL – ENVIRONMENTALISTS RALLY

They all join in for a group hug. Ruth comes out with some lemonade. She looks up.

> RUTH
> It's so nice to be out in the sun again
> without a fifty block and an umbrella.

Close on paper – the wind blows paper to page 2 – the headline reads:

OBAMA AND BIDEN MEET WITH NEW CABINET

The CAMERA PANS up to the SKY. It's a deep, rich, blue.

> GOD (O.S.)
> Try and keep the planet nice, huh?
> Take it away, Jimi.

As Jimi sings, the CAMERA PUSHES INTO some CLOUDS as the CREDITS ROLL.

> JIMI (O.S.)
> If a six turned out to be nine, etc.

> GOD (O.S.)
> What's that suppose to mean?

> HENDRIX (O.S.)
> Don't ask.

FADE OUT

DÉJÀ VU DÉJÀ VU

a comedy a comedy

Written by Pat Mulligan

FADE IN:

THE 1984 OLYMPICS

It's EARLY EVENING at the LOS ANGELES COLISEUM. After a day of pomp and circumstance, the final ceremony is the icing on the cake. A multitude of FLASHING LIGHTS flicker throughout the stands as people snap this historical event.

From his seat, BRAD WESTLAKE, age 31, finishes his beer and takes out his field glasses. From the POV of the field glasses, the show in the stadium. He moves his glasses up to the stands, randomly panning at a row of people. He passes an attractive woman, TIFFANY SILVER, age 31 and goes back to focus in on her.

> BRAD
> Holy shit.

He lowers the field glasses, gets an over view of the section she's in and scurries off in pursuit. Brad is now below Tiffany's section. Above her section is a huge BUDWEISER SIGN. Brad looks at her through the glasses. She notices and seems annoyed. She then takes out her binoculars and stares back at him. Brad drops his glasses and smiles. He then indicates to her to wait a second as he writes a note. He holds the note up.

You have a nice set...of binoculars.

Tiffany lowers her binoculars and laughs. He beckons to her to come down. She does. There's an awkward moment.

> BRAD
> Ah, I haven't seen a crowd this big
> since Woodstock.

> TIFFANY
> Oh, my God, you were at Woodstock?
> So was I.

> BRAD
> Cupid's a good shot today.

> TIFFANY
> Two hearts with one arrow.

MUSIC - JIMI HENDRIX'S, *BOLD AS LOVE*

A SHOT of the sky above. Speeding through the upper atmosphere to the stratosphere, we are now zooming towards the stars. Suddenly we do an about-face as our world is shrinking. Our planet is now projected on a large SCREEN.

The images on the screen change as if someone were switching channels on a television. The CNN logo appears with some of the events of the day.

THE FOURTH DIMENSION

The screen is in a classroom. Beings similar to humans watch. They are androgynous and differ only in size. An alien TEACHER steps in front of the screen and addresses the class.

> TEACHER
> Welcome to Interdimensional Socio
> 101. We've learned about cultures on
> different worlds. Some years ago we
> discovered another dimension.

As the teacher continues, images from the screen behind him project a rapid trip through history. From the DINOSAURS to NEIL ARMSTRONG setting foot on the moon.

> TEACHER
> We found a galaxy in the Third
> Dimension. The beings on a planet
> known as Earth have become textbook
> study because of their complexities. In
> today's lesson we'll visit two typical
> Americans from the Nineteen Eighties
> whom we have monitored.

More images. The SEVENTIES. VIETNAM, WATERGATE and JIMMY CARTER.

> TEACHER
> We were fascinated with a generation
> called Baby Boomers, a very dynamic
> group. They experienced a diverse
> shifting of values. From their youthful
> protests and anti-establishment activities
> of the Sixties.

On screen, there's a shot of ABBIE HOFFMAN smoking a joint in front of the Capital building in Washington DC.

126

TEACHER

To self the self-serving of the Seventies.

JOHN TRAVOLTA'S famous disco pose from *SATURDAY NIGHT FEVER.*

TEACHER

To the materialistic, greed oriented
adults of the Eighties.

In court, IVAN BOESKY is being indicted. The next image is a man at a THINK TANK
SESSION. It's Brad, a few years after we first saw him. On a blackboard behind him
are the words, "Operation Clean Bomb."

TEACHER

The year is Nineteen Eighty Seven.
This is one of our subjects. His name
is Brad Westlake, age thirty-four. The
company he works for, Rand Mac,
develops high-tech weapons.

BRAD

And I believe the ray, from the right
projectile could wipe out a whole
city without any residual radiation
or toxicity. And the best part is, it
won't make any racket. Now our
enemies can get a good night's sleep
before they're annihilated.

TEACHER (O.S.)

This is the same human who protested
a war they had fifteen years prior.

A shot of a YOUNGER, HIPPY-CLAD BRAD at a peace rally.

Back at the think tank session, there are several other MEN. One of them is Dick
JENNINGS, Brad's boss. He sits at the head of his corporate, mahogany table. He
flashes Brad an envious gaze.

JENNINGS

Clean Bomb? We tried to sell them on
the Neutron Bomb ten years ago. It
bombed.

                    BRAD
          Yes Mr. Jennings, but this bomb is a
          kinder, gentler bomb. Congress will
          love it.

Some other men at the table.

                    MEN
          Yeah! Here, here!

Jennings glares at them.

OUTSIDE OF RAND MAC, NEW YORK HEADQUARTERS it's a beautiful October
day. TWO GUARDS toss Brad into the street. Jennings bids him farewell.

                    JENNINGS
          You'll never build bombs in this town
          again, pal.

Brad picks himself up and dusts himself off. Across the street he looks up at SAINT
LUKES CHURCH.

INSIDE OF THE CHURCH. Brad enters A CONFESSIONAL BOOTH. He kneels and
blesses himself.

                    BRAD
          Bless me Father for I have sinned. It's been
          years since my last confession. In fact, the
          last time I was in a church was for my mother's
          funeral. I've broken *all* of the commandments.
          Including the big one, number six. Well, I didn't
          kill anyone directly, see. I used to design bombs.
          They kill. And I drink too much. I guess it's guilt
          from building all of the bombs. But the money
          was so good, Father. I guess I'm also guilty of
          greed and ah…

From the other side of the screen there's a SNORING sound.

                    BRAD
          Father? Father!

                    PRIEST (O.S.)
          Zzzzzzzzzzz.

Brad leaves the booth dejected.

TWO WEEKS LATER

OUTSIDE OF A WALL STREET OFFICE BUILDING. PEOPLE enter and exit. INSIDE, an office door reads: TIFFANY SILVER - MARKET ANALYST.

In her office, Tiffany, an immaculate business woman, is at her computer. She looks worried. She cleans her ear with a Q-Tip.

> TEACHER (O.S.)
> This is Brad's significant other of
> three of their years, which is about
> eighteen minutes to us. She is, to use
> some parlance of the time, a "yuppie
> weasel." Prior to this, Tiffany, oddly
> enough was a humanitarian.

The teacher projects some slides of a YOUNGER TIFFANY working with disadvantaged children. The CAMERA PUSHES IN and the slides are now LIVE ACTION.

In her class, Tiffany has a LITTLE BOY with Cerebral Palsy sitting on her lap. There are other CHILDREN sitting on the floor. They are all happily singing. A WOMAN enters the room and takes Tiffany aside.

> WOMAN
> Well, Tiffany, they've finally done
> it. They've cut this program. We
> couldn't get funding. I'm sorry.

A tear comes to Tiffany's eye as she hugs the little boy.

> TEACHER (O.S.)
> Soon Tiffany got caught up in the
> establishment that she once deplored.

From the screen Brad enters Tiffany's office building. INSIDE, Brad takes an elevator.

> TEACHER (O.S.)
> It's October Nineteenth, Nineteen Eighty
> Seven. "The Crash." A day that marked
> the epitome of the greed that ran rampant
> in America in the Nineteen Eighties.

As Brad enters Tiffany's office, the action continues in the Third Dimension.

BRAD
(sweating it)
Tiffany, love, you look fabulous! Hey,
got a great tip on some junk bonds.

She sensuously saunters up to Brad and slaps his face.

BRAD
I'd turn the other cheek, but I just
had some orthodontia.

TIFFANY
You slimy weasel.

BRAD
In what respect?

She gets ready to whack him again.

BRAD
I've been swamped.

TIFFANY
For two weeks?!

BRAD
(the truth)
Trouble at the bomb store. I got
fired and went on a little binge.

TIFFANY
Must be some hangover.

Brad favors his stinging face. In the background some BODIES drop down past the windows. The phone RINGS. Tiffany picks up.

TIFFANY
Not again! How many points? A
complete crash? Sell what's left.
(hangs up)
The market just tumbled. I'm ruined.

BRAD
Welcome to the club.

Tiffany weeps. Brad takes her in his arms.

> BRAD
> Come on, Honey. The hell with this
> rat race. Let's sell *your* BMW and hit the
> interstate. Let's let our hair down for a
> change, lay back and get back to our roots.
> (looks at her hair)
> And speaking of roots. You're about
> due for a touch up.

Tiffany looks in the mirror and laughs. She then pulls out several Kleenex tissues from a drawer marked "tissues," folds them up and wipes her tears.

> TIFFANY
> We worked so hard. For what?
> (a beat)
> Why did they let you go?

> BRAD
> Jennings liked my ideas. Enough to steal
> them and fire me. Hey! Let's drive up to
> the Catskills?
> (flashes peace sign)
> It's like near Woodstock, man.

> TIFFANY
> Do you know where I can score some
> Acetylsalicylic acid, man?

> BRAD
> That's aspirin.

> TIFFANY
> I know. I've got a headache.

THE NEXT DAY ON A COUNTRY ROAD IN UPSTATE NEW YORK.

INSIDE Brad's car, Brad and Tiffany are engaged in their own version of Trivial Pursuit.

> TIFFANY
> August Tenth, Nineteen Eighty Four.

                    BRAD
Let's see. The L.A. Olympics. No Russians,
so we kicked ass in gymnastics. The stock
market entered two thousand, plus. And the
press coins the phrase "Star Wars" for SDI.

                    TIFFANY
What else?

                    BRAD
That's it.

                    TIFFANY
                  (nudging)
Brad! That's the day we met.

                    BRAD
Big deal.

Tiffany playfully bites Brad's ear.

                    BRAD
Hey!

Brad puts his free arm around Tiffany's shoulder. Tiffany waxes misty. A tear drops
down on Brad's hand, which is gently caressing her ample breast.

                    BRAD
Tiffany, did you have your hooters
augmented?

                    TIFFANY
No, dearest.

                    BRAD
No, no. These babies are huge. Are
you pregnant?

                    TIFFANY
I was going to tell you.

                    BRAD
Who's the mother?

                    TIFFANY
          I don't know, but you're the father.
          I think.

                    BRAD
          That's what I get for letting you
          carpool with five other guys.

                    TIFFANY
          But, they used protection. You don't.
          It's got to be yours, honey.

                    BRAD
          Ah, so a kid. Clothes, puberty, college.
          That's going to take money, honey and
          we be broke.

WHITE LAKE - LATE AFTERNOON. Brad pulls off of the road. They both exit Brad's
BMW and stroll towards the lake.

                    BRAD
          Later on, what do you say we drive
          over to Bethel and bask in our old
          Woodstock memories. Hopefully
          we'll have an acid flashback or two.

                    TIFFANY
          Does that mean we have to pay the
          guy we scored it from a residual?

                    BRAD
                    (laughing)
          I never get a flashback when I want
          one. They usually occur when I'm
          operating heavy machinery.
                    (a beat)
          What's the matter?

                    TIFFANY
          I think it's morning sickness.

AN AERIAL VIEW OF THE OCTOBER COUNTRYSIDE

                    BRAD
This is why I love the East. But in
about a month, I'll be missing L.A.

                    TIFFANY
So, what are we going to do?

Brad takes out a joint.

                    BRAD
Well, first I'm gonna smoke this doob…

                    TIFFANY
No, I mean, with our lives. What are
we going to do for cash?

                    BRAD
Don't have a clue darlin'. My high tech
weapon days are over. Undoubtedly,
Dick Jennings has stolen my doomsday
idea. Ah, I should've stayed in show-biz.

                    TIFFANY
Show-biz? You were on the *Dating
Game*. Once. You lost.

Brad grimaces while Tiffany fusses with her purse. She pulls out a ROLL OF FILM
and puts it back.

                    TIFFANY
Everything's come to a head so quickly.
A few days ago we were successful
yuppie weasels.

                    BRAD
And now we're the scorn of our
generation.

                    TIFFANY
Oh, God. I'd give anything to go back
to a simpler time. No responsibilities,
no deadlines…

                    BRAD
No money.

                              TIFFANY
                    It's always something.

Brad lights up the joint. We now SEE this from the screen in the classroom. Suddenly
Brad and Tiffany FREEZE as the teacher stops the action from the control panel.

                              TEACHER
                    All right class. This is where our
                    experiment begins. You are about
                    to experience something that few
                    before you have witnessed. We are
                    going to eject Brad and Tiffany from
                    their time and insert them into another.

A student named ZWEETHANE interrupts.

                              ZWEETHANE
                    How is that possible?

                              TEACHER
                    Well, Zweethane, there are different
                    parallels of time relationships between
                    our two dimensions. The Third
                    Dimension is more transparent and
                    is easier to manipulate. Ironically, we
                    couldn't do this in our own dimension.

The teacher is about to set the INTERDIMENSIONAL TIME MODE, when he
asks…

                              TEACHER
                    What year should we send them to?
                    Perthud.

A student named PERTHUD smiles mischievously.

                              PERTHUD
                    Let's send them back to their Prehistoric
                    Age and see if they can fast-talk a
                    Tyrannosaurus Rex.

                              TEACHER
                    Interesting, but let's keep it in the realm
                    of Brad and Tiffany's own past. A time
                    that would be more relevant to them.

ZWEETHANE
Their generation had an extreme values
swing from the Sixties to the Eighties.
Brad and Tiffany just spoke of going back
to their roots and visiting this Woodstock
place. Let's put them back to when they
first went there.

TEACHER
Excellent. Let's see…

The teacher refers his computer. He projects it on the screen. THIRD DIMENSION
-EARTH - TWENTIETH CENTURY - 1969 - WOODSTOCK FESTIVAL - AUGUST
15TH, 16TH, & 17TH.

TEACHER
Let's give them a day to get there.

He sets the Interdimensional Time Mode.

TEACHER
August Fourteenth, Nineteen Sixty Nine,
at say, 11:30 A.M.

On the panel there are several time altering mechanisms. Near the VORTEX key is
the REVERSE key. He hits reverse.

On the screen, Brad and Tiffany DISSAPEAR and then REAPPEAR as they pass
through time. The jolt knocks them unconscious. The camera PUSHES INTO the
screen.

Brad and Tiffany start to come around and are a bit dazed and confused. Brad is
still holding the joint that he lit. He looks at it and then tosses it. He then rises, picks
Tiffany up and straightens her.

BRAD
What the hell was that? Are you okay
honey?

TIFFANY
I'm jonesing for some Haagen-Daz.

BRAD
Mmm, you're okay. Was that an earthquake?
Wow! Better get back to the car.

Brad looks around, bewildered.

>   BRAD
>   Wait a minute. Tiffany, look at the trees.
>   They're all green. A minute ago everything
>   was in full October drag. And it's hot as
>   hell. When we left the car, it was cool.

Brad checks his Rolex.

>   BRAD
>   My watch says three P.M. But, look at our
>   shadows. It's not even noon yet. Maybe
>   we were unconscious all night.

>   TIFFANY
>   All night and several months.

>   BRAD
>   If it were months, I'd have a beard.

>   TIFFANY
>   And I'd have a baby.

>   BRAD
>   This is way, weird.

Brad and Tiffany walk back towards the car when they notice something very odd.
They're not the only ones walking on this desolated road, deep in the boonies. There
are several groups of people, mainly YOUNG ADULTS. They all look as though
they're going to some kind of Sixties revival. Brad addresses one of the kids.

>   BRAD
>   Hey, what's going on? Where are
>   you guys going?

>   KID
>   Where are we going?

Everyone in the group laughs.

>   KID
>   That's a good one. Where are we going?
>   Like, the same place you're goin', man.

137

                         TIFFANY
              Ah, like where might that be, man?

The group laughs again. A GIRL in the group comments on Tiffany's attire.

                           GIRL
              Far out threads. Where you guys from?

                         TIFFANY
              Originally, my mom.

The crowd has another chuckle. A BLACK DUDE with a huge Afro addresses
them.

                       BLACK DUDE
              If whatever you guys are smokin' is
              on the market, I wanna get me some.

The group passes on, laughing hysterically. Soon, a group of older looking HIPPIES
types catch up.

                         HIPPIE
              Far out threads, man.

                          BRAD
              Thanks. Hey look, we're lost.
              Where's everybody going?

                         HIPPIE
              Oh, wow, man. You *are* lost. We're
              going to the Woodstock Festival.

                          BRAD
              Oh, are they having some sort of
              revival?

                         HIPPIE
              Revival! Are you on ludes? Janis is going
              to be there. The Who, Hendrix, Santana.
              Everybody!

As the group starts off, Brad calls out.

                          BRAD
              Hey! I know this is going to sound stupid,
              but what's today's date?

                           138

                    HIPPIE
          The date. I donno…it's the fourteenth,
          I think.

Brad and Tiffany look at each other.

                    TIFFANY
          The fourteenth of what?

A CHICK in the group shows her a local newspaper that she has wadded up to roll joints on. Some pot spills out.

                    CHICK
          Here. It's today's paper.

Brad and Tiffany examine the paper. It reads:

BETHEL GAZETTE August 14th, 1969 Morning Edition

THOUSANDS EXPECTED TO INVADE REGION

The highly publicized festival originally scheduled at Woodstock has been moved to Max Yasgur's farm in Bethel.

                    BRAD
          This is today's paper?!

                    CHICK
          Fresh off the press. Keep it. You
          wanna join us?

                    BRAD
                  (stunned)
          That's okay, thanks.

The Hippies press on. Brad and Tiffany are flabbergasted.

                    TIFFANY
          All right, what's going on here?

From a distance, a big RED CHEVY comes rolling up the road. Tiffany waves it down. A straight looking FAMILY of locals sit gawking. The driver, DAD, speaks up.

                    DAD
          Howdy.

TIFFANY
Howdy. Ah…nice car. I…I know this
is going to sound strange, but what
year is this?

DAD
Nineteen Sixty Nine Chevy.

BRAD
Oh, ah, well. It's in mint condition.

DAD
Well, it better be. It's brand new. Can
we help you with something?

BRAD
Brand new? Come on! Are you trying
to tell us that this is Nineteen Sixty Nine?

DAD
Well of course it is. I think you folks
need to get out of the sun.

Dad drives off in a huff. As the car heads out, Brad spots the license plate tag. It
reads:

1969

BRAD
Oh my God. This can't be possible.
                    (pinches himself)
Tiffany, is this happening?!

TIFFANY
Far as I can tell. Do you think this
could be attributable to that earthquake?

BRAD
I don't know. Let's see. Nineteen
Eighty Seven to Nineteen Sixty Nine.
We're having an eighteen year
flashback.

                    TIFFANY
But this one's in living breathing
color. And a flashback that won't
stop. I wonder what Einstein would
call this?

                    BRAD
Déjà vu hell. This *has* to be a dream.

                    TIFFANY
Brad, but what if it isn't.

                    BRAD
Well, if it isn't, at least we get to
experience Woodstock again. Let's
leave the car where it is and hitch.

Brad and Tiffany have been walking for about an hour.

                    BRAD
                  (signing)
By the time we got to Woodstock,
we had a half a million blisters.
                  (speaks)
We've been thumbing for miles. I
wonder why nobody's picking us up?

                    TIFFANY
It must be these Eighties clothes.
We probably look like narcs. This
is so strange.

                    BRAD
Yeah. I just realized. I left my wallet
in the car, with all my credit cards.

                    TIFFANY
                  (facetious)
Who needs money, man. This is the Sixties.

Tiffany flashes the "peace sign" when a school bus/hippie wagon passing by comes
to an abrupt stop. The HIPPIE DRIVER opens the bus door.

                  HIPPIE DRIVER
Peace, man. Need a ride?

Brad and Tiffany climb aboard.

MUSIC - CROSBY, STILLS AND NASH - *WOODSTOCK*

Soon the bus gets caught up in a massive traffic jam as young people from all over the country head to Yasgur's farm.

INSIDE the hippie wagon there are ten full-fledged, hippies on board. FIVE CHICKS, FOUR DUDES and one we're not too sure of. They are all tripping and passing a joint. They AD LIB some introductions. One of the dudes addresses Tiffany. His name is GROOVE. He passes a joint to Tiffany.

> GROOVE
> Hey, you wanna ball?

> TIFFANY
> I'm sorry Groove, but I'm not into
> contact sports.

This elicits a LAUGH from the others. A chick named CLOUD addresses Brad.

> CLOUD
> Are like, you guys, like over thirty
> or something?

> BRAD
> Yeah, thirty something.

> CLOUD
> Wow, I dig older cats. Let's get it on,
> man.

As Cloud disrobes, Brad looks to Tiffany for a way out.

> TIFFANY
> Ah, Cloud. We're ah, married.

> CLOUD
> Like, so what?

> TIFFANY
> Well, Brad here is a...also gay!

Just then, the hippie we're not too sure of begins to strip. His name is EASY.

EASY

Gay? Where have you been all my life?

BRAD

Well ya see, Easy, I'm really into
gay...animals. Yeah.

EASY

Far out!

Easy gives a WHISTLE and from the rear of the bus, a huge GERMAN SHEPHERD
springs up and barks, WOOFY.

TIFFANY

Oh, my stars. This is our stop!

THE WOODSTOCK FESTIVAL

It's the NEXT DAY. Brad and Tiffany have secured themselves a spot about a
quarter mile from the stage. They have nothing but the clothes on their backs and
it's beginning to RAIN. THUNDER AND LIGHTNING permeate the surroundings.
From the speakers, the voice of WAVY GRAVY.

WAVY GRAVY

Stay away from the speaker towers.
You may get zapped by lightning.
And anybody who's taken the brown
acid report to the bummer tent.

MONTAGE - SANTANA. RICHIE HAVENS. COUNTRY JOE AND THE FISH. SHA
NANA. THE GREATFUL DEAD.

During the Dead, Brad looks around.

BRAD

You know, Tif. The only one here
older than us is Jerry Garcia.
(delirious)
I was here when this first happened. A
younger me could be here someplace.
Let's go look for me.

TIFFANY

I was here, too. But I wouldn't know
me if I saw me.

143

Some HIPPIES sitting near them hear this.

                    HIPPIE # 1
        Wow!

                    HIPPIE # 2
        Must be the brown acid.

MONTAGE - CROSBY, STILLS AND NASH. SLY AND THE FAMILY STONE. TEN YEARS AFTER. JOE COCKER. THE WHO.

It's now EVENING. Brad and Tiffany have been awake for about twenty four hours. They're tired, hungry and dirty.

                    TIFFANY
                (whining)
        I'm a thirty-four year JAP. What am
        I doing here? I've got to be the only
        JAP here.

THREE JAPANESE KIDS are sitting right in front of them. They turn around and glare. They, then take out their CAMERAS and take Tiffany's picture.

                    TIFFANY
        Oy vay, I'm so embarrassed. Brad, what
        are we doing here?

                    BRAD
        I don't know. When I was a kid this
        was phenomenal. As an adult, this
        sucks. I want my BMW.

                    TIFFANY
        I need a manicure.

They both nod off for a while.

DAWN. ON STAGE, JIMI HENDRIX is now playing *THE STAR SPANGLED BANNER*. The rocket-like sounds of Hendrix's guitar jar them awake.

                    BRAD
                (groggy)
        Tif, it's the National Anthem. We've got to
        stand now. It's Hendrix. He was so patriotic.

144

TIFFANY
What do you mean, *was.* Was is *now!*

They both scream. A delirious Brad exclaims.

BRAD
I want to go back to Nineteen Eighty Seven.

As Brad and Tiffany bolt off, the two Hippies look at each other. One of them comments.

HIPPIE # 1
Wow! I wish *I* were that fucked-up.

THE NEXT DAY our disillusioned time travelers wearily get out of a STATION WAGON that's filled to capacity. A MAN, his WIFE, MOTHER-IN-LAW and FIVE screaming KIDS wave good-bye as they drive off.

BRAD (O.S.)
I think it would have been more
enjoyable driving back with that
German Shepherd.

TIFFANY
My kingdom for a Diet Coke, some bagels
and cream cheese. A Calgon bath, a massage,
satin sheets, a Broadway show, a career.
Oh yeah, and a life in my own time!

BRAD
How 'bout oral sex?

TIFFANY
My throat's got a headache.

As they approach the spot where the BMW was parked, an exhausted Brad comes to a realization. His face drops as he looks at a vacant lot.

BRAD
The car's gone! Of course, it hasn't
been built yet.

TIFFANY
Deep down I knew it, but I kept
hoping hat that maybe I was having
a real long, bad dream.

                    BRAD
That means we haven't been here yet.
Which means...

They both scream.

                    TIFFANY
Our Beemer's gone! All of our stuff
was in the trunk!

                    BRAD
Our credit cards are gone!

They embrace each other and weep.

                    BRAD
Why us, Tiffany? What are we going
to do now? We're like two carp out of
water. We have no identity, no money.

                    TIFFANY
Wait, Brad, I have some money in my bag.

She takes out her billfold and whips out a fistful of dollars. The roll of film drops out
of her bag. She retrieves it. She then takes the money and kisses it.

                    TIFFANY
Oh, thank God! There's enough here
to take a cab back to the city.

                    BRAD
Cab? Tiffany, get yourself a merry
little grip. We're a hundred and fifty
miles from Manhattan. We're going
to have to take a bus.

                    TIFFANY
                    (freaks)
A bus?!! I've never taken a bus in my
life! I'm going to vomit.

As Tiffany vomits, Brad rolls his eyes.

                    BRAD
When you're done, we need to find
a place to sleep. It's getting dark.

It's the NEXT AFTERNOON. Brad and Tiffany stumble onto an old gas station/general store/Greyhound bus stop. Brad spots a poster for the Broadway Musical, *HAIR*.

                        BRAD
        I wonder if we're stuck in the past?

                        TIFFANY
        If that's the case, we'll have to get
        back to the future the old fashioned
        way. One day at a time.

                        BRAD
        And by the time we get to the present,
        we'll be too old to enjoy the future.

They enter the little hole in the wall bus depot. INSIDE, Tiffany reminds Brad.

                        TIFFANY
        And let's not forget, Buster, I'm
        pregnant. Are we keeping it? If so,
        we're getting married.

                        BRAD
        I think I'm gonna puke.

As Brad runs to the men's room, Tiffany rolls her eyes. She then addresses a TICKET CLERK.

                        TIFFANY
        When is the next bus to New York?

                        TICKET CLERK
        In about four hours.

                        TIFFANY
        Oy, fucking vay.

                        TICKET CLERK
        Beg your pardon?

                        TIFFANY
        Ah, two tickets, one way.

Later, INSIDE THE BUS, Brad and Tiffany sit, stewing. It's a typical bus ride down Route 17 to New York. Some OLD PEOPLE and a few SMELLY TRANSIENTS. Toward the back of the bus, a BLACK WOMAN is trying to control her FOUR KIDS. A MAN sitting in front of them, obviously hung-over, tries his hand at shutting them up.

MAN

Would you shut them fuckin' kids up?!

BLACK WOMAN

How would you like to kiss my big,
black, bubbly ass?

MAN

Okay.

Brad is now in an ugly mood and curses the world, while Tiffany sobs.

BRAD

How the fuck did this happen? Is
it sun spots? Or just a bucket of
bad karma. Now we're stuck in
this time travel turd-lock. So we
have to go through the…
                    (figures in head)
next eighteen years knowing what's
going to happen.
                    (a beat)
Son of a bitch!

His eyes light up as an idea hits him like a Sidewinder Missile blowing up a falafel
cart.

BRAD

This is fantastic!

TIFFANY

What are you talking about?

BRAD

Don't you see? This has all happened
before and provided it's all going to
happen again, we have an edge. We
know the future. As a market analyst
you should realize the implications.

                    TIFFANY
          But Brad, you an I doing *this* has
          never happened before.

                    BRAD
          True, but we were at Woodstock.
          and it was all in tact, just the way
          it happened before.

                    TIFFANY
          So us reliving this hasn't altered
          anything?

                    BRAD
          So far it hasn't.

From outside of a SAVARIN STATION, the bus pulls in for a rest stop.

INSIDE, in the cafeteria line, Brad and Tiffany load up their trays with food.

                    BRAD
          What's the date?

                    TIFFANY
          Ah, let's see. I think it's the twentieth.

                    BRAD
          August Twentieth, Nineteen Sixty Nine.
          Did anything historic happen on this date?

                    TIFFANY
          I'm sure I don't remember. You're the
          one with the long term memory.

                    BRAD
          Well, if my memory serves me, Charley
          Manson and the kids got busted right
          after Woodstock. I'm going to get a paper.
          Gimme some money.

She gives him a few dollars.

                    TIFFANY
          They only have lemonade and iced tea
          here. Get me a Diet Coke.

149

Brad takes the money and goes over to the convenience store section of the station.

INSIDE THE STORE, Brad cruises the soda selections and makes an observation.

> BRAD
> No Diet Coke. It's Nineteen Sixty Nine.

He spots the prices and chuckles.

> BRAD
> Love these 'Sixty Nine prices.

He grabs a Tab and goes over to the counter and gets a paper. The headline reads:

NIXON ORDERS WESTMORLAND TO BEEF UP AIR STRIKES

> BRAD
> (to himself)
> Let's see, this dumb war won't end
> for another six years.

At the counter, a redneck STORE MANAGER hears this.

> STORE MANAGER
> How the hell do you know?

Brad sets the Tab, a Mounds bar and the newspaper on the counter.

> BRAD
> Ah…because the Vietnamese breed
> faster than we can kill them.

> STORE MANAGER
> Six years, shit! With our air superiority,
> we'll wipe those gooks out faster 'n you
> can suck shit through a pipe. That'll be
> sixty cents.

> BRAD
> For all this? I love it!

Brad takes his change, bag and exits singing.

150

                         BRAD
Life is lovelier the second time around.

                   STORE MANANGER
Commie faggot.

Back in the cafeteria, at a table, Tiffany files her nails while Brad scans the paper
making sure all is in place with history.

                         BRAD
Here's a blurb about the Tate-
LaBianca murders…arrest hippies
at Spahn ranch…Helter Skelter.

                       TIFFANY
How's that?

                         BRAD
The Manson kids killed LaBianca
as a "copy cat killing" diversion, to
trip up the fuzz from the Tate
slayings. Sharon Tate was hot, too.

                       TIFFANY
Hmm. Psychos on acid.

                         BRAD
Ah! Here's something about Woodstock.

                       TIFFANY
Does it say anything about how
many nails I broke?

                         BRAD
No, but it coins the festival and it's
incredibly well-behaved participants
as the "Woodstock Generation."

                       TIFFANY
So, Mr. Westlake, is everything in
it's historical lot?

                         BRAD
Yes and we're going to cash in on it.

TIFFANY
Be careful. Messing around with the
future can get you in trouble.

BRAD
How do you know?

TIFFANY
I saw it in a movie.

Tiffany points to her tummy.

TIFFANY
Now, I guess we can support our
little package.

BRAD
Designer clothes, private schools.
Y'all come back now, rich.

MUSIC - THE BEATLE'S, *COME TOGETHER*

A SERIES OF SHOTS - DAY

A) Brad and Tiffany on the bus - New York City in the background.

B) Brad and Tiffany visit old haunts - They approach what used to be Brad's old work
place, OUTSIDE OF A CHURCH.

BRAD
Look, Tiff, there's no Rand Mac. It's
a church. From church to weapons
development. Armageddon, or what?

C) They visit Tiffany's old work place INSIDE, ON AN OFFICE DOOR reads: Mark
Silverman - Market Analyst.

TIFFANY
Not too much has changed here. Good
old Wall Street.

It's LATE AFTERNOON. Brad and Tiffany enter a HOTEL. INSIDE the LOBBY, Brad
and Tiffany walk over to a row of public phones. Brad takes a phone book and starts
scanning.

                          BRAD
          Well, we're eighteen years older in
          this time space. Nobody knows us.
          I'm going to check one more place.

Brad fingers a number, picks up the phone, deposits a dime and rotary dials.

                          BRAD
          Hello. Mrs. Popelsdorf, please. Mrs.
          Popelsdorf? I'm trying to locate Brad
          Westlake. Is he at the orphanage?

From the other line, MRS. POPELSDORF, a middle aged woman, speaks.

                     MRS. POPELSDORF
               (upset)
          No, he's not. He's not.

INTERCUT - BRAD AND MRS. POPELSDORF

                          BRAD
          Do you know where he is?

                     MRS. POPELSDORF
          No, he vanished a, a week or so ago. Is
          this the police?

                          BRAD
          No, I'm a friend of his mother, God rest
          her soul. You say he just vanished?

                     MRS. POPELSDORF
          Yes. He never came back from lunch
          break. He was always adventuresome.
          He talked to his friends about going to
          that Woodstock place. The police think
          he went there. I don't know why he
          hasn't come back.

She begins to cry.

                          BRAD
          Hey, now. Don't fret. Well, thank you
          and don't worry, I'm okay.

                          153

                    MRS. POPELSDORF
          Huh?

Brad hangs up.

                    MRS. POPELSDORF
          Hello. Hello!

GREENWICH VILLAGE - AN OUTDOOR CAFÉ

It's a week later. Tiffany is ordering coffee to a WAITRESS, while Brad looks at snapshots of the film that Tiffany had in her purse when they transcended time.

                    TIFFANY
          Cappuccino, iced, decaf. Do you have
          Equal?

                    WAITRESS
          Equal?

                    TIFFANY
          Oh, just make it Sweet N" Low.
                    (to Brad)
          I keep getting my future brands mixed
          up with past brands.

CLOSE UP OF PHOTOS - DATE ON PHOTOS - OCTOBER 1987

                    BRAD (O.S.)
          The future *is* the past, hon. So, did
          you meet anyone from your past?

                    TIFFANY (O.S.)
          Present dear.

                    BRAD
          It does get confusing, doesn't it?
                    (referring to snapshots)
          Jeez, we sure look cool in these
          Eighties clothes.

A PHOTO OF TIFFANY WITH TWO OLD FOLKS

TIFFANY

I miss my aunt Shirley. My uncle
thinks I ran away because of him.
He was such a schmuck.

BRAD

Well, Tiff, I think it's safe to go
ahead with the show. To be sure
there's no connection, I'm
changing my last name to Scott.

He takes an engagement ring from a small jewelry box and puts the ring on Tiffany's finger.

BRAD

And yours too.

TIFFANY
(overwhelmed)

Oh, Brad!

BRAD

It's about time, huh? *And* I got us
fake Social Security cards.

He gives Tiffany her card.

BRAD

Plus, our being married will help sell
the show.

Tiffany flashes Brad a dirty look. Brad gets a paper and grazes the headlines.

BRAD

I spoke with some hanchos over at
CBS last week and told them what
would be in today's paper. Look at
these headlines. NASA Launches
Apollo12. It's all here, just as I
brilliantly predicted. We meet with
them today. They're sure to bite.

OUTSIDE OF CBS HEADQUARTERS, Brad and Tiffany exit a cab and enter the building.

INSIDE OF A CBS BOARDROOM, Brad and Tiffany are being interviewed by some CBS BIG-WIGS. They all rise. One of the wigs shakes Brad's hand.

A FEW DAYS LATER, Brad and Tiffany exit a door marked DEVELOPMENT. Brad is jubilant. Tiffany seems worried.

> BRAD
> That went beautifully. One more set of
> predictions and we start shooting the
> pilot. Let's go do some homework.

> TIFFANY
> I don't know, Brad. Look, I know the
> stock market. I know what to buy and
> sell now. I could make us a fortune in
> the privacy of our own living room. Why
> do we have to let the whole world in on it?

> BRAD
> Show-biz, baby.

As they approach the elevator, there's a sign marked ELEVATOR OUT OF ORDER.

> TIFFANY
> Tsk. Now I have to walk down two
> flights in these heels.

Brad walks over to the stairwell and opens the door.

> BRAD
> Ladies first.

Tiffany walks through and as she does, her heel gets caught in a crack. She trips and as she plummets down the stairs, Tiffany screams out in pain. From behind the stairwell door, Brad cries out.

> BRAD (O.S.)
> Tiffany!!!

INSIDE A HOSPITAL ROOM, Tiffany is lying in bed with an IV hook-up. Brad has just walked in.

TIFFANY
(weeping)
Brad, I lost the baby.

Brad steps over to the bed and gently caresses her forehead. He then gently kisses her cheek.

BRAD
Oh, Tiffany, I'm so sorry. Don't
worry honey, we'll try again.

TIFFANY
The doctor said I'll never have children
again.

Tiffany tries her best to be stoic, but sobs uncontrollably.

The CAMERA PUSHES BACK as we SEE this action on screen in the CLASSROOM. The students seem perplexed. Zweethane raises her hand.

TEACHER
Zweethane?

ZWEETHANE
This pregnancy thing. Tiffany loses
the baby and Brad says, "We'll try
again." Do they need each other to
procreate?

TEACHER
Yes. Here in our world, when we reach
five feet, we divide individually into two
beings. One grows up and the other grows
down and starts again. On Earth, they
multiply by having sex.

ZWEETHANE
Sex?

TEACHER
Yes. They have genitalia which they
connect. A seed is planted and soon
after, the female divides.

                    ZWEETHANE
Sounds troublesome.

A student named AAALLLFFFEEE interrupts,

                    AAALLLFFFEEE
Do they have a name for that seed?

                    TEACHER
Well, Aaalllfffeee, I believe they call
it jizz.

                    AAALLLFFFEEE
I've noticed that some of the males of this
Earth-kind seem restless. What makes
them so irrational?

                    TEACHER
Testosterone. It's the male hormone. It
can drive him to walk on his moon. And
it can drive him to total destruction.

From the screen, NEIL ARMSTRONG takes a step on the Moon. Suddenly, a giant
MUSHROOM CLOUD from an H-Bomb fills the screen.

                    TEACHER
          War.

                    ZWEETHANE
What is it good for?

                    TEACHER
Absolutely nothin'.

                    AAALLLFFFEEE
Say it again.

                    TEACHER
          No.

While the class intervened for that moment, several months have passed for Brad
and Tiffany. They are now preening and primping in their DRESSING ROOM. A
CALENDER on the table reads: May 4, 1970. The CAMERA PUSHES INTO the
screen.

Tiffany is quizzing Brad as she reads off of Brad's list.

                         TIFFANY
               Okay, Nineteen Seventy Three. What
               horse wins the Preakness?

                         BRAD
               Let's see. Ah, Sham. No, no. Oh, stupid!
               Secretariat, of course!

                         TIFFANY
               Good. All right. What happened on
               December Eighth, Nineteen Eighty?

                         BRAD
               December eighth? Ah, Gary Coleman
               gets a herpe. No. Let's see. Reagan gets
               shot. No, that's 'Eighty One. Lennon.
               John Lennon gets shot. If Mark
               Chapman had only aimed a little
               bit to the left, he'd be a national hero.

                         TIFFANY
               Remember to call John in ten years. Okay,
               you still got it. We'd better get out there.

On the GAME SHOW SET, we HEAR a drum roll.

                         ANNOUNCER (O.S.)
               Ladies and gentleman. Live from Radio
               City in New York. They've been touted
               as prophets, soothsayers and descendants
               of Nostradamus.

A SHOT OF THE AUDIENCE

                         ANNOUNCER (O.S.)
               Their predictions are uncanny. Please
               Welcome Brad and Tiffany Scott, for...

DRUM ROLL

                         AUDIENCE
               The Wheel Of Future!!!

MUSICAL FANFARE - AUDIENCE APPLAUSE

BACK STAGE, just before Brad and Tiffany go on stage, a young, black COSTUME GIRL straightens Brad's tie. She smiles. Brad is smitten. Brad and Tiffany walk out on

STAGE

                    BRAD
          Thank you everyone. Last week we
          predicted what horse would win at
          Belmont Park. The race was last night.
                    (waves racing form)
          We predicted Pearl Necklace.
                    (opens form)
          Pearl necklace!!!

The audience CHEERS.

                    BRAD
          Now, let's go to the Big Wheel.

                    TIFFANY
          As we play The Wheel of Future!

Brad winks at Tiffany and spins a HUGE WHEEL that has years, months and corresponding days on it.

                    BRAD
          The Wheel Of Future spins around.
          Where it stops will be headline bound.

The wheel slowly comes to a stop.

                    BRAD
          August Ninth, Nineteen Seventy Four!
          The headline on that day will read.

As Brad and Tiffany huddle in conference, there's a drum roll.

                    BRAD
          What the hell happened that day?

                    TIFFANY
          How the hell should I know? You're
          suppose to be the total recall genius.

160

The audience waits while Brad tries to recall.

>   TIFFANY
>   (whispers)
>   Brad. Make something up for the
>   love of God!

Brad takes out a hanky and wipes his forehead.

>   BRAD
>   Okay. Summer, 'Seventy Four...
>   Air Force...couldn't afford college.
>   Afford...Ford is new President!
>   (to audience)
>   The headline will read. "Ford is
>   New president." Richard Nixon
>   steps down as Gerald Ford trips up.

>   TIFFANY
>   (picking it up)
>   Ah, let's see. Richard Nixon will
>   be involved in a scandal called,
>   "Watergate." To avoid impeachment
>   he'll step down, giving up the
>   position to Vice President Gerald Ford.

>   BRAD
>   Ford will replace the deposed Spiro
>   Agnew as Vice President. President
>   Ford will go on to trip and fall in
>   public, to keep the attention from a
>   tipsy First Lady, Betty Ford, who'll
>   go on to start a clinic for celebrity drunks.

Brad gets interrupted by a HECKLER in the audience.

>   HECKLER (O.S.)
>   You're makin' this crap up!

>   TIFFANY
>   Believe me, you couldn't make this crap up.

161

                              BRAD
It appears as though we have a
doubting Thomas. Last week on
the Wheel Of Future, we predicted
today's headline.
                    (to directors booth)
Bill, run the tape from last week's
show. People in the audience,
watch the monitors.

They play back a segment of last week's show. On the MONITOR there's a CLOSE
UP of the wheel as it stops on MAY 4TH 1970. The SHOT SWITCHES to Brad and
Tiffany.

                              BRAD
                    (on video playback)
On May Fourth, Nineteen Seventy,
that's a week from today, the headline
will read: "Four Students killed at Kent
State." Students protesting the Vietnam
War will be shot by National Guardsmen.

                            TIFFANY
                    (on video playback)
Four dead in Ohio. The Kent State
Massacre will give Crosby, Stills,
Nash and Young a top ten hit. Also,
Spiro Agnew watches will take the
market by storm.

                              BRAD
                    (on video playback)
Now you can watch time run out for
Spiro Agnew.

The screen goes black. On stage, LIVE, a messenger walks on and hands Brad a
newspaper.

                              BRAD
The evening edition just came in.
Ladies and gentlemen, unfortunately,
The headline *does* read.

NEWSPAPER

FOUR STUDENTS KILLED AT KENT STATE

The audience GASPS. Tiffany takes the paper.

> TIFFANY
> And here on page two.

Tiffany reads it aloud as she shows the headline.

AGNEW WATCHES SELL ONE MILLION

> TIFFANY
> Which out sold Mickey Mouse
> and Bullwinkle Moose.

The AUDIENCE laughs and cheers.

> BRAD (O.S.)
> Are you ready for more?

> AUDIENCE
> Yes!!!

MONTAGE

A) The show - Brad displays newspaper headlines

THIRTY THOUSAND AMERICANS DEAD AS VIETNAM WAR RAGES ON

JANIS JOPLIN DIES OF AN OVERDOSE

SECRETARIAT WINS DERBY

JIMI HENDRIX DIES ON OWN VOMIT

B) Audience - A woman stands up and asks.

> WOMAN
> If you know someone's going to
> die, why not try to avert it?

> BRAD
> We all know that men are going to
> die in the war. Why don't we try
> to avert that? What will be, will be.
> If we alter an event now, it could
> have a domino effect on history.

From the wings, the costume girl flashes Brad an admiring gaze. Brad returns it with a wink.

C) More shows -

WEATHERMEN BLOW UP BANK OF AMERICA - PHILIP BERRIGAN SOUGHT FOR QUESTIONING

JIM MORRISON DIES - DRUGS SUSPECTED

TEN THOUSAND PROTEST WAR AT WHITEHOUSE - NIXON THUMBS NOSE

END OF MONTAGE

EARLY MORNING - WASHINGTON D.C. - THE WHITEHOUSE

INSIDE THE WHITEHOUSE - NIXON'S OFFICE - DAY

> NIXON
> (on phone)
> Edgar. Have you been watching that
> damned show? Well, I want it stopped.

THE FEDERAL BUREAU OF INVESTIGATION - A sign on an office door reads: "Subversive Activities." INSIDE THE OFFICE, a man is cleaning his revolver. A plaque on his desk reads: DARRYL HANNA. He is speaking on an intercom.

> DARRYL
> We don't know where they're getting
> their information. We have no records
> on them either. It's like they came from
> nowhere. Don't worry chief, I'll be on
> them like flies on shit.

Meanwhile, OUTSIDE OF A WAREHOUSE - LITTLE ITALY

A LIMO pulls up to the curb. TWO MEN get out. One opens the rear passenger door. A heavy set man wearing a shark skinned suit and smoking a cigar shuffles out. He is DON CHOOCH. The men enter the warehouse.

INSIDE THE WAREHOUSE several MEN are sitting at a large table. As Don Chooch and the other two enter, the men rise. Don Chooch approaches the table while the two men take their places. Don Chooch sits. The men sit. Don Chooch puts the cigar out on his tongue, tosses it aside.

DON CHOOCH
Roll call.

The men around the table call out their names.

MEN (CONSECUTIVELY)
Carmine. Vinnie. Antonio. Guido. Nunzio.
Fabrizio. Cubbie. Jimmy. Roy. J.J. Annette.

DON CHOOCH
Gentlemen. It has been brought to my
attention that we have a tattle tale among
us.
(a beat)
Guido.

GUIDO
(sweating)
Yes, Don Chooch

DON CHOOCH
How come it's like fifty-five degrees
in here and you're sweatin' like a
rat, fuckin' pig?
(a beat)
Nunzio.

Nunzio rises and goes over to Guido. As Guido tries to escape, two men hold him
down. Guido CRIES OUT. Nunzio takes off his belt and wraps it around Guido's
neck. He then proceeds to strangle him to death. Guido drops over dead.

NUNZIO
By the way, Don Chooch, what did
Guido do?

DON CHOOCH
He told my sister I was off my diet.

NUNZIO
Don Chooch, he was married to her.

DON CHOOCH
A rat's a rat. Next order of business. Has
anybody been watchin' that show, The
Wheel Of Future?

No response.

DON CHOOCH

What are you fuckin' guys illiterate?
On this show, they predict the future.
Quite accurately, may I add. This guy
and this broad are on the money with
major horse races, too. Need I say more?

Don Chooch nods to Nunzio.

DON CHOOCH

I want you to talk to these people. Take
Annette with you.

ANNETTE rises. He's a hulk of a man.

LATER THAT AFTERNOON - OUTSIDE OF THE DAKOTA

INSIDE - BRAD AND TIFFANY'S LUXURY SUITE

Tiffany is reading fan mail. Brad fixes a cocktail while watching the news. The maid,
HENRIETTA is leaving for the weekend.

HENRIETTA

I'll see you folks on Monday. Bye, now.

TIFFANY

Thanks Henrietta. Enjoy your weekend.

As she leaves, Tiffany takes out another letter, while Brad gulps down his drink.

TELEVISION

NEWSMAN

"Where's Poppa?" It's my pick-flick of
the week. In other show-bits. The hit
show, The Wheel Of Future is stirring
up a lot of controversy. The hosts of the
show, Brad and Tiffany Scott, claim to
be able to predict the future. Well, so far
their predictions have come to pass. Today,
Janis Joplin overdosed on heroin, just as
the Scotts predicted. Janis's manager was
said to have warned her about this. She,
obviously ignored it. Some experts on
parapsychology think it may be "self-
fulfilled prophesies," merely power of
suggestion. Others say the Scotts indeed
possess some psychic prowess.

Brad shuts off the TV and fixes himself a "stiff one." Tiffany seems distressed as she hands Brad a special delivery letter.

                              TIFFANY
              Drop that drink and get a load of this.
              It's from Washington D.C.

                              BRAD
                            (reading)
              We're on to your Commie, Pinko plot.
              If you don't watch it, you'll be predicting
              the future in a federal compound.

As Brad downs his drink, the DOORBELL rings.

                              TIFFANY
              Who can that be?

                              BRAD
              I ordered some caviar.

Brad opens the door. Much to Brad's alarm, some fifteen to twenty PEOPLE await him. They bombard him with a slew of questions.

                              WOMAN
              Will I be married?

                              MAN
              Will I be famous?

                              TEENAGER
              Will I be rich?

                              BRAD
              Que sera, sera.

                              MAN
              Lose the levity, Doris!

                              WOMAN
              We have a right to know our future!

                              BRAD
              You're right. You do. Here goes.
              Eventually, you're *all* going to die!

167

Brad slams the door. There's a look of disillusionment on his face.

                    BRAD
          This is getting ridiculous.

Brad makes another drink.

                    BRAD
          Ah, for the good ol' days.

                    TIFFANY
          Unfortunately, the good ol' days
          were ten years from now.

The PHONE RINGS. Tiffany picks up.

                    TIFFANY
          Hello! What a pleasant surprise.
                    (covers phone)
          It's our producer.
                    (on phone)
          Should you invest in silver? Ah, yes,
          you should. Buy big and sell next
          year. Sure. You're welcome.

She slams the phone down.

                    TIFFANY
          That's it! The vultures are coming out
          of the woodwork. How could something
          that seemed like such a blessing, turn out
          to be such a curse.

                    BRAD
          Kinda like your cycle (hic!)

                    TIFFANY
          I think I'll have myself an elaborate cry.

Tiffany begins to weep.

                    BRAD
          And I think I'll have myself an elaborate
          drink.

Brad doesn't bother with the glass and just guzzles from the bottle of bourbon.

                              TIFFANY
                    Hey, save me some of that.

Brad walk over to the liquor cabinet and opens it, exposing numerous bottles of booze.

                              BRAD
                    Knock yourself out.

Meanwhile, in the Dakota LOBBY. Pandemonium. The building MANAGER is screaming at the group of people who just visited Brad. In the corner the DOORMAN is bound and gagged. The manager unties the doorman.

                              MANAGER
                    What happened?

                              DOORMAN
                    These dickwads wanted to see the
                    Scotts. When I went to clear it, they
                    tied me up.

                              MANAGER
                         (to the group)
                    Get out of here or I'll call the cops!

Some in the group are still lingering, checking out the roster. A MAN notices something.

                              MAN
                    Hey, look! Bob Barker lives here!

The Manager runs to the doorway and screams.

                              MANAGER
                    Police! Police!

Just then, two men enter flashing badges. It's Nunzio and Annette. The remaining people quickly make their exit. A grateful manager thanks the Johnnie-on-the-spot-cops.

                              MANGER
                    That was quick. Thank God ! If you
                    hurry you can arrest those people.

169

NUNZIO
Take it easy. What seems to be the
problem?

MANAGER
They were trespassing!

NUNZIO
They're gone now. Let me ask you.
Do you have a Brad and Tiffany Scott
residing here?

MANAGER
That's it! Those two have to go. What
have they done?

NUNZIO
I need to ask them a few questions.

MANAGER
You tell them I said they have to the
end of the month to vacate.

NUNZIO
I'll do that. What apartment?

LATER, inside Brad and Tiffany's suite - Brad and Tiffany are hanging upside-down
from the second level stair banister, bound and gagged. Nunzio and Annette are at
the kitchen counter making salami sandwiches.

NUNZIO
Pardon me, do you have any Grey Poupon?

From upside-down, Brad shakes his head, "no."

NUNZIO
(eating)
See, if you stay in that position long
enough, the blood'll come gushin'
through your freakin' eyeballs. You
don't wanna leave a messy corpse,
do ya'?

From upside-down, Tiffany shakes her head, "no."

                    NUNZIO
Here's the gaf. My boss wants you
guys to stop predicting horse races
on your show. You know why?

Brad and Tiffany shrug their shoulders.

                    NUNZIO
Well, ya see. By blabbin' the results
you fuck up the odds.
                    (takes a bite)
Here's your alternative. Just give *us* the
results. Nobody else and we'll cut you in.
If ya' don't, we'll cut your fuckin' hearts out.
Capise?

              BRAD AND TIFFANY
Hmmmm Hmmmm.

Nunzio finishes his sandwich, while Annette releases Brad and Tiffany from their
constraints.

                    NUNZIO
Oh, I hate to be the bearer of ill tidings,
but your manager wants you out of here
by the end of the month.

It's EVENING, as PEOPLE file into RADIO CITY MUSIC HALL.

INSIDE, it's a full house. ON STAGE, a nervous WARM-UP COMIC checks his
watch.

               WARM-UP COMIC
Okay. Now it's time for…

He gets a signal from the STAGE MANAGER to stretch.

               WARM-UP COMIC
…hey, do you like impressions?

A SMATHERING OF APPLAUSE

               WARM-UP COMIC
                    (sweating)
How 'bout John Wayne doing an
impression of Truman Capote?

171

BACKSTAGE, a frantic stage manager is flitting about.

> STAGE MANAGER
> Where the hell's Brad? Has anyone seen
> Tiffany? They're not in their dressing room.

Several other STAGE PERSONNEL are combing the premises. In the DIRECTOR'S BOOTH, a hysterical DIRECTOR yells into his headset.

> DIRECTOR
> Tell the warm-up to go longer.

> WARM-UP COMIC
> (stretching)
> So, how 'bout those Mets, huh? Do you
> think they'll go to the World Series?

A HECKLER interrupts.

> HECKLER
> Yeah, if they get tickets!

The audience LAUGHS. In the audience, Darryl Hanna, the FBI man is sitting next to an OLD WOMAN.

> OLD WOMAN
> Why are they starting so late?

> DARRYL
> (cryptically)
> I don't know. Why do fools fall in love?

The old woman looks puzzled.

It's THE NEXT DAY. An AERIAL SHOT of the TAPANZEE BRIDGE with the MANHATTEN SKYLINE in the background. On the bridge we ZOOM-IN on a U-HAUL TRUCK.

INSIDE of the truck, Brad is driving while Tiffany does her nails. A road sign, UPSTATE NEW YORK flashes by. They are in the throes of discussion.

> BRAD
> I know this was all my idea. I'm sorry.
> This messing around with the future,
> business is insidious and precarious.

TIFFANY
And it sucks, too. Seriously, we have to
make an oath to *never* mess with the
future, *ever* again. Really, Brad.

BRAD
It's brought us nothing but grief.

TIFFANY
We're financially secure now, so let's
just slip away to "anonymityville."

BRAD
And have a nice, quiet life.

AUGUST 1971

A nice, quiet COUNTRY ROAD in UPSTATE NEW YORK. It's a HOT SUMMER DAY.
There's a cobblestone driveway that leads to a nice, little COUNTRY HOUSE with
an OLD ABANDONED BARN in the background. A nice POSTAL JEEP pulls up to a
MAIL PICK-UP BOX that reads: Brad and Tiffany Miller. A MAILMAN deposits some
mail and then drives off.

Meanwhile, in a nearby, small college town there's a GENERAL STORE. It sets
between a BARBER SHOP and an ANTIQUE STORE.

INSIDE the general store, the proprietors, Brad and Tiffany go about their business.
Brad is now sporting a beard and Tiffany has died her hair.

From a portable radio, The Who's, *Won't Get Fooled Again* is playing. There are a
few PEOPLE shopping. Brad fills a coffee order while Tiffany rings up a sale. An old
man named MR. HUBERT flirts with her.

MR. HUBERT
You know, if you were a few years older,
I'd take a shot at ya'.

TIFFANY
Let's not let age come between us Mr.
Hubert. Okay, that'll be six, fifty-two.

Tiffany bags the items while Mr. Hubert flops several rolls of pennies on the
counter.

MR. HUBERT
Sorry about the pennies. My Social Security
check is late.

TIFFANY
I just cashed it for you the other day. Keep
the pennies. Here.

She pushes the rolls back to Mr. Hubert.

TIFFANY
You know those Steel Stocks I told you
to buy. Sell them. Tomorrow!

Brad flashes Tiffany a disapproving glance. Tiffany shrugs. Brad hands a bag of coffee to a young man in an Army uniform. His name is BILLY.

BILLY
Thanks Mr. Miller. Well, I'll be shippin'
out soon. Goin' to Nam. Got my orders
yesterday. Guess I gotta defend my
country, huh?

Brad looks at him pensively.

BRAD
Listen to me Billy. Don't go. You'll
come back in a body bag, I swear. Go
to Canada. President Ford will give
you amnesty in a few years.

BILLY
President who?

Tiffany gives Brad a look and then smiles. Brad shrugs. He then turns to Billy.

BRAD
Canada, live. Vietnam, body bag.

Billy takes the coffee. On his way out, he takes off his army cap and hands it to another man. He is one of TWO LOADIES who have just walked in the store. He salutes Billy.

LOADIE # 1
Hey, man, First Infantry, 'Sixty Nine.

Billy keeps going while the Loadie who is tripping rambles on.

174

                    LOADIE # 1
Nam was a trip, man. Did some window
pane during a raid on this village. Mortar
rockets left these trails, man. Fuckin'
beautiful.

The other Loadie, also tripping, hears the Who's song on the radio.

                    LOADIE # 2
Woooo! I'm really rushin'.

                    LOADIE # 1
Wow, I thought you were Italian.

                    LOADIE # 2
Woah! Whew! Fooof! Wooow!

                    LOADIE # 1
Damn! Wooof! Yeoow!

                    LOADIE # 2
Meoow! Shhoof! Yiikes!!! Look out
for that space ship!

                    LOADIE # 1
Whew! That was close, man.

Just then, a bare footed black girl of about twenty walks in. She is wearing short-
shorts and a halter top that barely cover her breasts. Her name is BECKY. The
Loadies take inventory.

                    LOADIE # 1
Boooiiinnng! What planet are you from?
          (referring to her breasts)
Can you get Mars on these babies?

Becky smiles, takes the Army cap that he's holding and puts it on her head.

                    BECKY
Okay, soldiers. I want y'all to get down
and give me twenty.

                    LOADIE # 1
How 'bout forty?

                         175

                    LOADIE # 2
How 'bout sixty?

                    BECKY
At ease, boys.

Becky saunters over to Brad as the Loadies split. Becky gives Brad a big smile.

                    BECKY
Hi Brad.

Brad drops his scoop and comes to attention.

                    BRAD
H-hi B-Becky. How'd-how did your
test go?

                    BECKY
Fine, thanks to you. How do you know
so much about aerodynamics?

                    BRAD
I was in the Air Force. Can I do you?
Ah, *what* can I do you, for?

Tiffany flashes Brad a dirty look.

                    BECKY
I need *lots* of stuff.

                    TIFFANY
Maybe *I* can help you.

Becky winks at Brad and then bounces over to Tiffany.

                    BECKY
Do you sell condoms?
                (a beat)
They're for my boyfriend.

Brad seems relieved while Tiffany fills the order.

LATER THAT NIGHT, OUTSIDE of a MOTEL. There's a FULL MOON. The sound of
CRICKETS fill the summer night.

INSIDE, of the MOTEL ROOM, light from the moon spills onto a bed. Brad and Becky are making love. They CRY OUT passionately as they both reach a climax. After a moment Brad turns on the light while Becky lights up a cigarette.

                    BECKY
        You're pretty good for a white boy.

                    BRAD
        I've never had a woman climax with
        me before. You weren't faking it were
        you?

She shakes her head, "No" and blows smoke in his face.

                    BRAD
        Can we do this again, sometime?

                    BECKY
        As soon as I'm done smokin', sugar.

Meanwhile, at the MILLER RESIDENCE, Tiffany sits in the living room, alone and dejected. She picks up the phone and dials.

                    TIFFANY
        Hello, Aunt Shirley?

INSIDE SHIRLEY'S KITCHEN

                    SHIRLEY
                  (on phone)
        Who is this?

INTERCUT - TIFFANY AND SHIRLEY

                    TIFFANY
        It's Tiffany.

                    SHIRLEY
        Tiffany? You don't sound like my niece.

                    TIFFANY
        Aunt Shirley. It's me. Really. How are
        you?

SHIRLEY
Why do you sound so different?

TIFFANY
Because I'm eighteen years older.

SHIRLEY
What?

TIFFANY
Yes, Aunt Shirley. After I ran away, I
went to college and got a job on Wall
Street. And then something happened
that I can't explain. I need to talk to you.

SHIRLEY
Tiffany?

TIFFANY
I've called many times, but Moisha
kept hanging up.

Tiffany hears another voice in the background. It's MOISHA. He takes the phone.

MOISHA
Who the hell is this?!

TIFFANY
Uncle Moisha, it's me, Tiffany.

MOISHA
This ain't Tiffany. If you call here
again, I'll hunt you down and rip
out your gallbladder and make you
eat it.

Moisha slams the phone down so hard that the receiver flies off and smashes into
several pieces.

MOISHA
Tiffany my tukhis! That was definitely
an older broad.

SHIRLEY
Why did Tiffany have to leave us?

                    MOISHA
It's this fercockta generation.

                    SHIRLEY
Who do you suppose that was?

                    MOISHA
The cops said a lot of kids run away
from home these days. (Belch!)

                    SHIRLEY
I was good to her.

                    MOISHA
You spoiled her. It must be the marijuana.
They smoke it, run off to Woodstock, wind
up in some gutter, live with a pimp, use
heroin and get Hepatitis. Ah, these kids
today got no Goddamn class. (Belch!)

Tiffany sits in a daze with the phone off the hook.

                    TIFFANY
                    (to herself)
I should have known she'd never believe
me. Who'd believe anyone who said they
went back in time eighteen years.

Meanwhile, in an OLD SHACK, nearby - Darryl sits in a dimly lit room with
HEADPHONES on, monitoring Tiffany's call. Another man with a headset on is taking
notes. He is BILL ORANGE.

                    BILL
Back in time eighteen years? She's
not subversive, she's crazy.

                    DARRYL
Look at this.

Darryl takes a set of finger prints from his briefcase.

                    DARRYL
These are Brad's finger prints. We got
them from his dressing room right
after he left the show.

179

He passes them to Bill.

                    DARRYL
          We traced these to an orphanage where
          he was raised. His real name is Westlake.
          Here are his prints from the orphanage.
          Look at the birth date.

                October 12th, 1953.

                    DARRYL
          According to this, Westlake should only
          be about eighteen years old. The same
          with the dame. They're obviously twice
          that age. You've seen excerpts from the
          show. They were right on the money with
          some forty predictions about Vietnam.
          They *must* have known the future.

                    BILL
          Well, they're not stirring up any trouble
          now. The show's been off the air for over
          a year. They're no threat. It looks like
          they've completely dropped out.

                    DARRYL
          Yeah, but you heard her. She said, "Who'd
          believe anyone who said they went back in
          time eighteen years."

                    BILL
          Well, I sure don't and if I were you, I
          wouldn't bring that point home to the
          Chief. He may be nuts, but he's not crazy.

                    DARRYL
          You've got to admit, that there's something
          strange here. And I'm going to find out
          what's going on if it kills them.

                APRIL 1972

A COUNTRY FIELD. It's a beautiful spring day. Under a shady elm tree, near a pond,
there's a blanket and a picnic basket. A bottle of wine protrudes from an ice bucket,
next to a portable radio. From the radio, Don McLean's, *AMERICAN PIE* is playing.

From behind the tree, a man and a woman are singing along. Tiffany backs up from behind the tree, laughing.

                    TIFFANY
          Hey. Thanks for fixing my car. It's so good
          to have a mechanic you can trust. About
          last night. I am a married woman you know.
          It's just that my husband's going through his
          second adolescence. It's been lonely for me
          and you've been very sweet.

RADIO

                    ANNOUNCER (V.O.)
          In political news: George McGovern,
          top contender for the Democratic
          Presidential nomination, said that if
          elected, he would end the war in Vietnam.

CLOSE UP of a hand switching off the radio. The mechanic is Darryl. He now sports a mustache and long hair.

                    DARRYL
                    (covering)
          I've never voted before, but I'm for
          McGovern all the way. Nixon's got
          to go. That war's got to go.

                    TIFFANY
          And I've got to go. My husband's
          getting suspicious.

                    DARRYL
          Why should you care, the way he
          treats you?

                    TIFFANY
          I know, but I told him to be home
          this afternoon so we could talk.

                    DARRYL
          Ultimatum time?

                    TIFFANY
          Something like that.

Tiffany starts to gather her stuff.

                    DARRYL
          I've known you for what, six months
          now? Yet I know so little about you.
          All I know is that I'm the other man.

                    TIFFANY
          And I'm sure that's really killing you.

                    DARRYL
          Yeah.

Tiffany gives Darryl a quick peck on the cheek. He folds up the blanket.

                    DARRYL
          When did you and your husband
          first meet?

                    TIFFANY
          Oh, we met in L.A. a long time ago.

                    DARRYL
          Really. Where?

                    TIFFANY
                 (she slips)
          The 'Eighty Four Olympics.

                    DARRYL
          Eighty Four?

                    TIFFANY
          No. Seventy, ah…The Seventy Two
          Olym…no! That hasn't happened yet.
          I can't remember. What difference
          does it make?! Come on, I've got to go.

                    DARRYL
          Okay. I don't know why you're being
          so secretive. I just want to know all
          about you.

                    TIFFANY
          Look, the past isn't important. If you've
          noticed, I haven't asked you anything
          about your past.

                            DARRYL
                    I noticed.

Packed up, they head to their separate cars.

A while later, driving on a COUNTRY ROAD on his way to town, Darryl spots Brad
cruising on his Harley and smoking a joint. Darryl pulls into a gas station. He gets
out, goes to a PHONE BOOTH and makes a call.

INSIDE PHONE BOOTH

                            DARRYL (O.S.)
                    Bill Orange, please.
                            (a beat)
                    Bill, Darryl. I can't get anything
                    out of her…What?!

INSIDE BILL ORANGE'S OFFICE

                            BILL
                    Look, we've wasted enough time on
                    this case. They're losing interest
                    upstairs. You've got to do something
                    expedient, now! This Brad character
                    likes to party. He's probably holding.
                    Whip up a phony search warrant, bust
                    him, torture him and make him talk.

                            DARRYL
                    Look. I just saw Brad. I'll take care of
                    this, now. Thanks.

Darryl hangs up.

INSIDE of Brad and Tiffany's house, an argument is in progress. Brad has been
drinking and being abusive.

                            BRAD
                    So you're saying it's my fault that
                    we're in this fucking time warp?

                            TIFFANY
                    No, I didn't. You're being paranoid.

BRAD
What do you mean by that?

TIFFANY
Look. We came up here to have
a nice, quiet life away from the rat
race. But for the last year, you've
been acting like a jerk. Grow up, will
you?

BRAD
Leave the rat race. It's a snails race
up here. This was your idea.

TIFFANY
And it was your idea to do that
damned show.

She spots some lipstick on his shirt.

TIFFANY
The least you could do was to wipe
it off before you came home.

She wipes it off with her thumb and shows it to him.

TIFFANY
I'm sorry I ever fuckin' met you.

BRAD
I'm sorry I ever met and fucked *you*.

TIFFANY
I'm sorry your father met your mother.
Who ever he may be.

BRAD
I'm sorry you're such a bitch.

TIFFANY
Why don't you go give your big titted
co-ed a good bang!

Brad makes a fist.

184

BRAD

Oh, you'll see something go bang,
alright!

TIFFANY

What are you Ralph Kramden?

Brad realizing the ridiculousness of the argument begins laughing. Tiffany joins in.
Brad gives Tiffany a big hug.

BRAD

Oh, honey I'm sorry. I have been acting
like a jerk. It's just that it's kind of boring
up here. No challenges. We need some
stimulation, some purpose.

TIFFANY

Why don't we start a family? I need a
child, Brad. Maybe there's a poor
little kid in the ghetto we can adopt.

BRAD

A family. Huh! That's going to be
expensive. Why don't we hit just
one more derby?

TIFFANY

No! We made a vow. That's when things
went sour for us, when we got greedy.
We're resourceful enough. We can make
a good living. And we're not exactly broke,
you know.

BRAD

When you're right, you're right, baby.
But let's go back to the City. There's
too much…

TIFFANY

…college trim up here?

BRAD

No, honey. Mosquitoes!

He pretends to slap a mosquito on his neck.

                    BRAD
These damn little blood-sucking, pain-
in-the-neck mosquitoes.

                    TIFFANY
                   (laughing)
          Let's cuddle.

OUTSIDE, Darryl pulls into the driveway, stops the car and gets out.

BACK INSIDE, Brad and Tiffany are cuddling on the couch when the door bell
RINGS.

                    TIFFANY
No more tutoring, mister.

                    BRAD
Maybe it's the Publishers Clearing
House Sweepstakes.

Tiffany laughs as Brad opens the door. Standing there with an FBI badge in hand, Darryl
smiles.

                    DARRYL
          Avon calling.

                    BRAD
          What is this?

                    DARRYL
This is a badge. May I come in?

                    BRAD
          No.

                    DARRYL
Brad Miller, alias Brad Scott, alias
Brad Westlake?

Tiffany springs from the couch and addresses Darryl.

                    TIFFANY
          Darryl!

                    BRAD
                  (surprised)
Darryl?

                    DARRYL
Yes. I'm an FBI agent and I have a
search warrant.

                    BRAD
Is this a joke?

Darryl pushes his way in and shows Brad the counterfeit SEARCH WARRANT.
Darryl kicks the door shut.

                    BRAD
Tiffany, who is this clown?

                    TIFFANY
                  (innocently)
I dunno.

                    BRAD
You called him Darryl. That's your
name isn't it?

                    DARRYL
Correctamundo, Brad. Now spread 'em.

Brad resists. Darryl kicks Brad in the groin.

                    DARRYL
Now, I did ask you nice. Don't fuck
with me for the rest of my stay or
you'll need a busboy to carry your
balls for ya'.

Brad is doubled over with pain.

                    BRAD
How do you know Tiffany?

Darryl searches Brad.

                    DARRYL
Why don't you ask her?

187

Darryl discovers something in Brad's shirt pocket and takes it out.

> DARRYL
> Lookie here. Looks like cannabis hemp.

Darryl opens the bag and sniffs.

> DARRYL
> Smells like cannabis hemp. Golly gee,
> it *is* cannabis hemp and you're under
> arrest!

> TIFFANY
> Why are you doing this? What have
> we done?

> DARRYL
> Well, for openers, Brad here is holding.
> It's an illegal substance. And the Bureau
> has reason to believe that you've been
> involved in some subversive activity.

> BRAD
> Tiffany, how do you know this guy?

> TIFFANY
> Well, Brad…Darryl introduced himself
> to me at the store. He seemed nice enough.
> I didn't know he was an FBI agent, for
> God's sake.

> DARRYL
> Yeah, Brad. We've been kinda dating.
> Your wife gives excellent head.

> BRAD
> That's not true!

Brad swings at Darryl and lands a punch to Darryl's nose. Blood shoots out. Darryl pulls out his gun. Brad dives on him, knocking Darryl off of his feet. Darryl loses control of the gun which slides across the floor. They both go for the gun. There's a struggle. Darryl elbows Brad in the stomach and grabs the gun. Brad tries to take it from him and Darryl shoots. Another wild shot hits Tiffany in the foot. Blood splatters from her shoe.

Enraged, Brad takes the gun and knocks Darryl down, causing him to slide across the floor, face first. Brad accidentally drops the gun. It goes off. The bullet ricochets from a wall and hits Darryl in the coccyx. Darryl CRIES out. He tries to get up, but is immobilized.

As the smoke from the heated gun dissipates, Brad stands over Darryl in shock. Brad picks up the gun and drops it in a waste basket. The gun goes off again. The bullet hits a chandelier, causing glass to fly everywhere.

> BRAD
>
> Christ!

Brad immediately tends to Tiffany's foot. He rips off his shirt and uses it as a tourniquet.

> TIFFANY
> Oh, Brad. I'm so sorry. I had no
> idea he was the law.

Brad kisses her forehead.

> BRAD
> Shhh. Take it easy, baby. I'm going
> to get you to the hospital and then
> I've got to get the hell out of here.
> If he's really a Fed, my ass is grass.
> I'm gonna hide out for a while.

He kisses her again, picks her up and takes her outside.

> BRAD
>
> I love you.

> DARRYL
>
> What about me?

> BRAD
>
> Not so much.

The CAMERA PANS to the bedroom where the TV has been left on.

TELEVISION

David Jansen, running from the law as a title comes across the screen.

THE FUGITIVE

A SERIES OF SHOTS - MUSIC - *BORN TO BE WILD*

    A) Brad riding down the highway on his motorcycle with a back pack tied the sissy bar.

    B) Brad checks into a sleazy motel.

    C) In the motel room, Brad shaves off his beard.

    D) At a used car lot, Brad trades in his motorcycle for a car.

    E) In the car, on the highway, Brad looks stressed.

    F) Another cheap motel, Brad sits on the bed with his hands cupped over his face.

THAT NIGHT Brad walks into a POLICE STATION. INSIDE, Brad, speaks to a DESK SERGEANT.

DESK SERGEANT
You shot an FBI agent in the ass? Hold on.

As the desk sergeant gets on the phone, he takes out a WANTED POSTER. It's a rendering of Brad with his beard.

DESK SERGEANT
Hey, Sam, I think I got the guy who shot
the Federalie. Yeah, he's right here.

It's a FEW WEEKS LATER at an FBI HEARING ROOM. Brad, Tiffany and their DEFENSE attorney are sitting together. On the other side of the room, agents Darryl Hanna and Bill Orange are with their COUNSEL. Darryl is standing. Because of his injury he cannot sit.

The JUDGE, a man in his late sixties, presides. Defense addresses the bench.

DEFENSE
Your honor. Agent Orange's testimony
reveals that he and agent Hanna acted
illegally by conspiring to concoct a
phony search warrant and enter my
clients residence illegally.

> JUDGE
> When agents Hanna and Orange started
> this case, J. Edgar Hoover was the head
> of the FBI. His obsession with subversive
> activities was tolerated. But there's a
> new order. Agent Orange...

ON BILL ORANGE

> JUDGE (O.S.)
> ...you will be suspended from the
> Department for duplicity, for a period
> of six months. Agent Hanna...

Darryl winces in pain.

> JUDGE (O.S.)
> ...the Bureau feels that your involvement
> with this case was too obsessive. Because
> of your injury you'll never sit again. You
> can collect your pension, but you'll never
> serve. We won't stand for it.

> JUDGE
> (to Tiffany)
> Tiffany Westlake, Scott, Miller, whatever.
> You will not be charged with anything.
> The Bureau feels that the injury you
> sustained during this episode is just
> enough punishment. You are free to go.

The defense attorney smiles a big one. Brad bites his nails awaiting his verdict.

> JUDGE
> Brad Westlake, Scott, Miller, whatever.
> Your actions have been cause for an
> agent of the FBI to be confined to a
> standing position for the rest of his life.

Darryl winces in pain.

> JUDGE
> However, in the eyes of this court, you
> were provoked into your actions. I
> sentence you to five years at Danbury...

DEFENSE
Your Honor!!!

JUDGE
Okay, three. *If* you're a good boy. This
hearing is adjourned.

A look of hate fills Darryl's eyes.

It's a FEW WEEKS LATER, outside of DANBURY FEDERAL PRISON. INSIDE, a
CELL for conjugal visitation, Brad and Tiffany are sitting on a bunk.

BRAD
What do you mean you've got a
headache?

TIFFANY
I'm sorry Brad, but this place has no
atmosphere. It's so unromantic.

BRAD
Well, maybe I can have the warden
send down some champagne and a
violin player.

TIFFANY
Look, Brad, you've got to get out of
here, soon. I'm losing it. Without you
I have no life. All my friends are in
another time zone. This is too depressing.

BRAD
Well, maybe this'll cheer you up. Ya
ready? Here goes.
          (clears throat)
I'm doing time and you're *not*. Happy?!

Tiffany fakes a big, cheesy smile.

It's the NEXT DAY, OUTSIDE of a BROWNSTONE in Manhattan. INSIDE of
TIFFANY'S APARTMENT, Tiffany sits in a chair staring into space. She begins to
weep uncontrollably. As the CAMERA PULLS BACK, we SEE this action on the
screen in the Fourth Dimension classroom.

Some of the students in class are teary eyed. The teacher freezes the action and shuts off the projection.

> **TEACHER**
> All right, class, we'll take a moment
> for our break.

Everyone closes their eyes for a second and soon everyone is floating horizontally. The teacher continues to conduct the class.

> **TEACHER**
> Four years have transpired for Brad
> and Tiffany. What is that in our time?
> Anyone?

Aaalllfffeee, still floating, looms vertical.

> **AAALLLFFFEEE**
> Twenty four minutes.

> **TEACHER**
> Correct. In our world we learn most
> of our lessons in our classrooms.
> Unfortunately, for Earth-kind, their
> lessons are learned within the life
> experience.

Zweethane looms vertical.

> **ZWEETHANE**
> What modus do they call that?

> **TEACHER**
> The hard way.

Everyone looms back to their original position. The teacher turns the Interdimensional Time Mode back on, and as the CAMERA PUSHES INTO THE SCREEN, we are back in the Third Dimension.

SUMMER 1973

It's a hot summer day. From an APPLIANCE STORE WINDOW, a row of television sets are on. The Watergate Hearings are being televised. JOHN ERLICHMAN is wiping his brow as Senator SAM IRVINE questions him.

SAM IRVINE
(on TV)
Did you or did you not, have any
knowledge of the break-in?

JOHN ERLICHMAN
(on TV)
No sir, I did not.

MUSIC - DAVID BOWIE'S, *SPACEODDITY*

The CAMERA PANS to the next door window display. Several MANNEQUINS are dressed in the fashion of the day - bell bottoms and platform shoes.

PANNING across the street to a liquor store, TWO BLACK DUDES bolt out. They have just robbed the store and are running as fast as they can. They're wearing platform shoes and aren't making very good time.

An older ASIAN MAN and WOMAN dart from the store and easily catch up to them. The woman hits the men with a broom. One of the black dudes throws the cash they have just stolen over his head. The bills flutter about, stopping the proprietors as they gather up their earnings.

From there, the CAMERA PANS down the street to a COFFEE SHOP. Through the window, a profile of a MAN leaning over the counter, gestures to the COUNTER MAN to refill his coffee. The counter man gestures to the man to have a seat. The man indicates that he cannot.

INSIDE the coffee shop we see that the man is Darryl. He looks dejected.

1974

IT'S NIGHTFALL OUTSIDE OF DANBURY PRISON. INSIDE of a PRISON CELL, Brad is lying on his bunk.

MUSIC - CHICAGO AND BEACHBOYS, *WISHIN' YOU WERE HERE*

There's a small TV in his cell. He is watching the Academy Awards. David Niven is presenting an award when a "streaker" runs across the stage.

THE NEXT DAY, OUTSIDE - PRISON. A huge iron gate opens as a black and white drives in. TWO MARSHALS step out of the car. One of them opens the back door and escorts a man in handcuffs from the back seat. It's Nunzio. A GATE GUARD in a booth nearby addresses Nunzio.

GATE GUARD

Well, well, look who's back. You broke a
lot of hearts when you left. What is that
a whole year now?

NUNZIO

How's your wife and my kids?

GATE GUARD

Huh! No wonder those kids are so ugly.

It's the NEXT DAY, OUTSIDE, in the PRISON YARD, Nunzio and a few other
INMATES are playing "paper, scissors, and rock" for cigarettes. Nunzio spots Brad
across the yard and smiles.

LATER THAT DAY several INMATES are tending to the laundry. Two of them are
Brad and Nunzio. A GUARD stands watch. Nunzio approaches Brad.

NUNZIO

Hey! Ain't you that famous TV star?
What happened, you try to beat the IRS?

BRAD

Oh, no! What are you doing here? No
wait, that's a dumb question.

NUNZIO

Hey, let's let by-gones be by-gones.
Seen any good races lately? We gotta
talk, ah, it's Brad, Brad…

BRAD

Miller, and we don't need to talk.

NUNZIO

Hey listen, Miller, I gotta lotta pull
around here. You wanna pull that
shit? You'll be pullin' feet out of
yer ass.

BRAD

So what do you want, a *Pulitzer* prize?

195

THE NEXT DAY in the laundry room, about fifteen to twenty INMATES are tending to the laundry. Brad takes some clothes from a dryer and hands them to the next man in the brigade. Nunzio makes an entrance. The GUARD leaves and locks the door behind him.

> NUNZIO
> Okay fellas, ya' work hard all day.
> Now, it's Miller time.

As if on cue, the other prisoners jump Brad and start beating him up. Nunzio takes some bleach.

> NUNZIO
> I think this creep needs a Clorox colonic.

A HALF HOUR LATER. The laundry room is vacant. The CAMERA PANS the room and stops at a DRYER. Inside of the dryer, Brad is spinning around. He's bleeding and unconscious.

A FEW MONTHS LATER - VISITING AREA. Brad and Tiffany are sitting at a table. A GUARD stands in the background.

> BRAD
> They've taken away most of my
> privileges. We can't even do
> conjugal. That creep Nunzio is
> ruining my life.

> TIFFANY
> My life's not much better. I'm not
> relating very well out there Brad. I
> wasn't crazy about the Seventies
> the first time around. If I fall off
> another pair of platforms, I'm suing.
> Without you I'm really lost, honey.
> Besides that, we're broke.

> BRAD
> Hang in Tif. I'll be out of here in
> about nine months. Why don't you
> play the market or hit a horse or
> something?

> TIFFANY
> You know I have a problem with That.
> I feel that all this is reincarnant pay
> back from bad karma we created
> when we weren't what we are now.

                           BRAD
              Baby, I think you've got too much time
              after time on your hands. Maybe you
              should hit the work force again.

                           1975

OUTSIDE of a Wall Street office building, PAINE WEBBER JACKSON & CURTIS

MUSIC: ELTON JOHN'S, *PHILADELPHIA FREEDOM*

INSIDE an office door sign reads: MARK KOPPERMAN - MARKET ANALYST

As the CAMERA PUSHES through the door, Tiffany is taking dictation. She seems
distressed. Mr. Kopperman seems annoyed.

                      MR. KOPPERMAN
              If I went any slower I could take my
              own dictation. Tiffany, I thought you
              had potential. That's why I hired you
              with no credentials. But you're
              deteriorating. I'm sorry, but I'm going
              to have to let you go.

As Tiffany leaves, she comments.

                         TIFFANY
              Thank you Paine Webber.

A WEEK LATER - OUTSIDE OF MADISON SQAURE GARDEN It's NIGHTFALL. A
marquee reads: EST SEMINAR WITH WERNER EARHART.

INSIDE of the auditorium there are some FIFTEEN HUNDRED PEOPLE seated.
One of which is Tiffany. She doesn't look well. Tiffany looks wide-eyed as WERNER
speaks from his podium.

                         WERNER
              You are all assholes. By the way, you
              must buy my new book. *How I took
              EST, Scientology, TM, Gestalt, and
              Electroshock Therapy and I'm still a
              big zero.* You're all living in the past
              because you have no future. And if you
              live in the future, you have no present.
              And presently, you'll be out several
              hundred dollars. You know why?
              Because you're a bunch of butt plugs.

Tiffany's face starts to twist. She begins weeping. Soon, she becomes hysterical. She is in the throes of a nervous breakdown. From the stage, Werner alerts security.

                    WERNER (O.S.)
          Security! Lose the lightweight.

OUTSIDE of the auditorium FOUR SECURITY MEN toss Tiffany from the Garden. She is now in a state of shock and falls onto the sidewalk. Tiffany goes into convulsions. She is having delusions that she is pregnant. SEVERAL PEOPLE gather around.

                    TIFFANY
          Help me. I'm going into labor!

A WINO bends down and opens Tiffany's coat, exposing an apparent flat tummy.

                    WINO
          That's one hell of a small baby. What
          you need is mouth to mouth. (Hic!)

A WOMAN stops him.

                    WOMAN
          Get away from her you skeeve.

The woman lifts Tiffany's eyelids. She then feels her pulse. Next, she puts her head to Tiffany's stomach. She then takes an emery board from her purse to use as a tongue depressor, when a MAN pulls the woman up.

                    MAN
          What the hell do you think you're
          doing?! Someone call an ambulance!

As the CAMERA PULLS BACK from the CROWD, no one budges an inch. The crowd starts WHISTLING taps.

A FEW MONTHS LATER, OUTSIDE OF DANBURY PRISON - DAY. The huge iron gate opens as Nunzio walks through. The gate guard, now used to this ritual, says his good-byes.

                    GATE GUARD
          On your way back, could you pick me
          up a pack of smokes?

                    NUNZIO
          Sure, after I'm done diddlin' yer wife.

                         198

A WEEK LATER, the gate opens as Brad walks through to freedom. It's a chilly Autumn DAY. The gate guard bids him farewell.

> GATE GUARD
>
> Stay in touch.

From across the street a CAR is parked.

From INSIDE the car, Nunzio stalks his prey. Brad gets about a block away when Nunzio starts following.

NUNZIO'S POV - Brad crosses the street when another CAR pulls up to him. There is some resignation, but Brad gets in the vehicle. The car peels off. Nunzio takes off after them. He soon catches up and tries to force the car off of the road.

From the other car, the driver pulls out a gun. He shoots. The bullet smashes Nunzio's windshield. In retaliation, Nunzio takes out his weapon and fires back. His shot shatters the other car's back window.

From THE STREET, Nunzio's car rams the other vehicle. Soon there's a full-out chase. The chase is interrupted by an oncoming BUS that forces the other vehicle to swerve into a pole. The impact stuns its passengers.

Nunzio pulls up to the car, gets out and with his weapon drawn, he signals the two men to get out.

> NUNZIO
>
> Okay, scumbags, out!

A dazed Brad gets out of the car. His nose is bleeding. The other man, who is sitting in a special car seat that allows him to maintain a quasi standing position is Darryl. He conceals his weapon and exits the car. He addresses Nunzio.

> DARRYL
>
> Take it easy, pal.

> NUNZIO
> (pointing gun)
> Gimme the gun.

Darryl is about to surrender his gun when he flips it upright, pointing it at Nunzio.

                              BRAD
                          (wiping blood)
                    Hey fellas, would you like some bean
                    dip with your Mexican stand-off?

                              NUNZIO
                           (to Darryl)
                    No sense in us shooting each other
                    over this piece of dirt. Maybe we
                    can talk it over.

                              DARRYL
                    I've waited too long for this asshole.
                    He's mine.

                              NUNZIO
                    Fuck you, I want 'im!

                              BRAD
                    Fellas, please. This is all very flattering,
                    but don't fight. Flip a coin or something.

                        DARRYL AND NUNZIO
                    Shut up!!

Just then, a PATROL CAR pulls up. Both men conceal their weapons. As the cop
car approaches, Brad takes this opportunity to escape. His nose is bleeding quite
profusely now. He walks up to the car and addresses the TWO COPS inside.

                              BRAD
                    Thank god you're here. We were just in
                    an accident. I think I'm hemorrhaging.
                    Could you take me to the hospital?

From inside the car, one of the cops responds.

                              COP #1
                    Sure.
                              (to Nunzio and Darryl)
                    Are you guys alright?

                        DARRYL & NUNZIO
                    Yes!

Brad gets in the back seat, while the other cop radios in the accident. As they drive off, Brad looks out the back window and slips the guys the finger.

                    NUNZIO
Madonna fungoole.

                    DARRYL
Hey, we'd better get out of here.

                    NUNZIO
What about your car?

                    DARRYL
It's still running. Can you follow
me to my mechanic? I'll buy lunch.
Spaghetti and meatballs?

                    NUNZIO
        Fuckin' A.

INSIDE - **WINDOWS OF PALERMO RESTAURANT** - BAR. Nunzio sits at the bar eating spaghetti and meatballs, while Darryl stands, drinking an espresso.

                    NUNZIO
        Sit.

                    DARRYL
Can't. That son-of-bitch shot my
tail bone off. He ruined my career.

                    NUNZIO
Wa ja do?

                    DARRYL
I worked for the FBI.

Nunzio spits out a meatball. The BARTENDER catches it and tosses it back in his plate.

                    NUNZIO
I'm sittin' with a fuckin' fed?

                    DARRYL
Not anymore. I'd do anything to catch
the bastard. He knows things.

NUNZIO

Tell, me 'bout it. I tried to get him to
sing in the joint. He's tough.

DARRYL

I think that there's only one way to
nail this guy. We've got to get his
confidence. But how?

NUNZIO

Hang out with him. Get his trust.

DARRYL

Yes! And then nail him with some
Sodium Pentothal!

NUNZIO

Bada-bing!

DARRYL

But, how can I hang? He knows my face.

NUNZIO

You want this guy?

DARRYL

More than life itself.

NUNZIO

Then you gotta change. I know just
the guy who can do it. He changed
guys faces who were on the Witness
Protection Program. He can prob'ly
fix your back, too.

EVENING - OUTSIDE OF THE WAREHOUSE IN LITTLE ITALY

INSIDE, Nunzio introduces Darryl to a PLASTIC SURGEON.

NUNZIO

Doc. Darryl. Take good care of *him* and
we'll all be sittin' on easy street.

DARRYL
Are you sure this is going to work?

PLASTIC SURGEON
Don't worry, son. I used to work for the
CIA. During the "Bay of Pigs" I did a
Castro look-alike to confuse them. It
worked. Except we confused the wrong
side and the Cubans kicked our ass. So,
who do you want to look like?

DARRYL
Surprise me.

A FEW NIGHTS LATER, INSIDE THE WAREHOUSE BACK ROOM. Darryl is lying
on a gurney, while the doctor slowly unravels the bandages from his face. Nunzio
stands nearby waiting with baited breath.

NUNZIO
Oooh, this is nerve racking. I can't wait
to see your new fatch.

PLASTIC SURGEON
As for your back. You'll be able to sit now.
Unfortunately, I had to shorten one of your
legs, so you'll limp. If you'd like I'll take
a little off the other.

DARRYL
(from behind the bandages)
What is this a fuckin' haircut? Come on!

The doctor takes off the last of the bandages and hands Darryl a mirror.

PLASTIC SURGOEN
All right now, open your eyes slowly and
look into this mirror.

DARRYL'S POV. As his lids let in more light, he sees before him, the spitting image
of CLINT EASTWOOD.

MUSIC- Hugo Montanegro's Theme from THE GOOD, THE BAD AND THE UGLY
MID AFTERNOON - OUTSIDE OF BELLEVUE HOSPITAL

INSIDE, a CORRIDOR, various PEOPLE of varying degrees of mental instability are wandering around. Some are accompanied by ATTENDANTS. A NURSE walks with Tiffany.

                        TIFFANY
                        (woodenly)
              God talked to me last night. He hasn't
              done that in a long time.

                        NURSE
              Tiffany, your recovery has been
              remarkable. When you first came here
              you thought that it was Nineteen Eighty
              Seven. You meet with the board today.
              Please, don't mention this episode with
              God. You could get out of here by
              tomorrow.

                        TIFFANY
              Well, I didn't exactly see God this time.
              It was in a dream. He said I should go
              out an help children in the ghetto.

                        NURSE
              Well, I guess that's not *too* nuts. And
              remember, when they ask you what
              year it is, you say, "Nineteen Seventy
              Six." Okay?

Tiffany nods.

A FEW WEEKS LATER, Tiffany enters a DAY CARE CENTER. INSIDE, she is cheerfully met by a group of GHETTO CHILDREN.

                        TIFFANY
              Okay boys and girls today we'll
              conjugate the verb, to be.

A spirited young, BLACK BOY chimes in.

                        BLACK BOY
              That *be*, cool.

Later that NIGHT, on the other side of town - AERIAL SHOT OF THE CITY.

INSIDE of a lavish DISCO, on the dance floor, PARTY PEOPLE are doing The Hustle to the tune of Van McCoy's, *THE HUSTLE*.

At the BAR, Brad looks on. He has a new look. Typically disco. Short hair, mustache, and tinted glasses. Brad, now age forty one, is older than most of the people there. He's had a few drinks. He signals to the SKIP, the bartender, to refill his drink.

> BRAD
> I can't find her anywhere. It's like
> she vanished. Probably got tired of
> waiting for me. Found another guy.
> I dunno.

It's a few hours later and Brad is in the bag. He throws a bunch of cash at Skip.

> BRAD
> Hey, who do you have to drink to get
> blown around here? Ha ha ha (hic!)
> Gimme another drink, Skip and this
> time put some friggin' booze in it.

Brad passes out face down on the bar.

Meanwhile, across the street, a movie marquee reads, *ALL THE PRESIDENT'S MEN*. A man descends from a staircase that leads to the theater. The man has a noticeable limp. It's Darryl. His resemblance to Clint Eastwood is uncanny. A COUPLE approach him for an autograph.

> DARRYL
> (Clint's voice)
> Take a fuckin' hike.

As they scurry away, Darryl goes to a pay phone and makes a call.

> DARRYL
> (own voice)
> Nunzio. It's me, Darryl. Bingo! This is
> the place. Disco Seventies. Give me a
> week. I'll get his confidence and then
> we'll nail him.

Inside the disco, the crowd has thinned out. Brad is still passed out. Darryl pulls up a stool next to him and orders a drink.

MUSIC - Diana Ross's *LOVE HANGOVER*

CLOSE ON BRAD. We now share with Brad, the DREAM that spins in his head.

> BRAD (V.O.)
> Oh, Tiffany. I miss the things we used
> to do, back in the Eighties, when we
> were yuppie weasels.

MONTAGE - BRAD'S DREAM

A) Brad and Tiffany looking at a computer screen, viewing some stock reports.

B) at an upscale health spa - they are working out on Nautilus machines.

C) a holistic center - on separate gurneys, they hold hands while they both get a high colonic.

D) in a fancy restaurant - while dinning, they mix their bottled water - Perrier and Evian.

E) at a campground, Brad hand washes the BMW as Tiffany sets up their tent. Brad is also watching baseball on a portable TV while listening to music on his Walkman.

F) at the 1984 Olympics when Brad spotted Tiffany with his binoculars.

Brad starts talking in his sleep.

> BRAD
> I haven't seen a crowd like this
> since Woodstock.

> DARRYL
> Where are you now, Brad?

> BRAD
> The Nineteen Eighty Four Olympics.

> DARRYL
> Where?

> BRAD
> About mid field. I can see the
> Budweiser sign.

Darryl takes note. Brad wakes up and looks in the bar mirror at Darryl's reflection. He then looks at Darryl, trying to place the face.

> DARRYL
> (as Clint)
> Hey, friend. I think you need a cup of coffee.

> BRAD
> This may sound strange, but have you
> ever seen *DIRTY HARRY*?

THE BI-CENTENNIAL, FOURTH OF JULY CELEBRATION

LATE AFTERNOON - BATTERY PARK - LOWER MANHATTAN. It's jammed as thousands of PEOPLE flock to New York to participate. From a loud speaker, there's an announcement.

> ANNOUNCER (O.S.)
> Later this evening, Macy's and the Disney
> Corporation are sponsoring the Nineteen
> Seventy Six, Bi-Centennial, Fourth of
> July fireworks celebration. It's a hot day
> in the park today. So be sure you pick up
> some George Washington sun block at the
> Betsy Ross Pavilion and enjoy our nation's
> birthday without getting skin cancer.

In a PHONE BOOTH, nearby, Darryl is on the phone. He's with Nunzio and his huge henchman, Annette.

> DARRYL
> (as Clint)
> Hey Brad! How's it goin' buddy? No
> problem. We all get a little drunk
> sometimes. You're also a little lonely. Well,
> Dr. Clint's got just the thing. I'm having a
> little party, later at my hotel. Why don't we
> meet at Clancy's bar first and have a few
> drinks. Okay, see ya.

Darryl hangs up. As the three men head towards the pier, Darryl confers with his cohorts. He seems impressed with Annette's bulk.

DARRYL
What do you eat for breakfast, furniture?
(a beat)
Annette. Is that Italian for something?

ANNETTE
Yeah, Annette.

DARRYL
Gotcha. Nunzio, did you bring the
Sodium Pentothal?

NUNZIO
Check. I can't get over your new mug.

ANNETTE
Yeah, you look just like the "High Plains
Drifter."

NUNZIO
Sorry about you leg.

DARRYL
At least I can sit now. Okay. I'll get
Brad drunk and then we'll meet you
at the hotel in a few hours.

OUTSIDE of the HOTEL, the CAMERA ZOOMS IN on a window on the tenth floor
and PUSHES INSIDE of the HOTEL ROOM. Annette goes to the window with a set
of binoculars and looks out. Nunzio is preparing a syringe with Sodium Pentothal.

NUNZIO
A good blast from this and he'll be
babbling like a brook.

ANNETTE'S POV - THROUGH BINOCULARS

Through a window in an adjacent building, an OLD WOMAN is sitting on the toilet.

ANNETTE (O.S.)
This is great.

PANNING to another spot on the street. A MAN is getting mugged by TWO
ASSAILANTS.

                    ANNETTE (O.S.)
Nice.

PANNING DOWN directly to the street below. Brad and Darryl get out of Brad's car.

                    ANNETTE (O.S.)
        And there's our boy. After he spills his
        guts, can I tune him up a bit?

BACK TO ROOM

                    NUNZIO
        You can kill him if you want.

                    ANNETTE
Fabulous.

INSIDE OF THE HOTEL LOBBY, Brad and Darryl head towards the elevator. The
HOTEL MANAGER, an elderly gentleman, makes a comment from behind the front
desk.

                    HOTEL MANAGER
                    (to Darryl)
        Ah, Mr. Eastwood. I loved you in *Play
        It Again, Sam*.

Darryl winces as they enter the elevator. INSIDE, as the elevator doors close, Brad
acknowledges the manager's apparent faux pas.

                    BRAD
        I think he meant, *Play Misty For Me*.

                    DARRYL
                    (as Clint)
        He's probably senile.

They enter the ELEVATOR. Darryl hits the tenth floor button.

                    BRAD
        Hey, I've got a great Alzheimer's
        joke.

                    DARRYL
        What's Alzheimer's?

Brad realizes that Alzheimer's hasn't been discovered yet.

                    BRAD
            I forgot.

Darryl gives Brad a strange look as they exit the elevator to the CORRIDOR. As they approach Darryl's room, he takes out his key and deliberately fumbles with the lock. Darryl raises his voice and drops the impression.

                    DARRYL
            Damn key's stuck.

Inside the HOTEL ROOM, Nunzio stands behind the door. As Darryl opens the door, a smiling Annette waits to greet him them.

                    BRAD
                (suspiciously)
            This is the party?

                    DARRYL
            This is Annette. He's your date.

Nunzio appears from behind the door.

                    DARRYL
            And you remember Nunzio. He'll be
            your chaperone.

Brad backs up, bumping into Darryl. Darryl attempts to push Brad into the room.

                    BRAD
            What the hell's going on?

Darryl holds Brad. Annette brandishes the syringe.

                    DARRYL
            Let's go in Brad. We just want to
            reminisce.

                    BRAD
            That voice. Darryl! But your face.
            Reminisce! About what?

DARRYL NUNZIO ANNETTE
The Wheel Of Future!

Brad looks as if he's seen a ghost. He pulls away from Darryl and darts down the corridor to a stairwell. He swings open the door and bolts down the stairs, soon to be followed by the unholy trio. After four flights, Brad decides to take some diversionary action. He opens the stairwell door to the sixth floor, runs down the corridor and slips into a broom closet.

INSIDE the CLOSET it's pitch black. The only sound is Brad's heartbeat. About thirty seconds later Brad decides it's safe to breathe. He catches his breath when the door swings open. Nunzio holds the door as a smiling Annette stands posed with the syringe. Darryl extends his hand.

                    DARRYL
          Come on, Brad, this'll make you feel
          better.

                    BRAD
          Nah, that's okay.

                    DARRYL
          Nunzio, hold him.

Just then there's a sound in the background. The service elevator door opens.

                    DARRYL
          Quick, everybody in the closet.

As they all pile in the closet, a MAINTENANCE MAN emerges from the service elevator with a mop, bucket and broom. He heads down the corridor towards the broom closet.

Inside the closet it's pitch black.

                    BRAD (O.S.)
          I feel a sneeze comin' on.

                    DARRYL (O.S.)
                    (whispering)
          Shut the fuck up.

From outside, the maintenance man sings with a Puerto Rican accent.

                    MAINTENANCE MAN (O.S.)
    I like to be in America.

He then swings the door open and sees the four men inside.

                    BRAD
    Broom service?

Nunzio pulls the maintenance man inside the closet while Darryl closes the door.

                    DARRYL (O.S.)
    One word out of you and you're dead.

                    MAINTENANCE MAN (O.S.)
    Don't keel me, mang. I juus ga my gdeen
    caad.

                    DARRYL (O.S.)
    What?

                    NUNZIO (O.S.)
    He just got his green card.

                    DARRYL (O.S.)
    Is there a fuckin' light in here?

Suddenly we HEAR a scuffle. Brad tries to escape.

                    DARRYL (O.S.)
    Annette. Stick him now!

                    BRAD (O.S.)
    Annette?!

Just then there's a scream. Brad bolts from the closet followed by Darryl, Nunzio and Annette. As the door slowly closes, the horrified maintenance man slides down the wall with the syringe of Sodium Pentothal stuck in his arm.

OUTSIDE of the hotel it's DUSK. Brad jumps in his car and peels out. From the entrance Annette jumps into his car and starts it up as Darryl and Nunzio pile in. They peel out after Brad.

An AERIAL SHOT of Brad's car heading south towards Lower Manhattan, where he hopes to get lost in the massive crowd waiting to catch the fireworks. Soon Annette's car catches up.

INSIDE Brad's car he checks out his rear view mirror and spots Annette's car on his tail. Brad swings west towards the docks. Something catches Brad's attention as he looks up.

BRAD'S POV - the fireworks have begun lighting up the sky.

Brad and Annette's cars weave in and out of traffic with the Bi-Centennial pyrotechnic display as a backdrop.

BACK AT THE HOTEL - LOBBY

The maintenance man sits in a chair. Huddled over him are the hotel manager MR. BERNBALM, a BELL CAPTAIN and a CHAMBERMAID. The chambermaid puts a band aid on the spot where he was jabbed with the Sodium Pentothal.

                    CHAMBERMAID
          There you go. How do you feel?

The elixir has taken full effect as the maintenance man begins to babble.

                    MAINTENANCE MAN
          How do I feel? Lemme tell ju mang. I am
          proud to a be a Puerto Rican. But I'm geeting
          seek 'n' tire of cleaning dees sheet! My piple
          hab been een dees city for generations, 'n'
          all we got to show for eet ees Rita Moreno.
          Mr. Bernbalm, you're a Jewish man. The
          Egyptians made ju work for nothin'. And
          while I'm on dee subject. How 'bout a
          fuckeen raise, mang?
                    (to chambermaid)
          Verna. Did I ever tell ju for jeers I wanted to
          have jur babies?

Astonished, Verna and Mr. Bernbalm give each other a look.

CUT TO THE CHASE

Annette's car is right on Brad's bumper. No matter what maneuver Brad initiates, Annette stays with him.

INSIDE Annette's car, Nunzio takes out a magnum and points it at Brad's car.

NUNZIO'S POV through the gun sight - The back of Brad's head. CLOSE ON Nunzio's trigger finger.

                    DARRYL (O.S.)
              Just shoot out his tire.

He squeezes the trigger. The gun goes off, followed by tires squealing.

The bullet has hit the trunk of Brad's car. In response Brad employs a power turn. Brad's car just misses Annette's car causing him to swerve onto an old dock that rests over the river. Annette slams on the breaks. His car then plows into several dock posts before it finally plummets into the Hudson River.

Now safely out of harm's way, Brad pulls over and gets out of his car. Shaken, he leans up against a building.

                        BRAD
                     (tearful)
              Oh, Tiffany. Where are you?!

He turns into the building to weep. In the background, the fireworks light up the sky.

On the river, the aftermath of Annette's car that has just submerged. As the turbulent bubbles subside, just one man surfaces. He swims a few strokes but cannot go on. He cries out.

                      DARRYL
              Help! Please help me!

ON SHORE, two men dressed in typically "Seventies" gay biker drag are cuddling. One looks up. He is LARRY.

                       LARRY
              Lester! Did you hear that?

Annoyed, Lester responds.

                      LESTER
              Now you've blown my concentration.
              No pun intended.

Darryl is going down for the third time. There are SPLASHING SOUNDS as Larry comes to the rescue.

                    LARRY (O.S.)
              Don't drown young man. Here I come.

                    LESTER (O.S.)
          No pun intended.

As Larry catches Darryl by the collar. He looks astonished.

                    LARRY
          Oh, my, God! It's Clint Eastwood!
          Hurry Lester. Help me save Clint!

ON SHORE

                    LESTER
          Ooooh! Mouth to mouth with Dirty
          Harry! Here I come. Pun intended.

Lester quickly disrobes and jumps in.

1977

OUTSIDE - CATHOLIC CHARITIES HOSPITAL - DAY

MUSIC - The Bee Gee's, *HOW DEEP IS YOUR LOVE?*

INSIDE the hospital, Tiffany is doing volunteer work. She is accompanied by TWO NUNS.

1978

MUSIC - The Commodore's, *ONCE, TWICE, THREE TIMES A LADY*

INSIDE of a West Village apartment. Through the window, there's a SUNSET. Darryl has an apron on and is doing the dishes while Larry and Lester are drinking cappuccino.

INSIDE of a private detective's office, Brad sits at a desk across from the DETECTIVE.

                    BRAD
          I've put ads in the classifieds in Chicago
          and L.A. as well. But I'm sure she's here
          in New York, somewhere. Can you help
          me find her?

The detective is reminiscent of Bogie. He takes a puff from his cigarette and wipes the corners of his mouth.

                              DETECTIVE
                    Sure, but it'll cost you a fortune.

Brad spots a newspaper on his desk. It's the sports page. A headline reads:

Horses warm up for the final race of the season

                                BRAD
                      Price is no object.

NIGHTTIME, INSIDE of a tavern, Brad is doing shots at the bar with several LOW-LIFES and a BARTENDER. From the juke box, Jimmy Buffett's, *MARGARITAVILLE* is playing. Above the bar there's a horse race on TV.

                                BRAD
                    I'll bet you guys the next round
                    that Kaka Adios is gonna win.

                              LOW-LIFE
                    Yer on pal (hic!)

From the TV the horses pass the finish line as the announcer calls out the winner.

                          ANNOUNCER (O.S.)
                    And the winner is Junior's Goose, by a length!

The low-lifes cheer. Brad is clearly confused.

                                BRAD
                    I must be losin' it.
                                (to bartender)
                    Set 'em up.

1979

OUTSIDE of a CONVENT, it's EARLY MORNING.

MUSIC - Supertramp's, *THE LOGICAL SONG*

INSIDE the convent Chapel, Tiffany is about to take her vows. SISTER BERNDADETH is at the pulpit.

SISTER BERNDADETH
We are a humble order. We work for God
in the ghetto. Today we have a new inductee.
Our first Jew. Let's hear it for Sister Silver.

About twenty NUNS watch from their pews as Sister Tiffany Silver makes her way to
the pulpit in full nun drag.

TIFFANY
Thank you Sister Berndadeth. What can
I say, but Oy Vay, Maria!

The nuns CHEER and WHISTLE.

OUTSIDE of an OLD SCHOOL in HARLEM - DAY. A placard above the entrance
reads:

THE MARTIN LUTHER KING JR. SCHOOL FOR DEAF, BLACK KIDS

INSIDE the classroom, Sister Tiffany Silver is trying to motivate the children. She
uses sign language as she speaks.

TIFFANY
Ray Charles and Stevie Wonder made it
big, blind. We now need a representative
from the black, deaf community.

A bright, but impetuous lad of about ten, yells out. His name is BUSTER.

BUSTER
Say, what?

TIFFANY
(misunderstands)
All right. What.

BUSTER
(can't hear)
What?

TIFFANY
I said, what.

BUSTER
Say, what?

217

TIFFANY

I just did. And buster, try not to
speak so loud.
(using sign language)
Today we are going to learn how
to whisper.

A cute little girl named CLORETTA speaks up.

CLORETTA
(yelling)
Whisper! What's a whisper, sister?

TIFFANY
(using sign language)
Well, when most hearing impaired
people talk, to compensate, they
usually speak quite loudly. Now, say
you're in church and you want to go
to confession. If you yell out your sins,
everyone will hear. So you must speak
softly so just the priest can hear you.
Okay, Buster, repeat after me in a
normal voice. "How now, brown cow?"

BUSTER
(loudly)
How now...Hey! Why does the cow
have to be brown? Why can't he be
white?

TIFFANY
(shouting back)
Buster, a cow can't be a he!
(catches herself - quietly)
Cows can just be a she.

BUSTER
And why does it have to be a cow?
I like pigs!

TIFFANY
Okay. How about a white, boy pig?

BUSTER
How old?

218

TIFFANY
Ah, say your age.

BUSTER
Well, in that case, he can be brown.

TIFFANY
So now we have a pig.

BUSTER
That's right.

TIFFANY
Boy pig.

BUSTER
Right on.

TIFFANY
Boy pig, brown.

BUSTER
Let's make 'im black.

TIFFANY
Black pig, boy.

BUSTER
Age ten.

TIFFANY
Age ten.

BUSTER
When's his birfday?

TIFFANY
(losing patience)
Ahh, let's say November eleventh.

BUSTER
That's Veteran's Day.
(starts to cry)
My uncle died in Vietnam!

                    TIFFANY
I'm sorry. November twelfth.

                    BUSTER
That's cool. But that makes him
a Scorpio.

                    TIFFANY
So what?

                    BUSTER
That's a bad sign.

                    TIFFANY
                 (almost losing it)
What sign would you like your
black, pig boy to be?

                    BUSTER
Pick one.

                    TIFFANY
Taurus!!!

                    BUSTER
Nope. Taurus be a bull and we be
talkin' 'bout a pig!

                    TIFFANY
Screw the damn pig!!!

                    BUSTER
Hey! Not so damn loud, nun!

                    CLORETTA
I hea dat!

Tiffany has reached another psychological break down. She looks around as if she's
stepped out of a cryogenic chamber.

                    TIFFANY
Where am I? Why am I dressed like
this? Where's Brad?
                 (to Buster)
Why don't you answer me!!

                      220

BUSTER

'Cuz I'm deaf, bitch!

Tiffany begins to weep. The children rally around her. Buster and Cloretta hug Tiffany.

BUSTER

What's wrong, sis?

Tiffany looks at Buster and smiles. She then looks at Cloretta for a moment.

TIFFANY

You're the sweetest little girl.

CLORETTA

I hea dat.

OUTSIDE an OLD BROWNSTONE - DAY. Tiffany walks up the steps to her former apartment building. She's a civilian again. She scans the apartment roster. CLOSE ON Goldstein - Manager - 103. She buzzes his apartment. From the speaker:

GOLDSTEIN (O.S.)

Who is it?

TIFFANY

Hello, Mr. Goldstein. My name is
Tiffany Silver. I lived here a few
years ago. I think it was in apartment
two-o-four.

GOLDSTEIN (O.S.)

I hope you've come to pay your back rent.

INSIDE Goldstein's apartment, Goldstein turns down the volume on his TV and goes to his desk as Tiffany explains her situation.

TIFFANY

I'm trying to put my life back together
and was hoping you might have kept
some of my things.

GOLDSTEIN

Well, you didn't have much. I sold...
I mean, gave most of your stuff away.
You rented under the name of Tiffany
Miller. Did you re marry?

TIFFANY
Don't ask.

GOLDSTEIN
I did save a picture album. What I found
so peculiar about it was the dates on the
pictures read Nineteen Eighty Seven. Here,
I'll show you.

Goldstein goes to his bookcase, pulls out the album and gives it to Tiffany.

TIFFANY
Nineteen Eighty Seven.
(covering)
Ah…Oh! That was a misprint.

From the kitchen there's a WHISTLE of a tea kettle.

GOLDSTEIN
There's the tea. Would you excuse me?

As she looks through the album.

TIFFANY
(to herself)
Brad, where are you? If there's a
God in heaven. Tell me where he is.

Something on TV inspires Tiffany as her expression changes dramatically.

CLOSE ON TELEVISION

The *BEVERLY HILLBILLIES* are on. The opening song:

SONG
Said *California* is the place you
oughta be. So they loaded up the
truck and moved to Beverly…

Meanwhile, at BRAD'S APARTMENT. Brad sits guzzling a beer and watches the
same show as the song continues.

SONG
…Hills that is. Swimmin' pools, movie
stars. Y'all *come back now* hear?

Brad is struck with the same inspiration.

                    BRAD
          California? (Hic!)

He passes out and slips into a DREAM:

A vision of the LOS ANGELES COLISEUM where Brad and Tiffany met at the 1984 Olympics. THE WOODSTOCK FESTIVAL as Brad and Tiffany sit in the rain. On the SET OF THE WHEEL OF FUTURE Brad makes a prediction.

                    BRAD
          December Eighth, Nineteen Eighty?
          John Lennon gets shot. Oh, my God
          I've got to save him!!!

OUTSIDE OF THE DAKOTA, MARK CHAPMAN is about to shoot LENNON when Brad kicks the gun from his hand.

TELEVISION

                    NEWSMAN
          John Lennon, who just escaped an
          assassin's bullet, said that the Beatles
          will reunite on the Isle Of Wyte, if
          it's not too dear.

INSIDE A PRIVATE JET, JOHN, PAUL, GEORGE and RINGO are harmonizing - Brad is floating above them. Suddenly one of the engines catches fire and the jet takes a nose dive - pandemonium - John looks up at Brad.

                    JOHN
          Now the world's going to lose all
          the Beatles. Ya can't screw with
          history, Brad.

As the jet plummets further, Brad slips through a black hole.

                    JOHN
          No one knows how many holes it
          takes to fill the Albert hall…

Brad wakes up.

                    BRAD
          I don't want to change history. All
          I want to do is find Tiffany.

                    1980

GREENWICH VILLAGE. It's LATE EVENING, OUTSIDE a GAY COWBOY BAR.

INSIDE - Everyone's an Urban Cowboy. Larry and Lester who sport leather pants
are shirtless and are wearing cowboy hats.

MUSIC - Boz Scaggs, *LOVE, LOOK WHAT YOU'VE DONE TO ME*

Hand in hand they walk to the dance floor and embrace. Darryl is also dressed in
full cowboy regalia, complete with chaps and butt exposed. He's at the bar drinking
a glass of milk and talking with the BARTENDER.

                    DARRYL
          They can be a little rough sometimes,
          but I owe my life to them.

                    BARTENDER
          Well, Clint, if I were you I'd go back
          to Hollywood.

                    DARRYL
          I'm *not* Clint Eastwood. Clint's a real
          cowboy. I don't know who I am. I
          have no recollection.

                    BARTENDER
                    (facetiously)
          Must be the milk of amnesia.

The bartender then reaches into his pocket and takes out an Amyl Nitrate.

                    BARTENDER
          Wanna do a popper?

Before Darryl can resist, the bartender snaps the popper into Darryl's nose. Darryl
gets the full effect as he holds onto the bar for dear life.

                    DARRYL
          Woah! What the fff…

He looks around.

                              DARRYL
              Where am I?

The popper has jarred his memory. Darryl has regained his memory. He looks into
the mirror in shock. He observes the clientele and wonders why he's here.

                              DARRYL
                            (to himself)
              I hope I'm undercover.

Larry approaches Darryl and puts his arm around him while Lester pays the
bartender.

                              LESTER
              Come on, honey. It's time to go home
              and vacuum.

                              LARRY
              Hopefully, the Electrolux still has good
              suction.

Horrified, Darryl jerks away. He takes his cowboy hat and tosses it aside. He
then punches Larry in the mouth. As blood comes pouring from Larry's lip, Lester
gets hysterical.

                              LESTER
              Oh, my God, Larry, are you alright?
              You bitch! Why did you do that?

                              DARRYL
              Drop dead, you queer.

                              LARRY
              That's the tea kettle calling the Teflon beige.

Darryl can stand no more. He runs from the bar as if he were on fire.

OUTSIDE on the STREET, Darryl picks up the pace. His cheeks bounce with
every stride. As he turns the corner, he collides with TWO COPS who are on
beat. He knocks one of them down. The other cop draws his weapon and pushes
Darryl up against a brick wall.

                                    COP
                    Okay, Tex, turn around and assume the
                    position. Holy shit, it's Bronco Billy!

JFK AIRPORT - AFTERNOON

It's a few days later. Darryl is on a payphone.

                                  DARRYL
                    Thanks Bill. I'll pay you back as
                    soon as my FBI pension kicks in
                    again. Bye.

He sits for a moment deep in thought as he slips into a

FLASHBACK

Darryl and Tiffany sitting on a picnic blanket when they were dating in 1972.

                                  DARRYL
                    When did you and your husband first
                    meet?

                                  TIFFANY
                    The Nineteen Eighty Four Olympics.

Darryl then flashes to 1976 when Brad was passed out at the bar and talking in his
sleep, at Disco Seventies.

                                  DARRYL
                    Where are you now?

                                   BRAD
                    The Nineteen Eighty Four Olympics.

                                  DARRYL
                    Where?

                                   BRAD
                    About mid field. I can see the Budweiser
                    sign.

END FLASHBACK

Darryl gets up and heads towards his terminal.

1981

BEVERLY HILLS - OUTSIDE of a HOLISTIC CENTER - MORNING.

MUSIC - Foreigner's, *URGENT*

Brad is on a payphone near the entrance.

> **BRAD**
> How about Tiffany Scott?
> (a beat)
> Maybe it's under Miller.
> (a beat)
> No. Okay thanks.

Brad goes INSIDE and up a flight of stairs. He enters a room. An AA meeting is in progress. A SPEAKER addresses a GROUP of rich drunks.

> **SPEAKER**
> And now I'd like to introduce you
> to our guest speaker. She drank
> herself into a gutter. Now she's back
> with a vengeance. Sharon, come on
> up and share.

SHARON comes up to the podium and practically pushes the speaker out of the way. She's a perky little princess.

> **SHARON**
> Hi! My name is Sharon, one day sober.
> And I'm a lying, cheating, gambling,
> back stabbing, two timing, drug addict,
> credit card abusing, child molesting,
> police informant, nympho, bi sexual,
> embezzling, sadist, insider trading,
> kleptomaniac, incestuous and grateful
> alcoholic.

> **BRAD**
> (to himself)
> I need a drink.

The CAMERA PULLS OUT OF THE ROOM, OUT OF THE WINDOW AND PANS TO THE OTHER SIDE OF THE BUILDING AND PUSHES INTO A WINDOW.

INSIDE, a group therapy session is now in progress. Tiffany and her GROUP sit in a circle. A PSYCHOLOGIST is rambling on about the inner child. Tiffany glances down at a newspaper she has on her lap.

CLOSE ON PAPER - Circled in the classified section is an ad she put in.

> PSYCHOLOGIST
> …so the inner child's insatiable libido sucks
> the life from all who…
> (distracted)
> Tiffany, please share what you're reading
> with us.

Tiffany, is completely removed from the group and unconsciously reads her ad.

> TIFFANY
> SWF seeks husband lost in time. Going
> back to the future is a drag without you.
> Brad, please rescue me. Love Tiffany.

The GROUP starts sucking their thumbs.

> PSYCHOLOGIST
> (annoyed)
> Shall I get everyone a blankie!

1982

MUSIC - Toto's, *ROSANNA*

It's SUNSET on SANTA MONICA BEACH. Brad sits with a group of HOMELESS people, sharing a bottle of wine. He soon passes out.

1983

MUSIC - Missing Person's, *NOBODY WALKS IN L.A.*

MAIN STREET - Santa Monica - MORNING. INSIDE A WOMEN'S BOUTIQUE. Tiffany is waiting on an overweight WOMAN with a slight mustache when she notices the woman's newspaper. The headline reads:

1984 Olympics Ceremonies Scheduled At Coliseum

                    TIFFANY
                  (cryptically)
          That's it! The Eighty Four Olympics.
          That's where we first met.

                    WOMAN
                   (whining)
          Could you please hurry. I'm late for
          my electrolysis appointment.

                    TIFFANY
          Would you like some Gouda with
          that whine?

Tiffany gets on the phone and calls information.

                    TIFFANY
          Yes, do you have a listing for a Brad
          Miller?
                   (a beat)
          How about Brad Scott or Brad Westlake?
                   (a beat)
          No? Thank you.

                      1984

THE LOS ANGELES COLISEUM - 1984 OLYMPIC CEREMONIES - NIGHT

MUSIC - Hall and Oats, *SAY IT ISN'T SO*

Tiffany sits in the stands with her binoculars, just as she did eighteen years prior.

At the ENTRANCE, Brad passes the turnstile and takes out his binoculars. He tries to get his bearings.

                    BRAD
          Let's see…

He walks by a CONCESSION STAND and spots a sign - BEER AND WINE. He watches as the spout from the draft keg oozes out beer. It flows smoothly into a big cup that leaves a big frothy head. Brad begins to tremble. He can no longer contain himself. He goes over to the stand and buys a large beer. He looks at the beer for a moment. Brad downs the beer and orders another and downs that.

It's the final ceremony of the Olympics. Brad is passed out in his seat. He comes to.

> BRAD
> Oh, shit!

He frantically takes out his binoculars and looks through them.

POV BINOCULARS, panning the stands.

> BRAD (O.S.)
> Come on Tiffany, you've got to be
> here.

He stops at a woman. Right above her is the Budweiser sign. It's Tiffany.

> BRAD (O.S.)
> Is that her? It's been so long.

Brad focuses in clearer. Tiffany raises her binoculars.

> BRAD (O.S.)
> It's her!!!

Just then, a man behind Tiffany taps her on the shoulder and says something to her. It's Clint Eastwood. He points to the exit. They both get up and leave.

> BRAD
> No! Tiffany. It's Darryl!!!

Brad tries to stay with them, but gets lost in the crowd.

STADIUM PARKING LOT - Darryl drives Tiffany to her car.

INSIDE THE CAR, Tiffany and Darryl/Clint Eastwood resume their conversation.

> TIFFANY
> So I thought maybe my long lost
> husband would be here. It was a
> long shot.

> DARRYL
> Would you like to have a cup of
> coffee, some place?

                              TIFFANY
                    Oh, I'm flattered, but I think I'm
                    just going to call it a night.

                              DARRYL
                    Where do you live?

                              TIFFANY
                    Beverly Glen near Wilshire.

                              DARRYL
                    I live near there. At least let me follow
                    you home and be sure you get in safely.
                    Helping a pretty lady makes my day.

OUTSIDE OF TIFFANY'S APARTMENT BUILDING, Tiffany parks her car. Darryl
pulls up behind her and they exit their cars. Darryl approaches Tiffany.

                              DARRYL
                    Can I see you in?

                              TIFFANY
                    That's very sweet Mr. Eastwood, but
                    aren't you married?

                              DARRYL
                    Oh, yeah. I guess a man's got to know
                    his limitations.

Tiffany extends her hand.

                              TIFFANY
                    Thanks, it's been an honor.

                              DARRYL
                    Good night.

He waits while Tiffany makes her way in and enters an elevator.

LATER THAT EVENING, INSIDE TIFFANY'S BEDROOM. Tiffany is in her bathrobe.
She wraps a towel around her head as she goes into the bathroom. On a dresser, near
the bed, a picture of Brad and Tiffany on the set of *THE WHEEL OF FUTURE*.

From the window there's a silhouette of a man. He jimmys the window open and
enters. It's Darryl. He takes out a flash light and scans the room.

He spots the picture of Brad and Tiffany. He then goes through the dresser drawers. He finds a picture album. He quickly brings it over to the bed and looks through it.

CLOSE ON PICTURES. Different photos of Brad and Tiffany. The electronic digital date on the bottom of the photos read SEPTEMBER 1987.

DARRYL
I knew it.

The SOUND of a toilet flushing as Tiffany exits the bathroom. Darryl quickly takes the album and moves to the window. Tiffany enters the bedroom, sees the intruder and lets out a blood-curdling scream. It startles Darryl as he drops the album. As he goes to retrieve it Tiffany gets a better look at him.

TIFFANY
Mr. Eastwood!

Darryl loses his footing and falls out the window. Tiffany then runs to the window.

TIFFANY'S POV - From four stories up, Darryl is lying face down on the pavement.

Later, on the street, an AMBULANCE and THREE POLICE CARS are now on the scene. From amidst the flashing lights, Tiffany is giving an account of what happened to one of the COPS as TWO PARAMEDICS scrape Darryl from the pavement.

PARAMEDIC #1
Whew! This guy's a mess.

PARAMEDIC #2
Now I know what they mean by a
sidewalk pizza.

PARAMEDIC #1
Hmm. I could go for a pizza now,
myself.

As they load Darryl into the ambulance, another PARAMEDIC starts sticking tubes in Darryl's arms and nose.

PARAMEDIC # 3
We're going to need more tubes.

PARAMEDIC # 1
Waddia say we get a pizza and
watch the tube at my place, later.

TIFFANY
Yes, officer, I'm positive it was Clint
Eastwood.

One of the cops looks over to the ambulance as one of the paramedics shakes his
head, "no."

COP # 1
I don' think he's going to make it.

COP # 2
He has no ID on him. See if Clint
Eastwood's home.

COP # 1
I loved *Every Which Way, But Loose.*

COP # 2
His Orangutan period was his best work.

1985

From a window in BRAD'S APARTMENT, there's a MOON LIT SKY. Brad is watching
MIAMI VICE on TV. CROCKETT and TUBS are beating up two drug smuggling
punks dressed in GOOFY and MICKEY costumes at DISNEY WORLD. Crockett
takes a bag of cocaine from Mickey.

CROCKETT
What are you goofy, pal?

MICKEY
No, he is. Ah, Mr. Crockett, shouldn't
you be in Frontier Land?

Brad shuts off the TV and heads out.

OUTSIDE, across from Brad's building there's a PARK. In the center of the park
there's a stage. Above the stage a banner reads:

**Let's raise money to buy cab fare for the people in Ethiopia so
they can get a ride to where the food is.**

There is a large crowd of people surrounding the stage. ON STAGE, a comedian
named LICE MUD is doing his act.

                              LICE MUD
              Y'know the difference between Sandra
              Bernhard and a bowling ball?

Brad finishes the joke.

                           BRAD & LICE MUD
              You can't get your fist into a bowling
              ball. Hoowah.

FLASHBACK of the first time this happened. A younger Brad and Tiffany laugh as
they watch the show with their arms around each other. A commotion in the back of
the crowd has taken attention from Lice's show.

                              LICE MUD
              What am I a fuckin' mirage?

Brad's flashback is interrupted by a voice. A MAN carrying a cooler calls out.

                                MAN
              Get your ice cold beer, here. Hey
              mister, cold beer, two bucks.

                               BRAD
              No thanks.

Towards the back of the crowd, Tiffany looks around hoping to find Brad at this event
that they attended twenty years prior. She spots him and calls out.

                              TIFFANY
              Brad!

Lice is so loud he can't hear her.

                              TIFFANY
              Brad!

TWO STREET TOUGHS standing in front of her turn around.

                           STREET TOUGH # 1
              Shut the fuck up. We can't hear Lice.

                              TIFFANY
              You're kidding.

STREET TOUGH # 2
I'll show you kidding.

They whisk her to the outer perimeter of the crowd and start roughing her up. Some of the people close by react, but no one gets involved. Brad notices the commotion.

BRAD
(looks around)
What's going on?

An OLD WOMAN standing next to Brad comments.

OLD WOMAN
It's probably just a bunch of homeless
bums fighting over some sushi.

Brad's curious and pushes through the crowd to see what's happening. He sees the thugs man-handling a woman and decides to get involved. They start to drag Tiffany towards some thick brush at the end of the park. Brad catches up.

BRAD
Hey fellas, why don't you pick
on someone your own gender?

TIFFANY
Brad! Help me!

When he realizes it's Tiffany he springs into action, diving on one of the punks. He then pummels him with a barrage of punches. The other punk releases Tiffany and kicks Brad in the head, knocking him down. Tiffany reaches in her purse and pulls out some pepper spray. Brad has disabled one. Tiffany sprays the other guy in the face. He runs away, whimpering. She's about to dose the other creep, when he crawls away.

TOUGH # 2
Please don't hurt me!

Tiffany immediately tends to Brad. Dazed, he tries to lift himself up. She holds him.

TIFFANY
Oh, my God, Brad. Are you alright?

He shakes it off and comes to life when he sees Tiffany.

BRAD
Did you kick their asses, honey?

They embrace hard and long, hanging on in fear that each may disappear.

> BRAD
> Oh, Tiffany! I thought I'd never see
> you again. I tried calling you. Why
> weren't you listed?

> TIFFANY
> Oh, I went back to my maiden name.
> I tried calling you, too.

A crowd starts to gather.

> BRAD
> You're fifty-one now and you look
> great, baby. How have you been?

> TIFFANY
> When you were in prison, I really lost
> it. I went altruistic for a while and went
> underground.

> BRAD
> I went underground, too. Booze. I was
> living like a bum. I didn't even have a
> phone, but I'm sober now.

Tiffany caresses Brad's forehead.

> BRAD
> I almost caught up with you at the
> Olympics, but you ran off with Darryl.

> TIFFANY
> Some guy posing as Clint Eastwood…
> …that was Darryl?

They kiss. From the crowd that's gotten bigger. A MAN asks.

> MAN
> Hey, mister, do you need any help?

> BRAD
> No thanks. Where were they a minute
> ago?

236

TIFFANY

Crowds.

She looks at his bump again.

TIFFANY

Let's take care of that.

BRAD

Okay, honey.
(a beat)
I miss New York. Let's go back.

Tiffany shakes her head, "yes." They hug again. The man in the crowd starts to sing.

MAN

Those little town blues, are melting
away.

Soon, the others start signing along.

CROWD

I want to be a part of it. New York,
New York.

From the STAGE, the crowd has shifted from Lice Mud to Brad and Tiffany.

LICE MUD
What am I, a fuckin' mirage?

1986

NEW YORK - RAND MAC - DAY

MUSIC - Art Of Noise, *PETER GUN*

Brad and Tiffany reminisce as they walk by Brad's old place of employment.

BRAD

It's hard to believe that I invented a
doomsday bomb here. I wonder what
mode of destruction they're coming
up with this time? Come on.

> TIFFANY

Huh?

> BRAD

Just playin' a hunch. Let's go in.

They walk up the stairs and INSIDE the lobby. Brad spots Dick Jennings getting a drink from a water fountain.

> BRAD

Talk about a déjà vu. There's the Dick who
fired me seventeen years ago. Come on.

Brad and Tiffany slip past a SECURITY GUARD and head down a CORRIDOR. A sign on a door, DEVELOPMENT marks his old office.

> BRAD

My old office.

They slip INSIDE. On a blackboard in the corner, written in yellow chalk are the words, OPERATION NICE BOMB, a variation of his own discovery.

> BRAD

Wow! The only thing that's changed
is one word.

> TIFFANY

Wasn't yours, Operation Clean
Bomb?

Just then a man of about thirty enters. He is PHILIP.

> PHILIP

What are you doing here? How did
you get past security?

> BRAD

I used to work here. My name's Brad.

Brad extends his hand, un welcomed by Philip.

> BRAD

Let me ask you. Ah, what's your name?

> PHILIP

It's Philip, now I must ask you to leave.

238

                    BRAD

Philip, please indulge me just one
moment. Operation Nice Bomb.
Is this your idea?

                    PHILIP

Yes.

                    BRAD

Amazing. I guess it's inevitable no
matter who's here.

                    PHILIP

What?

                    BRAD

I know this is going to sound crazy,
but your boss, Dick Jennings, will
steal this idea and fire you. Please,
you've got to scrub the project.

                    PHILIP

How do you know this?

                    BRAD

I just know.

                    PHILIP

You know, it's funny, I don't trust
him. He's taken credit for several of
my ideas.

Philip's phone RINGS.

                    BRAD

Philip, believe me, scrap this idea.
Annihilating people is not the answer.

Brad and Tiffany exit. Philip picks up the phone.

                    PHILIP

Yes. Mr. Jennings. I can't seem to get
out of the gate with this one. Sure. I'll
stay with it.

He walks over to the blackboard, takes an eraser and erases OPERATION NICE BOMB.

OCTOBER 19TH, 1987 - THE CRASH

INSIDE THE NEW YORK STOCK EXCHANGE - DAY

MUSIC - The O'jays, for the Love of *MONEY*

Brad and Tiffany stand, watching the Dow Jones numbers plummet, just as they did eighteen years prior. Suddenly a cacophony of ALARMS and BELLS go off as the Market closes. Pandemonium sets in as PEOPLE rush from the building. Brad and Tiffany are pushed outside by this human Tsunami.

OUTSIDE, the sea of people rush into nearby bars and pubs. A BODY drops from above.

> BRAD
> Well, there it is again.

> TIFFANY
> You know, we celebrate an anniversary
> tomorrow.

> BRAD
> Yeah, that's the day we went back in
> time. Call me crazy, but what do you
> say we take a ride upstate to
> commemorate.

> TIFFANY
> Sounds like fun.

UPSTATE NEW YORK. It's a beautiful October AFTERNOON. An AERIAL SHOT of Brad's car cruising down a COUNTRY ROAD. INSIDE the car Brad and Tiffany reflect.

> TIFFANY
> Getting shot in the foot and losing my
> mind wasn't much fun. Being without
> you for ten years was awful. But losing
> the baby was the worst.

> BRAD
> Having a child certainly would have
> changed things.

240

                              TIFFANY
                    Here I am at fifty-three with no kids.
                    I wonder if we're too old to adopt?

Brad puts his arm around her.

                              BRAD
                    We can try. We'd definitely make better
                    parents now. I can't believe we did this
                    eighteen years ago.

                              TIFFANY
                    If we didn't go back, it would be two
                    thousand and five. By then they'll
                    probably have electric cars, no foreign
                    oil…

                              BRAD
                    Automation, computers and robots, so
                    no need for illegal aliens. World peace
                    and harmony.

                              TIFFANY
                    Alright, now you're pushing it.

Brad fixes on his REAR VIEW MIRROR - Reflection of a CAR.

                              BRAD
                    This car's been following us since
                    the interstate.

Suddenly, the car pulls along side of them. A DEFORMED MAN waves a gun and motions
them to pull over. Brad complies. Both cars pull off to the side of the road. The man gets
out and motions them to get out. They do. The man then gestures to them to move behind
a huge OAK TREE.

                              BRAD
                    Look, mister if it's money you want,
                    she's loaded.

                              TIFFANY
                    Don't listen to him. He's the one with
                    all the money.

DEFORMED MAN
Shut the fuck up!

TIFFANY
Oh my God it's Darryl! You survived
the fall. Ah, you look great.

DARRYL
Never mind the bullshit. I don't want
money. I want *truth*. I finally have you
both together after all these years.

TIFFANY
Together after all these years? This isn't
going to be a menage-a-trois or anything is it?

DARRYL
Shut up!

BRAD
From Darryl Hanna to Clint Eastwood.
Let me guess. This week it's Lon Chaney?

DARRYL
I said, shut up!! Now you better tell me
everything or I'll cut you down right
now. Did you two go back in time?

BRAD
Don't be ridiculous.

Darryl shoots above Brad's head.

BRAD
Yes, we did. Can we go now?

DARRYL
Oh, you'll go alright. You stirred up a lot of
trouble with that show of yours. You've ruined
my life. My face! Look at my face!! Now I want
to go back in time and fix everything. How do I
do that?

TIFFANY
Take it easy. Really, we don't know.
We just wound up in the past. Honestly.

                         DARRYL
              You've got about five seconds to tell
              me how to go back or you're dead.

CLOSE ON DARRYL'S WATCH as the seconds melt away. DARRYL'S TRIGGER
FINGER as he SHOOTS.

The shot rings LOUD. As the smoke slowly subsides, the bullet exits the cylinder
in SLOW MOTION. The bullet is about to penetrate Brad's skull, when everything
FREEZES.

Back in the classroom, the teacher has hit the STOP BUTTON on the I.T.M. control
panel.

                      TEACHER (O.S.)
              That Darryl sure is persistent. Okay,
              let's send Brad and Tiffany back to
              when they transcended time.

The teacher sets the time mode back to the FIRST 1987, when Brad and Tiffany went back
to 1969.

Brad's BMW is cruising down a country road on that beautiful October day. Brad
pulls over and parks the car. A YOUNG Brad and Tiffany walk from the car just as it
happened eighteen years before. They resume their original conversation.

                         TIFFANY
              Oh, God I'd give anything to go back to
              a simpler time. No responsibilities, no deadlines…

                          BRAD
              No money.

                         TIFFANY
              It's always something

Brad and Tiffany are now FROZEN in space and time as the SCREEN goes blank.

                         TEACHER
              Well, class. Brad and Tiffany have gone full circle.
              Eighteen years have transpired for them. One
              hundred and eight minutes for us. That concludes
              our experiment for today. So, did we learn anything
              from their experiences?

ZWEETHANE
Yes, greed is not good.

AAALLLFFFIE
Too much knowledge is dangerous.

PERTHUD
And if you're going to look like Clint
Eastwood, you'd better back it up.

TEACHER
Good. All right, let's get some sustenance.

From the back of the classroom, a STUDENT points to the SCREEN.

Brad and Tiffany are knocked to the ground, unconscious. Brad and Tiffany start to
come around and are a bit dazed, just as it happened when they were zapped back
to 1969.

The teacher, puzzled, tries to reset the Interdimensional Time Mode to no avail.

TEACHER
Hmm. The I.T.M. seems to be
malfunctioning. We've exceeded one
hundred and eight minutes and for
some reason it's starting over again.

On the SCREEN, Brad looks a the joint he lit before the time jolt. He tosses it, just
as it happened the first time.

BRAD
What the hell was that? Are you okay,
honey?

TIFFANY
I'm jonesing for some Haagen-Daz.

TEACHER
I better check the coordinates.

He activates his computer and searches for the adjustment.

Meanwhile Brad and Tiffany are approached by the hippies on their way to Woodstock,
just as it happened before. Brad realizes that they're time tripping once again.

BRAD

Oh, no. We must be in déjà vu, flashback,
Retro Hell. Wow, we're thirty something
again. Maybe this is how life *is*. A series of
reincarnations. Only, each time we keep
coming back as ourselves.

TIFFANY

Look on the bright side. We're young
again. We've had two rehearsals. Maybe
this time we can get it right.

The teacher is making adjustments on the Interdimensional Time Mode. He checks
a page on his computer screen.

TEACHER

Oh, I didn't lock in the closing time.
Okay, go back three seconds. That
should put them back a few days.

At Woodstock, Hendrix is playing the *STAR SPANGLED BANNER*. He suddenly freezes and
disappears.

Brad and Tiffany are back at White Lake.

BRAD

What the hell was that? Are you okay,
honey?

TIFFANY

I'm jonesing for some Haggen-Daz.
Hey, didn't I just say that a minute
ago?

BRAD

What the hell's going on here?

TIFFANY

Here? Where's that?

BRAD

Déjà Vu Déjà Vu.

Tiffany rubs her stomach.

245

TIFFANY
Brad. I'm pregnant again!

BRAD
The way it's going here, he'll be
swimming around in my testies.

TIFFANY
She.

BRAD
(smiling)
Whatever. If we get out of this, you're
staying put. You're not going to lose
the baby this time.

They kiss.

The teacher locks in the CLOSING TIME and from the screen, Brad fondles Tiffany's
tummy. The class CHEERS.

TEACHER
In our next session we'll monitor
Darryl from when we first met him.

He sets the Interdimensional Time Mode for AUGUST 1970 - DARRYL HANNA -
WASHINGTON D.C.

On the screen, a YOUNG DARRYL in his office, cleaning his gun.

An ELECTRONIC HUM goes off signaling lunch break. As the class leaves, the
teacher, distracted thinks he's hit the OFF KEY. Unwittingly, he hits the VORTEX
KEY. The teacher gets up and hastily exits the class.

TEACHER
Boy, am I hungry.

On the screen, Darryl, gun in hand, caught up in a TIME VORTEX is speeding
through different periods of time. At one point, Darryl is standing on a GRASSY
KNOLL, gun in hand. The shock of being zapped to another environment causes
him to shoot. The bullet hits a MAN in a limousine. As PEOPLE turn to look, Darryl
vanishes.

Next, Darryl is tied to a crucifix next to JESUS CHRIST, gun in hand. Jesus turns to look at Darryl and then looks up to the heavens.

                    JESUS
         Forgive him father, he knows not
         where he's at.

A CENTURIAN standing nearby, raises his spear and says to Darryl.

                  CENTURION
         So, you're the son of God.

                    JESUS
                (to Centurion)
         Psst! Over here.

Darryl vanishes. He is now catapulted to a CITY OF THE FUTURE, beyond our time. He stands, gun in hand, looking on with amazement. He spots what appear to be TWO POLICEMEN. They see his gun and pull out their weapons. And just as they shoot, Darryl disappears.

He is now spinning around in a whirlpool, a BLACK HOLE.

Next, Darryl is being chased by a DINOSAUR. He turns and empties the gun into the beast. All that does is provoke it more. And just as the dinosaur is about to devour Darryl, we…

CUT TO BLACK

HOOSIER DADDY

Pat Mulligan

FADE IN:

1979

MUSIC: SISTER SLEDGE'S, *WE ARE FAMILY*

An AERIAL SHOT of an old Ford station wagon with a U Haul trailer hitched on back, hitting the highway. It's a hot, August, summer day. Up ahead a big sign reads: WELCOME TO INDIANA, THE HOOSIER STATE. INSIDE of the car, RONALD SWEENEY, age twenty four is driving. His Mother, MARGARET, age fifty and his eighteen month old daughter, JENNIFER, sit in the back seat. Margaret is holding another BABY, barely a year old. Ronald NARRATES.

> RONALD (V.O.)
> That little package Mom's holding
> doesn't really belong to me.

Upon a closer look we SEE the baby is black.

> RONALD (V.O.)
> An ol' school chum of mine left l'il Lightnin
> on my door step with a note saying that he'd
> be back soon to pick him up. Well, soon
> never came. And his mom…

1978 - NEW ORLEANS

NIGHTTIME - From a window, an outside street light provides the only luminous source INSIDE of this dark and smoky room. The back of a WOMAN'S LEG comes into view.

> RONALD (V.O.)
> This shapely leg belongs to Jasmine.
> She's a wiggler. That's colloquial for
> exotic dancer.

A MAN'S HANDS tie a catheter around Jasmine's leg, just above the knee. On the man's right hand is a tattoo of Jesus. A CLOSE UP of a spoon being torched by a lighter. A syringe comes into view, sucking out the contents of the spoon. The man's finger taps the works, Some of the elixir squirts from the needle. He then injects Jasmine's leg.

> RONALD (V.O.)
> She's also the mother of baby Lightnin.
> For the grace of God, he's a healthy boy.

251

The man then unties the catheter. Soon the leg drops OUT OF FRAME as Jasmine plummets onto a bed, sighing with pleasure.

Meanwhile, a high school basketball game is in progress. Some CHEERLEADERS are screaming frantically. A BELL sounds, signifying that the game is over. The score reads:

HOME 68 VISITORS 66

The home SPECTATORS cheer. The home TEAM rushes the coach, Ronald, put him on their shoulders and parade him around the court.

> RONALD (V.O.)
> It was nice winning the championship.

Later, that night on the other side of town - A neon sign in bright red, flashes the outline of a naked lady with the words CLUB SODA flickering across the rear end of this seductive configuration.

INSIDE, on STAGE, a young Nubian goddess goes through her paces, dancing and slithering across the floor. She smiles down on a middle aged, BLUE COLLAR GUY. He gratefully stuffs a wad of George Washingtons down her bikini top. A CLOSE UP of the back of her leg exposes some tracks. This is JASMINE COWIN.

From across the club a slick looking Hispanic dude named RODRIGO sucks the life from a cigarette he's finished. Smoke shoots from his nose as he crushes out the butt with his over shined slip-on. He flashes a big, toothy grin at Jasmine. She smiles back.

OUTSIDE, it is raining. An old pimped-out Cadillac spins, making a quick power turn in front of the club. The Caddy over swerves and then recovers.

INSIDE of the car, JOE FAVREAU, barely twenty one, drives down the street and parks. He takes his wallet from the glove compartment, flips it open, exposing a cops badge and then puts it in his jacket. He checks himself out in the rear view mirror. His reflection shows a handsome, Adonis-like black man. He then pulls out a pistol, checks the cartridge and flips it back shut and stashes it. Joe carefully exits the vehicle. As he walks towards the club, he changes his gait to a "jive-walk" as he slips on a beret.

INSIDE of the club, Joe swaggers down a few steps and heads towards the bar. He then spots Jasmine. His jaw drops. She returns the gaze, equally as smitten.

THUNDER AND LIGHTNING

Flashing lights emerge from the front window. The power goes off for a second, slowing the music and dowsing the lights briefly.

Rodrigo catches the exchange between Jasmine and Joe, whips out a Winston and lights it with a netted table candle. On his hand there's a tattoo of Jesus. Joe saunters over to the bar. BUTCH, is the manager/bartender/bouncer.

                    BUTCH
          What'll it be?

                    JOE
          Club soda.

                    BUTCH
          How apropos.

Butch fills a glass with ice and puts a bottle of club soda in front of Joe. Joe gawks at Jasmine.

                    JOE
          A little slow tonight, huh?

                    BUTCH
          It's early.

A few more patrons enter. THREE GUYS and A GIRL. Jasmine has finished her set. The EMCEE comes out applauding.

                    EMCEE
          Let's hear it for Jasmine. Our next dancer
          is working her way through law school.
          Ooo, Selena, you're leading the witness.

SELENA comes out while Jasmine steps off stage to a small but enthusiastic applause from some OLD GUYS up front. Jasmine approaches the bar and sits next to Joe.

                    JASMINE
          Got a cigarette?

                    JOE
          Smokin's for chimneys.

Butch gives her one of his smokes and lights it for her. Jasmine notices the soda.

                    JASMINE
You don't smoke, you don't drink. What's
your pleasure?

                      JOE
I like to wrestle.

Butch pours Jasmine a brandy. The two guys and the girl who entered earlier go
over to Rodrigo. They slip away into the back room. Joe and Jasmine look at each
other, trying to conceal the smarts from Cupid's arrows.

Meanwhile, in a driveway next to a MODEST LITTLE HOUSE in the suburbs of New
Orleans, Ronald's old station wagon pulls in. He gets out, holding his TROPHY and
an umbrella. He steps up to the porch light and checks his mail. He sifts through the
mail and stops at one. He stares at it for a moment and goes inside.

INSIDE, Ronald sets his umbrella and trophy down, and as he opens up the letter we
SEE its contents. It's an official letter from the State of Louisiana. In affect, it states
that Ellen Sweeney is serving DIVORCE PAPERS. From the other room, Margaret,
calls out.

                  MARGARET (V.O.)
        Ronald?

                    RONALD
                 (preoccupied)
        Mmm-hmm.

Margaret enters the living room holding five month old Jennifer. On her pajamas in
big pink letters is the LUCKY 13.

                   MARGARET
        Any news?

Ronald automatically gives his mom a quick peck on the cheek while he reads on.

                    RONALD
                  (quietly)
        Money talks. Bullcrap walks.

He spots the pajamas.

                    RONALD
        Mom, why thirteen?

MARGARET
It was your father's lucky number.

RONALD
Lucky? He was run over by a garbage truck.

MARGARET
Well, when he was alive he was lucky.

As Ronald finishes reading the notice The CAMERA PANS over to the fireplace façade. On the mantel are several pictures of Ronald with his wife, parents, the baby and a couple of photos of some high school buddies. We get a CLOSE UP of Ronald and Joe Favreau.

BACK AT THE CLUB, Jasmine's back on stage, showing off for her new, future-ex-boyfriend. The house is starting to fill up. From the back of the room, the guy who entered earlier comes floating out. Rodrigo and the girl remain. Jasmine is burning up the stage. Joe goes to take a sip from his soda. He's mesmerized. He misses and slobbers the drink all over his jacket. Soon, Rodrigo and the girl exit from the back room. The girl can barely walk as Rodrigo holds her up. Joe is transfixed and doesn't notice.

The NEXT DAY, outside of a POLICE PRECINCT, COPS enter and exit. INSIDE, the CAMERA PUSHES though a door marked CAPTAIN SULLIVAN. A stocky, red faced, middle aged man is pacing and ranting. Joe sits humbly.

CAPTAIN SULLIVAN
God damn it, Joe! You didn't pop 'em? My
mother could have made that collar and she's
a cripple. Maybe I got you undercover too
soon.
(a beat)
I knew your ol' man well. He told me what
happened before he took his life. Joe, I'm
sorry. That's why I gave you an advantage.
But maybe you need to pay some dues.

JOE
Gimme another shot, will ya captain?

CAPTAIN SULLIVAN
Forget it. The commissioner wants that club
shut down. They're gonna hit 'em tonight.

Joe slowly heads out.

Outside of Club Soda, there's a line to get in. It's Friday night. As Joe approaches the club he slips into his pimp walk. Butch is checking IDs. He spots Joe and waves him over.

                              BUTCH
              Hey, Romeo, what did you do to my
              wiggler? Better hurry, she's on stage.

Butch lets Joe in ahead of the long line of people. Some MEN in front aren't too happy.

INSIDE, the place is packed. Jasmine's burning up the stage to the tune of *THE STRIPPER*. Jasmine makes fools of some horny OLD MEN up front. WOMEN in the audience go wild. Rodrigo, TWO PLAYERS and THREE HOOKERS are sitting in a booth in the center of the room. They're all obviously loaded and smoking in unison. One of the hookers nods out in her Mai Tai. Jasmine spots Joe at the bar. She immediately jumps off stage, runs up to Joe and plants a big kiss on the mouth. The CROWD goes nuts.

                              JOE
              Meet me out back after your set.

                           JASMINE
              I'm glad you came.

The crowd is still cheering. CAT CALLS permeate throughout the house. Butch steps in to see the commotion. He sees Jasmine off stage with Joe. He shakes his head disapprovingly and goes back outside as Jasmine runs back on stage. Joe heads out back. The Emcee staggers on stage.

                             EMCEE
                            (loaded)
              Let's hear it for the fabilis Jasmine (hic!)
              Guys, you can see her again in your next
              wet dream. Don't get too excited, I'll be
              there, too (hic!) Hey! Welcome to "fucked-
              up Fridays."

A WIZE-ASS in the audience heckles.

                           WIZE-ASS
              You suck!

He gets a big laugh.

                            EMCEE
Hey, pal! I'm just trying to make a living
up here. I didn't bug you when you were
blowin' all those guys in the men's room.

                          WIZE-ASS
And I appreciate that.

Everyone including the Emcee crack-up. Jasmine heads out back. The Emcee brings
on the next act.

                            EMCEE
Our next act puts on a nice spread. And she's
a good cook, too. Let's hear it for Cookie!

Cheers and whistles from the crowd as COOKIE comes out wearing just a Chef's
hat and an apron.

OUTSIDE, a loading platform and a few cars adorn the back of the club. The only
light comes from a FULL MOON. Joe jumps down from the platform. Jasmine exits
the club, lights up a cigarette and takes a drag. She looks down at Joe and smiles.

                             JOE
           C'mere.

Jasmine flicks the cigarette, walks to the edge of the dock and jumps. Joe scrambles
to catch her. She lands in his arms. They start making out. Joe breaks away.

                             JOE
Jasmine, are you using?

                          JASMINE
                        (innocently)
Using what?

                             JOE
Oh, please. Listen, I know some people
who want to shut this place down. Lay
low.
                         (a beat)
Why do you associate with Rodrigo?

                          JASMINE
Low self-esteem.

They resume making out.

Inside the club, Cookie is still cooking. Suddenly, several VICE COPS rush in, followed by UNIFORMED COPS who have Butch in hand cuffs. The vice cops rush Rodrigo's table. One cop flashes his badge while the others cuff Rodrigo and company. The hooker who nodded out earlier has apparently OD'd and is carried out.

Pandemonium ensues as people get up from their tables. The Emcee comes out and tries to take control.

                    EMCEE
          Folks! Hang out! Phyllis is a great
          orator. (Hic!) Please, a nice Club
          Soda welcome for Phyl Aysheeo.

It's useless. The crowd scrambles to leave as WAITRESSES try to collect checks. A uniformed COP takes the stage. He adjusts the mic and speaks into it.

                    COP
              (clears his throat)
          Good evening. Alright people, this party's
          over. Don't forget to tip your waitress.

A WEEK LATER. It's EARLY MORNING. Some WORKERS take down the club's sign.

During the next SERIES OF SHOTS, Ronald NARRATES.

                    RONALD (V.O.)
          The club went under new ownership.

Workers put up a new sign which reads: CLUB SEAL.

                    RONALD (V.O.)
          Club Seal wasn't much different than
          Club Soda. It was still a wiggler joint
          with the same staff.

Jasmine is dancing, to *THESE BOOTS WERE MADE FOR WALKIN'*. There's a full house, mostly a younger crowd.

                    RONALD (V.O.)
          Maybe a different clientele. The
          stakeout on the club had rescinded,
          but Joe had a stakeout of his own.

258

Joe is sitting at the bar still maintaining his pimp disguise. Jasmine shoots him grind shots in sync with the bass licks from the song.

> RONALD (V.O.)
> Joe and Jasmine's love affair was in full
> bloom. There was even a courtship.

In a RESTAURANT, at a table, Joe summons the WAITER. The waiter has a patch over one eye. Joe puts out Jasmine's cigarette, sprays Binaca in her mouth and gives her a kiss. Jasmine won't break away and the kiss gets steamy.

At the table, the waiter becomes impatient. While still in this very sensual, soul kiss, Joe opens one eye and looks at the waiter. He points to some items on the menu lying on the table. And as the waiter writes it down, Joe then gives him the "okay sign." The waiter rolls his eye, takes the menus and leaves.

In the PRODUCE SECTION of a grocery store, Joe and Jasmine are shopping. Joe fondles two ripe, juicy melons while Jasmine caresses a long, thick zucchini. They drop the items and start making out, catching dirty looks from TWO OLD LADIES and a PRISSY STORE MANAGER. One of the old ladies comments.

> OLD LADY
> Oh my! Two Negroes kissing in
> public. Someone call the police.

IN CHURCH, Joe sits next to Jasmine. He hears something. He looks over to see Jasmine nodded out and snoring.

> RONALAD (V.O.)
> Joe and Jasmine's love was passionate.
> They loved each other madly. However,
> they were diametrically opposed in every
> way. She was a strung-out stripper and he
> was a Presbyterian, vice cop.

In Jasmine's BATHROOM, she's about ready to inject herself with heroin when Joe walks in on her. He takes the works from Jasmine and shows her his badge.

> RONALD (V.O.)
> Joe, sternly scolds Jasmine and confesses
> to her that he's a cop.

Joe goes to shoot himself up, but stops and laughs.

259

                    RONALD (V.O.)
"Just kidding" he says. Joe can be a
caution.

Joe destroys the syringe with his bare hands. It's made of glass. He cuts himself.
Jasmine takes Joe's cut finger and puts it in her mouth, soothing the wound.

                    RONALD (V.O.)
Apparently, she was out of band-aids.

In Jasmine's LIVINGROOM, she puts Joe's hands on her tummy. Joe is deeply
moved.

                    RONALD (V.O.)
When Jasmine announced her
pregnancy, Joe proposed marriage.
Jasmine declined but, promised that
she would stop using.

In a HOSPITAL BED, Jasmine holds her new born, BABY BOY. Joe sits on the bed,
hugging them both. Jasmine is teary eyed.

                    RONALD (V.O.)
Having the baby seemed to have a
profound affect on Jasmine. They
name the baby, Lightnin.

FLASHBACK of the lightning storm at Club Soda when Joe and Jasmine first laid
eyes on each other.

In JASMINE'S BEDROOM, Joe puts some of his clothes in her closet, while she
breast feeds the baby.

                    RONALD (V.O.)
Joe moved in with Jasmine. It seemed
like they had become a normal, happy
couple.

                    JASMINE
Joe, I need to get back to work. Dancers
make good money and we need money,
honey.

                    JOE
Well, I work nights, too. Who's going to
watch Lightnin?

                  JASMINE
How about a baby sitter?

                    JOE
A stranger? No way. I'll call a friend.

A SHOT of Ronald sitting on his sofa feeding the baby. Little Lightnin clutches
Ronald's finger.

                   RONALD
                 (to Lightnin)
You got some big hands. Yes, you
gonna make a great basketball
player someday. Yes.

Ronald sniffs the air, checks out Lightnin's diaper and then looks at the baby bottle.

                   RONALD
What the heck is in this milk?

NIGHT - INSIDE Club Seal, Jasmine misses a step going on stage. Rodrigo and two
men are sitting in a booth: TANK, a hulk of a man and CARLOS, a young Hispanic.
Rodrigo winks at Jasmine. Joe is at the bar thinly maintaining his pimp act. Butch
automatically opens a bottle of soda and pours it in Joe's glass.

                   BUTCH
How's it goin'?

Joe glares at Rodrigo.

                    JOE
Same ol' shit, same ol' flies.

Jasmine finishes her set and goes out back for a smoke. Joe follows. Rodrigo signals
for Tank and Carlos to follow.

On the LOADING PLATFORM, outside, Joe is scolding Jasmine.

                    JOE
Are you nuts? You've got a little
baby, now. You're quitting this job!

Suddenly, Rodrigo's henchmen appear and confront Joe. Tank grabs Joe, while Carlos searches him. He pulls out Joe's wallet, flips it open, exposing Joe's badge.

                              TANK
                  Carlos, he's a fucking cop!

Joe recoils and pulls out his revolver. Tank pulls out his piece aiming it at Joe. Carlos chimes up.

                             CARLOS
                Are you loco, Tank! He's the law, esse.

Tank gets the message and puts away his piece. Jasmine runs to Joe, startling him, causing him to fire his gun. Jasmine catches the bullet and she falls off the platform. Joe, immediately jumps down to assist her as Tank and Carlos scramble from the scene.

                               JOE
                  Jasmine! Jasmine! Oh, God, no!!

The NEXT DAY at the precinct, Joe turns in his badge and gun. Captain Sullivan looks on in disdain.

Later, in a HOSPITAL ROOM, Joe enters. Lying in bed with an IV connected to her arm, Jasmine is recovering. On her shoulder, a large bandage protrudes from her gown. Rodrigo is at her side.

                            JASMINE
                 I'm leaving you, Joe. Rodrigo's my
                 man, now.

                              JOE
                 What about our son?

                            RODRIGO
                 We'll take care of him.

Joe glares at Rodrigo.

                              JOE
                 Over your dead body.

That NIGHT in Ronald's living room, Ronald and Margaret console Joe, who is holding Lightnin. The baby starts crying.

                              JOE
                    What am I gonna do now?

The NEXT DAY at JOE'S APARTMENT. He sits with the baby. Joe FLASHES BACK
to when he was a kid...

Joe is seven years old. He's sleeping when JOE'S DAD enters his room, drunk. He
takes off his police uniform and climbs in bed with Joe.

                           JOE'S DAD
                 Hey, boy time for your back rub.

                          YOUNG JOE
                    Where's Momma?

                           JOE'S DAD
                      She left us, Joe.

Joe's dad starts to weep. He then starts to fondle Joe and soon goes under the
covers. Joe cries out.

                          YOUNG JOE
                    Momma? Momma?!

BACK TO PRESENT

Joe stares at a picture of Jasmine. Her bikini clad pose is powerful. Joe FANTISIZES.
He is on stage with her. They embrace and become one.

THAT NIGHT, on the loading platform behind Club Seal, Rodrigo and Jasmine are
having a smoke. Someone approaches. It's dark and they can't make out the figure,
below. Suddenly, Joe appears and hoists himself onto the platform. Rodrigo senses
that a threat to him is eminent and he kicks Joe who is now on his haunches.

                            JASMINE
                     Joe!

Joe intercepts Rodrigo's foot and twists it around causing him to fall. Joe pulls
Rodrigo up and the two men engage in some fisticuffs. Rodrigo's a skillful boxer and
pummels Joe with some stinging combos. Joe's nose is bleeding. Joe blocks the
next series of punches and attempts to lay a haymaker on Rodrigo's noggin. Rodrigo
ducks and Jasmine catches the punch. It knocks her up against the building. She
barely recovers.

JASMINE
Joe, you're killin' me.

Joe sees red. With all his might, he swings at Rodrigo and connects. The blow knocks him off the platform and onto the pavement below. Joe jumps down and pulls Rodrigo up. Rodrigo is limp as his body crumbles into a heap. Joe realizes that his opponent is out for the count.

JASMINE
(screaming)
Joe! What the hell have you done!

Joe slips into the darkness.

The NEXT MORNING, OUTSIDE of Ronald's house, Joe carries a wicker basket. Inside of the basket, Lightnin, sleeping, is wrapped tightly in a flannel blanket. Joe sets the basket down in front of the door and re-examines a note that he has written which reads:

Ronald, Please take care of Lightnin. I'll be back, soon. Joe

He then rings the doorbell and scurries off.

RONALD (V.O.)
Well, soon never came. Rodrigo, later died
from a cerebral hemorrhage. Joe was tried
for third degree murder. Or as Joe put it…
"pimpslaughter."

Inside a COURTROOM, Joe approaches the bench. The JUDGE addresses Joe.

JUDGE
Although, I believe that your crime
was a service to our community, the
law must prevail. I sentence you to
eight years in Angola State Prison.

ON THE ROAD - INDIANA - DAY - INSIDE of Ronald's station wagon and we're BACK TO WHERE THE STORY BEGAN.

Margaret is sweating profusely. She sets baby Lightnin down while she wipes her face with a towel.

MARGARET
Ronny, the heat here is unbearable.

RONALD
Well, rural Indiana wouldn't've been my
first choice either, Mom, but they're
offering me way more than I was making
back home. Plus, we have another mouth
to feed.

Just then Margaret starts gasping for air. She chokes and then croaks, hunching forward in her seat.

RONALD
Mom! Mom!

The NEXT MORNING, at a GRAVE YARD behind an old church, a teary eyed Ronald holds Lightnin while standing with little Jennifer. A PASTOR throws dirt on Margaret's grave. An old wooden cross subs as a tombstone. The pastor is in the middle of a long winded speech.

PASTOR
…and Jacob who begat his son who
begat…

Baby Lightnin starts wailing as Joe looks up to the heavens in thanks. He then signals to the pastor to wrap and hands him some money. The Sweeney's then make their way to the car.

RONALD
(to camera)
Okay, now I have one *less* mouth to feed.

1995 - KUKAISION INDIANA

THE TRYOUTS

AN EXTERIOR SHOT OF TEIU HIGH SCHOOL

MUSIC: COOLIO'S *GANGSTA'S PARADISE*

INSIDE, on the BASKETBALL COURT, there are about TWENTY SIX BOYS trying out for the team. Also in attendance are some FACULTY and STUDENTS.

Lightnin, now sixteen is trying out for The Beavers, Varsity team. He's the only black kid attending Teiu High. An announcement is heard over the PA SYSTEM.

ANNOUNCER (V.O.)
Next in the foul shot drill, number
thirteen, Lightnin Sweeney.

Ronald winces, wondering how Lightnin got that number. Lightnin nervously dribbles for a moment. He shoots and misses. He has two more shots. The next ball bounces twice on the rim before it sinks. The third…Swish. CHEERS from Ronald, head coach and Jennifer, now seventeen. Silence from everyone else. TIM, the sub coach, yells out enthusiastically. Tim is handicapped and sports a wheelchair. Attached to his chair is a "Ahooga horn" which he applies when he's excited.

AHOOGA!!

ANNOUNCER (V.O.)
Next up, number fourteen, Blaine Coleman.

BLAINE is Tall, blonde and self-assured. As he leaves the bench he quips to his FELLOWS bunched up with him.

BLAINE
(sotto voce)
Looks like I'm going to have to show
Fudgie how it's done.

He throws thrice and "swishes" thrice. CHEERS from the crowd and

AHOOGA!!

During the rest of the tryouts each player is maneuvering, dribbling, passing and shooting hoops. Lightnin shines. He gets "wows" and applause from the people in the stands. With his back turned from mid court he throws the ball and "swish." The crowd goes wild. A CLOSE UP on Blaine's eyes as they turn bright GREEN.

The last drill, rebounding. Lightnin goes up for a rebound and is pushed by Blaine. Lightnin's subsequent fall causes an injured knee. As lightnin hobbles off the court, Blaine and his cronies snicker, off court. Frustrated, Ronald looks on.

The NEXT DAY, OUTSIDE OF SCHOOL, students entering and exiting.

INSIDE - A door marked "Principal Coleman." Inside the office, Ronald and the Principal, HARVARD COLEMAN, are in conference. Harvard examines a list of the new team.

HARVARD

Good. I have high expectations this year.
Our tradition here at Teiu High, as you
are well aware, is to get our basketball
champs off to Indiana University to become
Hoosiers. We both have sons on the team,
as well. Ah, and I hope there's no problems.

RONALD

What do you mean, sir?

HARVARD

Nothing, really.

Harvard shuffles some papers on his desk.

HARVARD

I understand you just bought a new home.

RONALD

Yes, I did.

HARVARD

Congratulations.

He extends his hand. The two men shake.

HARVARD

Keep up the good work.

It's a hot Saturday AFTERNOON. On the outskirts of Kukaision, in a quiet little
neighborhood, the SWEENEY HOME is nestled in between two big Oak trees and
surrounded by a white picket fence. In front is a driveway that leads to the garage.
On the garage door is a basketball hoop. Lightnin, sweating, is shooting baskets. His
knee is wrapped. Ronald steps out, brandishing a pitcher of lime Kool Aid.

RONALD

Thirsty?

LIGHTNIN

Hey, dad, I think I finally mastered
my hook, right *and* left. Wanna see?

RONALD

Why don't you take it easy. Save your knee.

267

Lightnin hooks one more as Ronald goes inside.

INSIDE, Jennifer sits at the dining room table playing solitaire and sipping on her frosty beverage. From the TV, a re-run of *Diff'rent Strokes*.

> JENNIFER
> The girls in my dance class have
> been exceptionally rude. They say
> we have different mommas, one
> white, one black. If our family were
> to have a sitcom, it would be called,
> "Diff'rent Storkes."

Ronald shuts off the TV and raises his glass.

> RONALD
> On the road to Hoosierville, there's
> bound to be some obstacles, but we
> all know that people are the same
> where ever you go.

> LIGHTNIN
> There's good and bad in everyone.

> JENNIFER
> Let those girls be catty. Here's to a great
> guy.
>   (a beat)
> Hoosier daddy.

Lightnin misunderstands.

> LIGHTNIN
> I don't know.

> JENNIFER
> No! To *our* dad. The Hoosier Daddy.

> RONALD
> Hey! Lightnin made the team. You are
> now a Beaver!

They clink glasses and cheer. Ronald looks at Lightnin's knee.

                        RONALD
              However, you won't be able to play in
              the first two games scheduled next week.

                       LIGHTNIN
              Hey, dad. Have you ever heard from my
              real daddy?

                        RONALD
                       (nervously)
              As I told you he was, ah, in the Army. He
              trained as a Green Beret and was injured
              badly. He was admitted at a V.A. hospital
              and I've never heard from him since.

                       LIGHTNIN
              Where was the V.A. hospital?

                        RONALD
              Ah, Washington.
                       (looks at watch)
              Hey, gotta run.

Ronald downs his Kool Aid and then takes his keys from the dining room table.

                        RONALD
              Okay, guys, I'll be back, later. I've got to
              take care of a couple of things.

CLOSE UP of two large breasts, covered with a tight yellow sweater. Soon, they
bounce as the woman bearing them picks up two dishes from a kitchen window and
walks towards a table at a busy restaurant, THE GREASY PLATTER.

The gum chewing waitress is BETSY. As she sets the two plates in front of Ronald,
she makes a point of brushing her ample bosom against his head.

                         BETSY
              Here ya go honey. Hey, you gonna join
              the poker tournament?

She points to a big sign near the entrance.

SIGN - POKER TOURNAMENT. COME RAISE MONEY FOR DEAN'S KIDS. FRIDAY, OCTOBER, 21st AT 7 P.M. IN THE BRILLO ROOM. DANCE CONTEST. PRIZES! BE HERE OR BE QUEER!

                         RONALD
          Not much of a card player, but I think
          my daughter may be interested.

                         BETSY
          More coffee? Looks like yer outta
          cream, too.

Betsy takes a pot from a passing WAITRESS and a creamer from another table. The TWO TRUCKERS gawking at her hardly object.

                         BETSY
          Got a couple-a-jokes.
                    (puts on little girl's voice)
          Daddy, where do babies come from?
                    (voice of a man)
          Well, baby girl, they come from the
          the stork.
                    (girl's voice)
          Well, then who fucks the stork?

Betsy laughs insidiously, complete with snorting. Ronald feigns amusement.

                         BETSY
          Hey, what's black and dribbles?

Ronald's almost afraid to hear the punch line and sips his coffee.

                         BETSY
          Your son.

Ronald spits out his coffee, Betsy snorts up a storm while the two truckers fall off their chairs from laughing. Ronald smarts from the joke, but the pain soon subsides when Betsy brushes her 38-double-Ds against his head on the way back to the kitchen.

INSIDE, Teiu High Basketball arena, Lightnin burns up the court as he scores big time. His grand standing doesn't sit too well with the other players, especially Blaine. Blaine waves his arms to Lightnin to pass the ball to him. Lightnin scores another basket. CHEERS from the home team as the scoreboard reads:

BEAVERS 28 CLAMDIGGERS 16

During the break, Blaine complains to Ronald.

                    BLAINE
         Coach, you've got to tell yer boy, there
         to stop hogging the ball.

Later, after the game in the LOCKER ROOM, Ronald addresses the team.

                    RONALD
         Good game boys. The Beaver's are
         six and 0 so far. Blaine, nice defense.
         Lightnin, please share the ball. This
         is a *team*! Okay, team shake!

The guys roll their eyes and half heartedly shake their bodies.

                    RONALD
         C'mon boys, more spirit.

                    BLAINE
         Coach. Is it okay if we slug each other
         instead.

                    RONALD
         Well, alright.

What starts to be a playful punching of each others arms evolves into a group slugging. Lightnin being the object of the slug-fest.

                    LIGHTNIN
         I think I liked the shake, better.

                    BLAINE
                  (sotto voce)
         Fag.

The other guys laugh it up. Ronald, frustrated, shakes his head.

                    RONALD
         Practice tomorrow, seven thirty.

THE NEXT DAY during lunch period at the school CAFETERIA, Lightnin is having lunch with Jennifer. He takes a salt shaker, shakes some salt on his food when the whole lid comes off dumping the remains all over his lunch. From a table nearby, Blaine and the boys laugh it up.

Later, in the SCHOOL CORRIDOR, Lightnin opens up his locker to find a big watermelon inside.

THE NEXT NIGHT, before the game in the LOCKER ROOM, Lightnin sets down his under things. He then retrieves his sneakers from his locker, while one of the BOYS shakes some hot sauce in his jock strap. Later, on the BASKETBALL COURT, Lightnin nurses the discomfort he feels in his crotch area which elicits laughter from the stands and prompts Tim to hit his

AHOOGA!

AT ANOTHER GAME, Blaine goes up for a rebound when his pants drop to the floor. A huge LAUGH from the spectators. An embarrassed Blaine pulls up his shorts and sees that the elastic has been cut. Blaine spots Lightnin smiling ear to ear.

AHOOGA!

LATE AFTERNOON, INSIDE of class, a TEACHER, standing in front of a black board, highlights the greater points of the Emancipation Proclamation. Near the list is a rendering of Abraham Lincoln. Jennifer listens intently. The rest of the class isn't as involved. One STUDENT makes faces behind Jennifer's back.

> TEACHER
> This was a difficult time for Lincoln. He
> fought within his own party, he fought
> deep depression and he fought the rigors…

> STUDENT
> (quietly)
> …of niggers.

The CLASS breaks out laughing which brings Jennifer to near tears. The teacher, unaware of the comment scolds the class for the disruption.

> TEACHER
> What seems to be so hilarious?
> (noticing Jennifer)
> Jennifer, what's wrong, child? Did
> someone say something hurtful to you?

Jennifer stands and is about to blow the whistle. She thinks better of it.

                         JENNIFER
               Oh, it's nothing, I just, ah, am...

                          STUDENT
                          (quietly)
               ...having my period.

                         JENNIFER
                     (absent mindedly)
               ...having my period.
                          (a beat)
               No!!!

More LAUGHTER, and just as the teacher is about to reprimand...

CLASS BELL

The class rushes out for the end of the school day. Jennifer slowly gets up from her desk. A tall, lanky boy wearing thick glasses approaches Jennifer. His mouth is full of braces causing him to speak with a lateral lisp. He is RALPH.

                          RALPH
               Hey, don't let those creeps bug you.
                       (humorously)
               They're ignornant.

Jennifer smiles.

                          RALPH
               I better walk you out. Never know
               what The Klan may be up to.

They head out of class and out of the building.

OUTSIDE, the ice has been broken and Jennifer has cheered up considerably. They continue walking.

                          RALPH
               Hey, do you play chess?

                         JENNIFER
               Not really. I'm more of a card player,
               especially poker.

Ralph, excited, pushes Jennifer.

                    RALPH
          Get out!

She drops her books. Ralph immediately picks them up.

                    RALPH
          Sorry. Hey, you know they're having a
          fund raiser, poker game and dance
          contest at the Greasy Platter this Friday
          night.

                    JENNIFER
          Poker. Isn't gambling illegal?

                    RALPH
          It's for charity. They raise money for
          The Dean Hospital Children's Wing.
          The winners get lots of prizes and junk.
          Hey, you wanna be my partner for the
          dance contest? You should just do it.

                    JENNIFER
          Hmm. Maybe I just will.

They continue walking past the track field. In the center of the field, the TEIU HIGH
TRACK AND FIELD TEAM, a pumped up, testosterone based group of lads are in
rows doing squat thrusts. The COACH calls out the drills, keeping them in rhythm.

                    COACH
          One, two, three. look at Mr. Lee.
          Three, four, five. Look at him jive.

A beautiful October day in full autumn drag, showcases the campus foliage with
radical colors of red and yellow and green. Some leaves blow off of an Elm tree and
lightly drift past the head of a bruiser named BILLY BILL. He punches at the leaves
and accidentally smacks a BOY standing next to him.

                    BILLY BILL
          Whoopsie.

The boy stops, reeling from the hit.

COACH

One, two, buckle my shoe.

BOY

Fuck!

COACH

Three, four, shut your mouth. Okay,
guys, once again. One, two, three,
four. What are we fightin' for...

From behind the stands, Lightnin has been running and is out of breath. Soon, Blaine
and crew catch up to Lightnin. Blaine starts thumping Lightnin and Judo kicks his
knee. Lightnin yells out in pain and drops to the ground when Billy Bill, who sees the
ruckus yells out.

BILLY BILL

Hey! What are you guys doin'?
Let's get 'em!

The Field and track team are in pursuit. The basketball team is no match and they
scramble like roaches. Lightnin is horizontal and is in no shape to run. Billy Bill picks
him up buy the scruff of his jacket as if he were a rag doll.

BILLY BILL

Lookie here, we got us a fudgy. Looks like
your teammates did a number on ya, boy.

The coach intervenes.

COACH

Okay, boys, calisthenics. Billy Bill, take
this boy to the infirmary.

BILLY BILL

What???

COACH

Do it!!

Billy Bill reluctantly assists Lightnin as the coach and team jog back to center field.
Billy Bill has his arm around Lightnin's waist.

LIGHTNIN

People will say we're in love.

Billy Bill releases his hold as Lightnin drops to the ground, groaning in pain.

                    LIGHTNIN
          Okay, I asked for it. Please, help me up.

Billy Bill complies.

                    BILLY BILL
          Okay, Fudge. Just watch it.
               (a beat)
          So how come the Beavers star player
          is gettin' whopped by his teammates?

                    LIGHTNIN
          If you have to ask that question, you're
          as dumb as you look.

Billy Bill is ready to pounce. He looks over at the coach who is watching and changes course.

                    BILLY BILL
          I told you to watch it, boy.

Lightnin stumbles. Billy Bill retrieves him.

                    BILLY BILL
          Hey, I gotta admit, you're one heckava
          good athlete.

                    LIGHTNIN
          And so are you, if you want to call track
          and field a sport.

                    BILLY BILL
          You know what?

                    LIGHTNIN
          What?

                    BILLY BILL
          I'm gonna kill you for that.
               (smiles)
          But, later.

Lightnin laughs as they enter the campus INFIRMARY.

276

AN HOUR LATER, Lightnin limps down the infirmary steps with a bandage on his face and his knee wrapped up when he's met by Ronald, who pulls up in a campus utility cart.

                    RONALD
What happened, son?

                    LIGHTNIN
I ah, tripped. Fell into some brush.

                    RONALD
Get in.

Lightnin hobbles on the cart as they head out towards the parking lot.

                    RONALD
Are you alright?

Lightnin nods.

                    RONALD
We've got a big game this Thursday.
Will you be up to it?

                    LIGHTNIN
Sure.

It's THURSDAY EVENING. The Beavers are being hosted by the Badgers. On the COURT, above the players the SCOREBOARD reads:

BADGERS 50 VISITORS 50

It's the fourth quarter with one minute left.

Blaine has the ball, goes for a lay-up and misses. A BADGER takes the ball and dribbles quickly back down court with Lightnin hot on his tail. Lightnin keeps up, but is favoring his injured knee. The Badger goes up for the basket, but the ball is intercepted by Lightnin, who dribbles it back to the Visitors hoop. Lightnin's knee is quitting. He looks for an opening to pass. Nothing. He goes for a long shot and is pushed by another BADGER.

A REFEREE blows his whistle for the foul. Lightnin takes his place for the foul shots with five seconds left. He slowly dribbles, gaining composure for the shot. He shoots and misses. CHEERS from the HOME SCHOOL. A SHOT of the VISITORS stands.

Ronald and Jennifer look on. A tense moment. Silence. Lightnin, sweating, nervously dribbles for his last chance to win the game. Blaine looks on with anticipation.

Lightnin shoots and SWISH.

CHEERS.

BADGERS 50 VISITORS 51

With three seconds left, a BADGER makes a gallant attempt to score. He throws mid-court and misses. The BUZZARD SOUNDS, CHEERS from the visitors stands. The BEAVERS go wild. They all give Lightnin congratulatory pats on the back. Blaine fakes a big smile then turns away with a scowl.

THE GREASY PLATTER. It's a chilly OCTOBER EVENING as PEOPLE FILE IN for the Friday night festivities.

INSIDE, to the left is The Brillo Room, to the right, the dining room. It's a busy FRIDAY EVENING and a low roar permeates throughout restaurant. Every seat is filled except one spot at the end of the COUNTER. Ronald enters and fills it. Betsy flies out of the kitchen carrying five big platters. She spots Ronald.

> BETSY
> Hey, stuff! I'm busier than a pimp
> at a hooker convention.

Ronald hides his face in a menu.

At The Brillo Room entrance there's a large table ala ticket booth. Above the table a big sign reads: DEAN'S KIDS POKER GAME $10 ENTRY FEE, SPECTATORS $5. DRAWINGS FOR PRIZES - RANDY AND THE REAMERS - DANCE CONTEST. The CHAIRMAN is handing out the forms. There are about THIRTY PEOPLE left in line. Lightnin and Jennifer enter.

Inside the restaurant, sitting at a booth, Blaine and three of his Mafia spot Lightnin. In a booth nearby, Billy Bill and three of his chums are chowing-down. Billy Bill eats without using his hands. Blaine's pal, ARNIE pulls out a box of paper clips and a big rubber band and hands it to Blaine. The boys yuk it up.

Back in line, Jennifer nudges Lightnin.

> JENNIFER
> Are you sure you won't enter the dance
> contest? It'll be fun.

LIGHTNIN
My knee's been buggin' me. And besides,
who would dance with the colored guy?

JENNIFER
I would but, I'm taken.

She points to her gawky looking date, Ralph. They both laugh.

Inside THE BRILLO ROOM, BALLOONS, STREAMERS and PRIZES decorate the
STAGE. Members of the BAND are setting up. In the center of the room there are
five tables. One is empty and the other four have FOUR PLAYERS and a DEALER.
Against the walls, bleachers have been set up for spectators. The competition is
about to begin. Jennifer is issued a badge and takes her place at a table. About
ONE HUNDRED PEOPLE are seated. More PEOPLE file in from the restaurant. At
each table, an OFFICIAL stands to judge the competition, one of which is Ralph. The
CHAIRMAN is now on stage and speaks into the mic.

CHAIRMAN
The player with the most chips at the
end of the first round wins the heat.
The other three players are eliminated.
The four remaining players go to the
center table for the next competition.
At the end of that heat, the winner with
the most chips wins the game. The
grand prize, one hundred dollars. The
rest of the proceeds go to The Dean
Hospital Children's Wing. After the
game, Randy and the Reamers, and
the dance contest.

Big CHEERS from the audience. From another table, Ralph waves at Jennifer. She
waves back.

CHAIRMAN
Now for our first drawing.

He shakes up a basket and pulls out a ticket.

CHAIRMAN
This will be for a 1995 toaster! Ticket
number, 90210.

A young GIRL goes ballistic.

279

GIRL
I never win anything!

She runs from the bleachers to the stage and claims her prize.

GIRL
(into mic)
There are so many people to thank…

Inside the restaurant, Betsy delivers Ronald's burger. As he turns to thank her, she leans in and grabs a bottle of ketchup for him. In doing so, she smothers his face with a sweater full of bosom.

BETSY
Better chow down Hon or you'll
miss the festivities. I'll be gettin'
off early.

She pulls away.

RONALD
Me too.

Billy Bill and his boys finish up, exit their booth and head into the Brillo Room, soon to be followed by Blaine and company. Ronald wolfs down his burger as he walks up to the cashier and pays.

MONTAGE:

    1.) SHOT OF CARD GAME - Jennifer wins the first round.

    2.) ANOTHER DRAWING - Boy runs off with a RAT TRAP.

    3.) SHOT OF BLAINE IN STANDS - He sits just above Billy Bill.

Blaine looks both ways, pulls out a rubber band with a paper clip attached (ala sling shot) and flings it at Lightnin. It hits him in the forehead. Lightnin cries out and cups his hands over the wound. When he looks back up, he spots Blaine smiling a big one as he shrugs his shoulders.

    4.) SECOND ROUND - Ralph announces the winner of the poker game.

RALPH
The winner is Jennifer…

Jennifer looks up with anticipation.

                              RALPH
                    …Smith.

JENNIFER SMITH is a house wife with THREE SMALL CHILDREN who are sitting in the audience with an OLDER WOMAN. She quickly runs up to the stage and claims her money.

                         JENNIFER SMITH
              I want to thank all the little people…

A SHOT of her kids.

    5.) A SHOT of Betsy joining Ronald in the stands as some BOYS remove the poker tables from the floor.

END OF MONTAGE

The Chairman takes the mic.

                            CHAIRMAN
                 And now, folks, pick your partner for
                 the dance contest. Everyone's invited.
                 let's get the ball rollin' with Randy and
                 the Reamers!

As the band strikes up their first tune, Lightnin runs off to the restroom to tend to his cut forehead. Blaine and company follow. BILLY BILL TAKES NOTICE. Ronald and Betsy join Jennifer and Ralph. Ronald hugs Jennifer.

                            RONALD
              Sorry you didn't win, baby.

                            RALPH
              That's okay, cuz we're gonna win the
              dance contest.

                           JENNIFER
              Dad, this is Ralph.

                            RONALD
              Hi, Ralph. Oh, you know Betsy?

                       JENNIFER AND RALPH
              Hi.

Betsy grabs Ronald's hand and tugs him on the dance floor.

INSIDE THE MEN'S ROOM, Lightnin is tending to his cut. He reaches for a paper towel to dry off. From the mirror, he sees Blaine and company enter.

> BLAINE
> Hey, hot shot. We got a big game
> coming up next week. We're tired
> of your grand standing and hogging
> the ball.

> LIGHTNIN
> Well, if you want the ball so bad,
> why don't you just take it.

They approach Lightnin. Lightnin scrambles and slips through them quickly while pulling the door open. Blaine catches Lightnin and grabs his collar and pulls him outside of the building. Lightnin yanks loose and runs off into the night, followed closely by Blaine and his henchmen.

Meanwhile, the dance contest is in full swing. Jennifer and Ralph are stealing the show. As the band plays a medley of tunes from the Forties to the Eighties, Jennifer and Ralph perform the dance step of that day. Right now, it's a SWING TUNE. Ralph lifts Jennifer up and then swings her between his legs, She slides off into a split, wowing the crowd. Ralph slides over, picks her up and they start to Jitter Bug.

> RALPH
> (a bit winded)
> Where did you learn how to dance?

> JENNIFER
> Dance class. How about you?

> RALPH
> Raw talent.

They laugh and slip into the next era. The Twist.

OUTSIDE, two blocks from the restaurant, Blaine and the boys are starting to gain on Lightnin. His knee is giving out. Soon, Blaine catches up to Lightnin and tackles him. The other guys catch up and they drag Lightnin off the street and onto an empty lot.

> BLAINE
> (winded)
> Okay, Jungle Bunny, no more hoppin'
> for you.

BACK AT THE DANCE CONTEST - The band plays a DISCO TUNE. Jennifer and Ralph slip into a Disco routine. The female contestants gather around them, cheering them on while their male partners gather around Betsy. Betsy is putting on a show of her own. Ronald drops out. Betsy hardly notices. With every hop, skip and jump, the contents of her sweater bounce, jostle and shake, hypnotizing the men. Ronald embarrassed, shakes his head with a blush.

BACK TO FIGHT - Blaine kicks Lightnin's knee. Enraged, Lightnin screams out and lunges at Blaine, choking him. The three other guys pull Lightnin off and start to pummel him. They have him down when Blaine comes over for the coupe de gras. He's about to jump on Lightnin's leg. We SEE the hate in his eyes when a LARGE, THICK HAND appears, grabbing a big hunk of Blaine's hair. As Blaine's head snaps back, Billy Bill punches Blaine's head with his other hand. The blow knocks him to the ground. Billy Bill's entourage have the other three at bay. Billy Bill picks Blaine up. He appears to be half conscious.

> BILLY BILL
> Go ahead, Lightnin, take your best
> shot.

> LIGHTNIN
> That's okay.

> BILLY BILL
> After all the shit he's done to you. Do it!

The temptation is too much. Lightnin makes a fist, swings and hits Blaine on the jaw. Billy Bill lets Blaine drop to the ground.

BACK TO DANCE - The contest is over as the crowd gathers around the stage. The JUDGES make their final tally and hand the chairman the results.

> CHAIRMAN
> And the winners are. As if you didn't
> know. Jennifer and Ralph!

CHEERS from the crowd. A SHOT of Betsy's sweater.

> CHAIRMAN
> Second and third place. Betsy!

Jennifer, Betsy and Ralph all run to the stage for their prizes.

BACK TO THE FIGHT.

                    BILLY BILL
          Okay, jack-offs, this party's over. Take
          this piece of crap home. Come on guys,
          let's go.

As they head out, Blaine's crew tries to get Blaine up.

                    BILLY BILL
          Lightnin, you comin'?

Lightnin tries to walk, but his knee is injured badly. As Billy Bill's boys help him, Arnie
tries to wake Blaine. Blaine is unconscious.

                    ARNIE
          Blaine. Blaine!
                    (slaps his face)
          Blaine, wake up. Hey, man, Blaine's
          out. Somebody call an ambulance.

Lightnin hobbles over to Blaine.

                    ARNIE
          Get away from him. Somebody get help!

They all scramble.

The NEXT DAY, outside of THE DEAN HOSPITAL, Harvard Coleman and his WIFE
enter. INSIDE of an Intensive Care Room, Blaine lies in his bed unconscious.

It's a WEEK LATER, outside of the KUCAISION POLICE DEPARTMENT. It's a cold,
cloudy day and it's snowing a bit. Ronald, Lightnin and Billy Bill enter.

INSIDE of the Police Chief's Office, CHIEF MULLIGAN interviews the boys.

                    CHIEF MULLIGAN
          So let me get this strait, Billy Bill. Oh, by
          the way, how's your dad?
                    (to Ronald)
          We fought in Nam together.

                    BILLY BILL
          He's fine, chief.

The chief continues.

CHIEF MULLIGAN
Alright, you hit Blaine Coleman first
and then Lightnin struck the final blow.

BILLY BILL
Affirmative.

CHIEF MULLIGAN
Well, Principal Coleman is pressing
charges. Blaine is now lying in Intensive
Care in a coma.
(a beat)
Lightnin, I'm going to have to hold you in
Juvenal Hall until the hearing.

RONALD
Wait a minute Chief. Blaine and some
team members have been abusive.
They've been harassing my son for
months, now. They provoked this fight.

CHIEF MULLIGAN
Yes, but didn't...
(rolls his eyes)
your son, here, hit Blaine on the jaw?

RONALD
Well, Chief, from what I'm told, Billy
Bill punched Blaine first.
(to Billy Bill)
No offense, but you're a big fella.
(to Chief)
How do you know it wasn't Billy
Bill's blow that did the damage.

CHIEF MULLIGAN
He who strikes last, strikes best. Anyway,
it'll all come out during the hearing. We'll
set it for...
(looks at his desk calendar)
...the 24th, no that's Thanksgiving. The 28th,
...no, I'm going hunting...ah, the 5th of
December.

BILLY BILL
That's my dad's birthday.

CHIEF MULLIGAN
Oh, poo, then it's the Holidays…Hmm, looks
like we'll have to wait until January. Sorry.

RONALD
You're going to hold Lightnin in Juvenal
Hall during the Holidays?!

CHIEF MULLIGAN
Sorry Ron, but Lightnin could be a flight
risk.
                    (to Lightnin)
I've seen you run, son. You're fast.

The chief laughs it up while Lightnin rubs his knee.

LIGHTNIN
Not anymore.

During the next SERIES OF SHOTS, Ronald narrates.

LATE AFTERNOON - Lightnin is in Juvenal Hall, moping the corridor floor.

RONALD (V.O.)
He spent the Holidays in Juvenal Hall.

LATER, In the GUEST LOUNGE, Lightnin opens some gifts that Ronald and Jennifer
brought, one of which is a cake. Lightnin brings it over to the counter. A KITCHEN
ATTENDANT hands him some plates, a fork and a knife. Lightnin cuts the cake and
discovers a file inside. He pulls it out. The all have a good laugh. The attendant,
good naturedly takes the file, licks off the frosting and tosses it.

RONALD (V.O.)
Juvenal Hall wasn't such a bad place and
Lightnin took it in stride. Jennifer brought
him his studies so he could keep up with school.

Blaine lying in a coma in a HOSPITAL BED.

                    RONALD (V.O.)
I couldn't help but feeling bad about Blaine.
He was bad, but he's only sixteen. He has
so many more years left to be evil.

The Beavers at a HOME GAME. The scoreboard reads:

HOME 0 VISITORS 29

                    RONALD (V.O.)
I suppose I didn't see the gravity of the
situation. And now two young lives have
been seriously effected. Not to mention,
how our team has suffered without
Lightnin and Blaine.

EARLY MORNING - KUCAISION COUNTY COURTHOUSE. It's snowing. TWO
MARSHALS escort Lightnin from the courthouse into their vehicle. One marshal
opens the rear door for Lightnin as he gets in while the other marshal gets in and
starts the car.

                    RONALD (V.O.)
There was a hearing and it was as ruled
that Lightnin was the guilty party, being
that he struck the last blow. Lightnin was
sentenced to one year at Christian Brothers
Reformatory.

LATE AFTERNOON - Blaine leaving the hospital. He's assisted by Harvard and
Arnie. Blaine's walk is different and his face is expressionless.

                    RONALD (V.O.)
Blaine pulled out of his coma, but his
injury left him a little slower than he
used to be.

                    ARNIE
Don't you worry Blaine, we'll get that
jungle bunny, someday.

                    HARVARD
I should have never hired that slave
lovin' Sweeney.

EARLY MORNING - Ronald entering the EMPLOYMENT OFFICE.

RONALD
(to camera)
And I'm looking for another job.

SIX MONTHS LATER

AFTERNOON - It's mid July. Green trees surround an old gothic style building. Above the cathedral-like portal reads: CHRISTIAN BROTHERS REFORMATORY. Below the placard, etched in stone, "Leave The Chip On Your Shoulder At The Door." Some JESUIT BROTHERS enter and exit the building. INSIDE the reformatory a long, dark corridor leads the way to classrooms. Rays of light shine down from Mosaic glass windows above.

Summer school is in session. A loud CHURCH BELL RINGS signaling a class period change. TEENAGED BOYS file along the walls and methodically walk to their next class. Lightnin is now seventeen. A BOY across the hall calls out to Lightnin.

BOY
Psst. Lightnin. What was the answer to
the last question on the test?

As Lightnin passes a door, slightly ajar, marked THEOLOGY, he replies.

LIGHTNIN
(whispers)
Shakespeare.

From the slight opening, an arm protrudes, grabs Lightnin by the collar and pulls him into the room. He simply vanishes from line. INSIDE the room, BROTHER OGDEN chastises him.

BROTHER OGDEN
Talking in line, Boy?

LIGHTNIN
No, Brother O.

He then gets Lightnin in a head lock.

BROTHER OGDEN
It's Brother Ogden. And the answer on the
test was Francis Bacon, you dolt.

He squeezes harder.

                    BROTHER OGDEN
Who loves you?

                    LIGHTNIN
Jesus.

                    BROTHER OGDEN
Did Jesus talk when he was up on the cross?

                    LIGHTNIN
Yes.

Brother Ogden squeezes harder.

                    BROTHER OGDEN
What did he say?

                    LIGHTNIN
I can see Paul's house from here?

He then lets go of Lightnin and slams him up against the black board face first. On the black board are the words, "Forgive them Father they know not what they do."

                    BROTHER OGDEN
No, wise guy.
                    (points to black board)
He said this.

He gets Lightnin back in a headlock.

                    BROTHER OGDEN
I'm going to forgive you because you don't
know what you do.

He squeezes harder.

                    LIGHTNIN
                    (choking)
I'm not sure, but are you forgiving me
right now?

Brother Ogden lets go. Lightnin catches his breath and looks around the classroom that is cluttered with artifacts and paintings of Christ. In the back corner of the room, the rendering of the anatomical man by DaVinci dominates the wall.

On a table below it, some books are strewn about. A CLOSE UP of two books reads: *You Broke It, You Fix It.* and *Sports Medicine Through Christ.* Both authored by Brother Ogden O'Roark.

> BROTHER OGDEN
> We all have a purpose in life. What's yours?
> They say you were an excellent basketball
> player at Teiu High. I coach a basketball
> team here at CBR. Will you tryout?

Lightnin shakes his head, "no." Brother Ogden goes to enforce another headlock.

> LIGHTNIN
> I have a bad knee.

Brother Ogden looks him up and down.

> BROTHER OGDEN
> Report to practice tomorrow, after school.

The next MORNING, in the back of the building there's a BASKETBALL COURT for practice. It's a hot, sunny day and all of the PLAYERS are sweating profusely. Brother Ogden who wears his heavy, wool Jesuit investiture is as cool as a cucumber. He blows his whistle, indicating a start to the next drill.

> BROTHER OGDEN
> Alright, fellas, form two lines.

While the boys side up, Brother Ogden throws the ball up for the toss ball.

> BROTHER OGDEN
> (to Lightnin)
> Let's see what you got.

Lightnin instinctively grabs the ball and dribbles toward the hoop. As the game progresses, Brother Ogden observes Lightnin's ability. Lightnin makes each basket with ease. His lay-ups and rebounds are impeccable. However, he has some trouble running and soon he starts limping. Bother Ogden blows his whistle.

> BROTHER OGDEN
> Okay, fellas, time out. Go get a drink.
> Lightnin, come with me.

He takes Lightnin over to a bench.

                    BROTHER OGDEN
              Lie down and raise your right leg.

Lightnin complies while Brother Ogden manipulates his leg, up and down. He pushes
Lightnin's foot which brings his knee to his chest.

                       LIGHTNIN
              Ahh!

                    BROTHER OGDEN
              Have you seen a doctor about this?

                       LIGHTNIN
              Yes, the school doctor said I'll probably
              need an operation.

                    BROTHER OGDEN
              Horse manure. What you need is therapy.
              Brother O-style.

In a SERIES OF SHOTS we see Brother Ogden and Lightnin working his rehabilitation
program.

BROTHER OGDEN'S QUARTERS a make-shift whirlpool is humming. The swift,
swirling, warm waters bring circulation back to Lightnin's knee. Brother Ogden hands
Lightnin Rosary beads as he heads out.

                    BROTHER OGDEN
              Say three of these and call me in the
              morning.

As Bother Ogden closes the door.

                       LIGHTNIN
              But I'm not Catholic.

In the LOCKER ROOM, Brother Ogden shows Lightnin how to work and stretch his
leg, to strengthen his knee.

                    BROTHER OGDEN
              Say a good act of contrition while you
              stretch.

                       LIGHTNIN
              What the hell's that?

                    BROTHER OGDEN
          Just pray, heathen.

After THEOLOGY CLASS, Brother Ogden hands Lightnin a device that he's concocted to support his knee.

                    BROTHER OGDEN
          Now you can get on your knees when
          you pray.

During BASKETBALL PRACTICE Lightnin's performance has noticeably improved. He can now run without pain.

                    TWO MONTHS LATER

It's early EVENING as PEOPLE enter CBR. INSIDE the small gym, bleachers have been erected for the first game of the new semester. Ronald and Jennifer take the seats. Brother Ogden makes an announcement.

                    BROTHER OGDEN
          Thank you, everyone for coming. Excuse
          our Spartan set up. There's no frills. No
          cheerleaders. We don't even have a score
          board. But we have a great team. And now
          a word for our sponsor.

BOTH TEAMS assemble mid court as everyone stands while Brother Ogden leads them in the LORD'S PRAYER.

DISSOLVE TO:

With a minute left, Lightnin dunks the ball as Brother Ogden erases the old score on a blackboard

HILLBROOK 54 CBR 56

In the stands, an exuberant crowd CHEERS their team on. Ronald comments to Jennifer.

                    RONALD
          Lightnin's dominated this whole game.

                    JENNIFER
               (facetiously)
          How unusual.

RONALD
And his knee is holding up miraculously.

Hillbrook scores. Lightnin retrieves the ball and with five seconds left he throws mid court and swish. Brother Ogden blows his whistle ending the game as the crowd CHEERS on. He then proudly chalks up the new score.

HILLBROOK 56 CBR 58

OUTSIDE of CBR, Lightnin walks with Ronald and Jennifer to their car.

RONALD
Great game, son.

JENNIFER
Hey, dad got his job back at Teiu High.

LIGHTNIN
Wow. They couldn't top the best, huh?

RONALD
Well, Harvard Coleman took a higher
paying job in Nevada. The school board
called me back. You're graduating soon.
Have you thought about where you'd like
to continue your education?

LIGHTNIN
You know, I haven't. I'm not sure what
I'm doing when I get out of here.

RONALD
Well, it's obvious. You have a brilliant
future as a basketball pro.

LIGHTNIN
Thanks. I think what I'd like to do is to
get out of Indiana.

RONALD
Well, they have great schools back East
or even California.

                    LIGHTNIN
          I don't know. I think I'd like to get away
          from school for a while. See the world.
          Maybe spend some time in New Orleans,
          my birth place.

During the next SERIES OF SCENES Ronald narrates.

                    RONALD (V.O.)
          After Lightnin graduated from CBR he
          took a job at the Greasy Platter as a cook.

INSIDE THE KITCHEN, Lightnin puts up plates of hot food. He burns his hands.

                    LIGHTNIN
          Ooowww!

Betsy tries to help.

                    BETSY
          Get some ice on that Hon and use some
          profanity. It helps.

                    LIGHTNIN
          Shit!

                    BETSY
          You call that profanity?

                    LIGHTNIN
          Cock sucker!

                    BETSY
          That's what I'm talkin' 'bout.

The CHEF rolls his eyes.

                    RONALD (V.O.)
          He saved up enough money and by June
          he was ready to spread his wings. I bought
          him a car to commemorate the occasion.

MORNING - The Sweeney's, driveway. Lightnin puts two suitcases in the trunk of his
1978 Chevy Caprice. Ronald hands him the keys and an envelope.

RONALD
Here's a little something extra and a list
of some people you can contact in Norlins.

They have a group hug. Lightnin gets in the car, starts it up, drives up to the end of
the driveway and waves good-bye.

JENNIFER
Call us every day, ya hear?

DISSOLVE TO:

MID MORNING - A highway sign reads - INTERSTATE 65 SOUTH - NASHVILLE
200 MILES

INSIDE of the car, Lightnin tunes the radio station to Willy Nelson's, *ON THE ROAD
AGAIN.*

It's a hot, sunny day. Lightnin spots a black man hitchhiking and pulls over.

The hitchhiker grabs his bag and saunters to the car and gets in. He's mid-thirties,
wearing a flashy three piece suit, well shined shoes and a hanky in his lapel. His
name is ELI.

ELI
Thank you, brother. It's tough for a
black man to thumb a ride in these
parts.

LIGHTNIN
Where you headed?

ELI
Nashville, then Vegas, baby! How
'bout you, bro?

LIGHTNIN
New Orleans.

ELI
(singing)
Way down yonder in New Orleans.
We can trim some Dixie Queens.
(laughs)
Hey, my name's Eli.

He extends hand. Lightnin shakes his hand and notices the huge rocks on Eli's fingers.

                        LIGHTNIN
Lightnin. What's in Vegas?

                        ELI
The land of opportunity, my brother.
I have some associates there who are
involved with some money making
enterprises. You dig?

                        LIGHTNIN
I dig.
                    (a beat)
Are these your hitchhiking clothes?

                        ELI
                    (chuckles)
You see, what had happened. On my
way down from Chi Town my car
went bust...a few miles back and I
didn't want to wait for the redneck
mechanics to fix it.
                    (lights up a cigarette)
I'll have plenty of money when I get
to Nashville to buy a new one. Mind
if I smoke.

                        LIGHTNIN
Ah, no.

Eli takes a couple of drags and flicks the cigarette out of the window. He then stretches and yawns.

                        ELI
Hey bra, if you don't mind, I'm gonna
cop me a few zzz's, ya dig?

                        LIGHTNIN
I dig.

It's a FEW HOURS LATER and from inside the car they pass a sign that reads:

NASHVILLE 20 MILES TO INTERSTATE 40 WEST - OKLAHOMA CITY - ALBUQUERQUE - LOS ANGELES

Eli is snoring away. Lightnin gently shakes him. He wakes up with a start.

> ELI
> Not guilty.
> (comes to)
> Oh, hey. How long have I been out?

> LIGHTNIN
> A couple of hours. We're almost in
> Nashville. Where do you want to
> me to leave you off.

> ELI
> Oh, ah, (sniff). Tell you what. You
> have done me a huge solid, ah,
> Lightnin, right? Lightnin, what the
> fuck kinda name is that?

> LIGHTNIN
> What do you mean?

> ELI
> Lightnin was a character on Amos 'n'
> Andy. He was one shufflin' nigga, bra.

> LIGHTNIN
> Amos 'n' Andy?

> ELI
> Ah, never mind. Look-a-here. Give me
> a ride to my lady's crib. We'll feed ya,
> you can crash and get you a fresh start
> for your trip to Norlins.

> LIGHTNIN
> Oh, I couldn't.

> ELI
> No, no, no! I insist.

DISSOLVE TO:

The Chevy pulls into a driveway, past a house. There's another house in back. They park, get out and stretch. From inside the house a lady emerges wearing a robe. RONDELLE, attractive, age twenty-eight, runs up to Eli and showers him with kisses.

                    ELI
          Easy, baby. Your makin' an African
          specticle outta yo' self.

                    RONDELLE
          You know how I get.

She then turns her attention to Lightnin with a big smile.

                    ELI
          Hey, baby, I want you to meet
          my ol' friend Lightnin.

                    RONDELLE
          Lightnin? I bet you fast.

                    LIGHTNIN
          Well, actually I'm pretty fast on
          the basketball court.

Rondelle comes up to Lightnin and looks him up and down.

                    RONDELLE
          You look black, but choo don't
          sound black. Where you from?

                    LIGHTNIN
          I just came from Indiana.

                    RONDELLE
          Well, come on in. I cooked up ribs
          and corn bread. Hope y'all hungry.

INSIDE, the house is cluttered. On the couch, TWO KIDS, age six and four sit watching a blaring TV.

                    RONDELLE
                    (yelling)
          Turn that TV down!

ELI

Rondelle, get us a drink, baby.

Eli signals Lightnin to follow him. They enter a BEDROOM. Eli fires up a joint, takes a hit and passes it to Lightnin.

ELI

This is good shit.

LIGHTNIN

I'm sorry, but I don't smoke.

Eli exhales. The smoke blows in Lightnin's face. He coughs. Rondelle enters with two beers and a drink for herself. Her robe slips open, exposing her undergarments. Eli takes the beers and hands one to Lightnin. Lightnin tries his best not to look at Rondelle's equipment.

LIGHTNIN

No thanks.

RONDELLE

Now, shugga, you gotta have a taste
with us, c'mon.

Lightnin reluctantly takes the beer. From the living room the PHONE RINGS.

ELI
(excited)
I betcha that's Leroy.

He hands Rondelle the joint and leaves. Rondelle takes a hit and passes it to Lightnin. Lightnin declines. She blows residual smoke in his face. Lightnin can't help but noticing Rondelle's mocha colored cleavage.

RONDELLE

Here's a toast. To new friends.

She drinks. Lightnin, politely sips his beer. Rondelle approaches Lightnin and rubs his stomach.

RONDELLE

Mmm-mm-mm. You in shape, boy.

Lightnin is now woozy from his contact high. He nervously takes a gulp from his beer.

LIGHTNIN
Thanks. So are you.
(giggles)
I'm sorry. That was rude.

RONDELLE
That's okay. Drink up, shugga.

Lightnin takes another sip. He now feels the effect of the beer.

LIGHTNIN
So, how long have you and Eli been
married?

RONDELLE
(laughs)
We ain't married.

Just then, Eli pops his head in.

ELI
Hey, I gotta run an errand. Lightnin,
is it okay if I borrow your car for
a minute?

LIGHTNIN
Jeeze, I don't know…

ELI
That's okay. Don't fret. Throw me
your keys.

Lightnin's a bit overwhelmed. He reluctantly tosses Eli the keys.

ELI
See you in about an hour.

Eli quickly exits. Rondelle gets up and locks the door.

RONDELLE
Another toast. To you, shugga.

She finishes her drink. Lightnin laughs nervously and takes another sip. He is now
substantially buzzed. Rondelle, takes Lightnin's beer, sets it down and puts her arms
around him.

                    RONDELLE
         Ooh, Honey, you nice.

She leans her head back and purses her lips.

                     LIGHTNIN
         You sure have nice lips. (hic!)

They laugh as she pulls him down for a soul kiss. Rondelle feels something.

                    RONDELLE
         Is that a grenade launcher in your pocket
         or are you just glad to see me? Take off
         your clothes, shugga.

Lightnin complies. Rondelle removes her robe and panties. She, then turns around
displaying her very round derriere. Lightnin begins to quiver.

                    RONDELLE
         Undo my brassiere.

Lightnin tries to unhook, but his hands are shaking. Rondelle pulls the bra over her
head and turns to Lightnin. Her large, round bosom brushes up against Lightnin who
has everything off but his shoes and socks. She pushes Lightnin on the bed and
removes his shoes. She then moves up, kissing his thighs.

                     LIGHTNIN
         Are you sure this is alright?

                    RONDELLE
         Yeah, baby.

She pulls the covers over her head and goes down on Lightnin. He is in the throes
of ecstasy and begins to moan.

                    RONDELLE
         Take me baby.

                     LIGHTNIN
         Take you where?

                    RONDELLE
              (chuckles)
         Put it in me.

Lightnin turns her around and gets on top of her. She pulls the covers over them. He fumbles for a bit.

                        LIGHTNIN
            I'm not sure where to put it.

                        RONDELLE
            Oh my God, we have a virgin.

She reaches down and guides him in.

                        RONDELLE
            Go, baby. Go in and out.

Lightnin pumps in and out with staccato speed. Rondelle cries out with pleasure. Lightnin cries out too, as he finishes. He gasps for air, sighs and collapses.

                        RONDELLE
                     (disappointed)
            Now I see why they call you Lightnin.

She pushes Lightnin to the side, grabs some cigarettes on the night stand, lights up and has a smoke. Lightnin is fast asleep. Rondelle puts out her cigarette and nods off.

DISSOLVE TO:

It's about an hour later. The SOUND of a key unlocks the bedroom door. Rondelle awakens and shakes Lightnin.

                        RONDELLE
            Eli's comin'.

Eli enters.

                        ELI
            What the fuck?! I can't leave you
            alone for a minute.

                        RONDELLE
                     (looks at watch)
            It was an hour.

302

                           ELI
              Don't get smart, bitch.
                      (to Lightnin)
              And you! Get dressed.

As Lightnin goes for his pants, Rondelle lights another cigarette.

A few minutes later, OUTSIDE, Eli reprimands Lightnin.

                           ELI
              What the fuck am I gonna do with you?
              I show you hospitality. I turn my back for
              an hour and your bangin' my woman. What
              kind of animal are you?

                        LIGHTNIN
              Well, Eli, she said it was alright.

                           ELI
                       (mocking)
              Oh, she said it was alright. Are you out
              yo' mind? She has her two babies in the
              next room, I'm out tryin' to raise money
              to pay you for the ride and that's alright?!
              What am I gonna do with you?

                        LIGHTNIN
              Eli, I've never done anything like this before.

Eli thinks for a minute. He pulls out a small knife from his jacket.

                        LIGHTNIN
              Oh, no. Please, don't.

Eli puts the knife back in his jacket.

                           ELI
              Don't worry. You wanna make it up?

                        LIGHTNIN
              Yes, anything.

ELI
Here's the kick. I need a ride to Vegas.
As I said, I have a friend who's startin'
a bidness. I'm a little short right now
or I'd fly. Take me there and then you
can get on with yo' bidness, you dig?

LIGHTNIN
I dig.

ELI
Now, let's grit.

LIGHTNIN
Hmm?

ELI
Eat, man, eat! Are you sure you black?

Rondelle is at the door.

RONDELLE
Oh, he black, alright.

As Lightnin enters, Eli and Rondelle wink at each other.

THE NEXT MORNING an AERIAL VIEW of the car entering ROUTE 40. INSIDE
THE CAR Eli drives. Lightnin's a bit hung-over.

ELI
(chuckles)
What's a matter sport, the party
too much fe' ya'?

LIGHTNIN
Uhh, hmm.

ELI
Busted yo' cherry and everythang.
Ha, ha.

DIFFERENT SHOTS of car entering different cities and states.

MEMPHIS - OKLAHOMA - TEXAS - NEW MEXICO - FLAGSTAFF - KINGMAN

A HIGHWAY SIGN READS: ROUTE 93 NORTH - LAKE MEAD - BOULDER DAM - LAS VEGAS.

It's DUSK. From inside the car, the sky line of the LAS VEGAS STRIP with all it's lights, glittering. Lightnin's now driving. Eli's asleep.

                         LIGHTNIN
          Wow! Eli!

Eli wakes up with a start.

                         ELI
          Not guilty!
                    (comes around)
          There it is my bra. Las Vegas, Sin City,
          The Meadows, Lost Wages, The Pearl
          In The Desert and our ticket to fame and
          fortune.

                         LIGHTNIN
          Ours?

                         ELI
          It's there if you want it. Tell you what.
          Hang for a couple of days and I'll show
          you the lights.

                         LIGHTNIN
          Well…

                         ELI
          You in a hurry?

                         LIGHTNIN
          Well, no…

                         ELI
          Take a left here at Tropicana Boulevard.

Lightnin seems intrigued.

                         LIGHTNIN
          Alright.

A SHOT of the car pulling into THE TROPICANA HOTEL.

Two VALETS open their doors. Lightnin opens the trunk as one of the Valets takes out their bags.

INSIDE THE HOTEL ROOM, the LIGHTS of the strip and the Excalibur Hotel across the street catches Lightnin's attention. A ROOMSERVICE WAITER brings in a tray of food and beverages. The waiter waits for his tip.

                         ELI
              We'll catch you next time, man.

The waiter rolls his eyes and leaves. Lightnin is on the phone.

                      LIGHTNIN
              Yes, Las Vegas. Yeah, me and this
              guy named Eli came to check out
              some business opportunities.

Eli signals to Lightnin to cut the call short.

                      LIGHTNIN
              I'll call you tomorrow, okay. Gotta
              go. Tell Dad I miss 'im. Bye.

Lightnin hangs up the phone and grabs a sandwich.

                         ELI
              Look-a-here, Lightnin. Don't tell
              anyone about our bidness, man.
              Not until I'm sure where we're at.

Eli opens a beer and takes the phone. Lightnin turns on the TV. An advertisement for a local cabaret is on.

TELEVISION

A line-up of EXOTIC DANCERS are on stage.

                   ANNOUNCER (V.O)
              Tonight at the Crazy Pony Saloon, the
              hottest act in Vegas burns up the stage.
              "Transgression." At the world famous
              Flamingo Hotel.

Eli plugs one ear as he speaks quietly into the phone. Lightnin is glued to the TV.

The featured dancer is an older, but attractive BLACK WOMAN surrounded by FOUR young, hot WHITE GIRLS all dressed in a bikini thong. Lightnin is transfixed on the black woman.

> ANNOUNCER (V.O.)
> In the fourth sensational year at the Crazy
> Pony Saloon, Jo Mamma heads up what
> The Las Vegas Sun called, "The wildest
> strippers on The Strip." Transgression.
> Call now for reservations.

A NUMBER flashes across the screen.

Eli hangs up while Lightnin turns down the TV.

> LIGHTNIN
> Hey, you want to catch a show tonight?

> ELI
> Sure, man.
> (a beat)
> I'm gonna slide down and cop some
> squares, maybe toss some bones, you
> know, get my pockets full-grown.

> LIGHTNIN
> Huh?

> ELI
> (sarcastically, very white)
> I'm going to the lobby and purchase
> a package of cigarettes. Then, perhaps
> I'll procure some extra capital in a
> game of chance known as craps.

No stranger to sarcasm Lightnin retorts with...

> LIGHTNIN
> Okay, bra, I'm gonna horizontal, cop
> some zzz's, dream about trim 'n' hode
> my Johnson.

Eli's eyes bug out.

                                    ELI
                        Scared-a-you.

Eli leaves, laughing out loud.

In the CASINO, at a CRAP TABLE, Eli is on a losing streak. He throws the dice.
SNAKE EYES. ANOTHER SHOT, snake eyes. He reaches in his pockets. Nothing.

Later that EVENING, in their room, Lightnin emerges from the bathroom, with a
towel around his waist. Eli lies on the bed watching TV.

                                LIGHTNIN
                        Okay, Eli, you're next for the
                        bathroom.

                                    ELI
                        I don't think I'm goin', man.

                                LIGHTNIN
                        Why not?

                                    ELI
                        I didn't do so well at the tables. I'm
                        gonna try to hold off, 'til this deal
                        comes through.

                                LIGHTNIN
                        Look, Eli, I don't want to go out
                        alone. Besides, I'm under age. If
                        you're with me I have a better
                        chance to get in. I'll sponsor.

                                    ELI
                        That's what I'm talkin' 'bout.
                        I'll be ready in a snap, you dig?

                                LIGHTNIN
                        I dig.

THE FLAMINGO HOTEL CASINO. To the right of the tables is THE WILD PONY
SALOON. There's a line of PEOPLE to get in. Eli looks around, crushes his smoke
on the carpet and puts the ash on his finger. He then smudges some of the ash
above Lightnin's lip, creating a mustache.

ELI
You need some maturity.

INSIDE the crowded club, Lightnin and Eli are at their table. They order a drink from a scantily clad WAITRESS.

The LIGHTS DIM and fanfare music permeates the room.

MUSIC: *THUS SPAKE ZARATHUSTRA*

SMOKE FILLS THE STAGE. From the PA system:

ANNOUNCER (V.O.)
And now Ladies and gentlemen! From the thing that makes the world say, "Damn!" From the stage to your eyeballs. Please fasten your erotic seatbelts and give a warm welcome for Jo Mamma and the craziest Transsexuals on the Las Vegas Strip. Ladies and gentlemen, it's "Transgression."

The CROWD, WHISTLES and CHEERS.

MUSIC - Creedence Clearwater Revival's *SUZIE Q*

LIGHTNIN
(whispers)
Eli, these aren't women?

ELI
That's right.

One by one, the TRANSGRESSETTES file out on stage bumping and grinding. Eli waxes giddy.

ELI
(giggles)
And who cares.

Soon, JO MAMMA hits the stage. She's tall, dark and built like a brick shipyard. The dancers in the background perform on their poles while Jo Mamma does her Voodoo.

ELI
Hey, look at Jo Mamma, bro. She looks like he could be yo mamma.

Lightnin is transfixed on this transsexual.

> LIGHTNIN
> Wow!

From the stage, Jo Mamma looks down at the AUDIENCE and spots Lightnin. She stops for a second and continues her dance.

> ELI
> Shit, I left my smokes in your short.
> Gimme the keys, I'll be right back.

> LIGHTNIN
> Can't you buy em here?

> ELI
> Yeah, if you wanna pay ten bucks.

Eli takes the keys and splits.

Back on stage, the boy/girl show gets hotter as they start to strip down. Lightnin is overwhelmed, but intrigued.

DISSOLVE TO:

It's the end of the show as Jo Mamma and the Transgressettes exit the stage. Lightnin realizes that Eli hasn't returned. A WAITRESS drops the check. Lightnin looks around for a minute.

> LIGHTNIN
> Oh, shit.

He goes for his wallet. It's gone.

> LIGHTNIN
> Oh, shit!!!

He then runs out of the club, through the CASINO and to the exit.

OUTSIDE, in the parking lot he panics. He doesn't see his car.

> LIGHTNIN
> Eli! Eli, you son-of-a-bitch. He stole
> my car, too! Ahhhh!

Lightnin runs back INSIDE. He then frantically gestures to a SECURITY GUARD. Soon a BOUNCER from the club grabs Lightnin. The security guard gets on his Walkie-Talkie and literally, seconds later a COP CAR pulls up to the exit. One COP gets out and enters the casino. Lightnin tries explain, when COP # 2 enters.

COP # 2
Could I see some ID, sir.

Lightnin checks for his wallet again. He frantically checks all of his pockets.

LIGHTNIN
He took my wallet, too!

COP#1
What's the guys name?

LIGHTNIN
Eli.

COP# 1
His last name?

Lightnin thinks for a few seconds.

LIGHTNIN
God, I don't even know.

The two cops look at each other.

COP # 2
Okay, what kind of car?

LIGHTNIN
It's a 1978 Chevy Caprice, four
door sedan. Gold color.

COP # 2
License number?

LIGHTNIN
Shoot, I don't know.

Just then, Jo Mamma and another dancer exit the club. She stops to eves drop.

COP #1
What's your name, son?

311

                              LIGHTNIN
                              Lightnin Sweeney.

Jo Mamma's jaw drops.

                              BOUNCER
                              What about the check? How are we
                              suppose to know this ain't a scam.
                              This shit happens a lot, officer.

                              COP # 2
                              We're going to have to hold you.

                              LIGHTNIN
                              Oh, God.

Cop #1 cuffs Lightnin.

                              COP # 1
                              You have a right to remain silent…

Jo Mamma approaches the bouncer.

                              JO MAMMA
                              What's up?

                              BOUNCER
                              This guy tried to walk out on the
                              check.

The NEXT MORNING, OUTSIDE a police precinct, COPS enter and exit.

INSIDE a JAIL CELL, Lightnin sits on his bunk, dejected. A GUARD appears, jingling
keys.

                              GUARD
                              Mr. Sweeney, you're a free man.

                              LIGHTNIN
                              What?

                              GUARD
                              Your bail has been posted.

The guard opens the cell door and escorts Lightnin out.

                              LIGHTNIN
        By who?

                               GUARD
        That, I don't know.

At the FRONT DESK, Lightnin collects his private belongings which includes a watch
and his hotel key. He addresses the DESK CAPTAIN.

                              LIGHTNIN
        Have they found my car yet?

                           DESK CAPTAIN
        Not that I know of.

He hands Lightnin a card.

                           DESK CAPTAIN
        Check back with us tomorrow.

OUTSIDE, Lightnin walks down the steps wondering what to do next. He looks at
his hotel key. As he makes his way towards the Tropicana, he hears a CAR HORN.
From the driver's side of a new CADILLAC he sees someone beckon him over. He
walks up to the car. Inside, Jo Mamma is in her street clothes.

                             JO MAMMA
        Need a ride?

                              LIGHTNIN
        Ah, yeah.

He gets in.

INSIDE The car.

                             JO MAMMA
        Where to?

                              LIGHTNIN
        Hey, aren't you the dancer at the Crazy
        Pony?

                             JO MAMMA
                              (smiles)
        Mmm, hmm.

LIGHTNIN
I'm ah, staying at the Tropicana Hotel.

Jo Mamma swings the car around and heads for the Trop.

LIGHTNIN
Did you bail me out?

JO MAMMA
Mmm, hmm. Walkin' out on the
check. Shame on you.

LIGHTNIN
No, I was with this guy. He said he
had to get something from my car. I
gave him the keys and he never
returned. He must've taken my wallet,
too. I have some money back in my
room. Christ, I hope it's still there.

JO MAMMA
Well, let's go see.

LIGHTNIN
Why are you being so nice?

JO MAMMA
(changing the subject)
You should have known somethin'
was up when this guy leaves in the
middle of *my* show.

A SHOT of the car pulling into the Tropicana.

INSIDE of the hotel room, Lightnin checks the closet and drawers while Jo Mamma
opens the drapes.

LIGHTNIN
Well, he took my clothes and my
money, my wallet *and* my car!

JO MAMMA
Where did you meet this guy?

LIGHTNIN

I picked him up hitch hiking. We
stopped at his place in Nashville.
Hey, at least I know where he lives.

JO MAMMA

What's his name?

LIGHTNIN

Eli.

JO MAMMA

Eli what?

LIGHTNIN

I don't know. I never thought to ask.
I have to get back to…
(realizes)
Shit! I wouldn't even know where to
look in Nashville. I'm screwed.

JO MAMMA

Well, it seems that you are. Maybe
they'll find your car. He can't keep it.
We'll call your DMV for the registration.
What state?

LIGHTNIN

It's in Indiana. God, my dad will think I'm
an idiot. I just left home. Now, four days
later, I'm broke without a car or a wallet.

JO MAMMA

Well, maybe you don't have to tell him
right away. Look, I know some people.
We can get you a place to stay and a job.
You can get caught up and then do what
you have to do.

Lightnin still has a wisp of ash on his top lip. Jo Mamma wipes it off with her thumb.

JO MAMMA

Hey, let's get some breakfast.

INSIDE of the Tropicana's coffee shop. A WAITRESS serves Lightnin and Jo Mamma breakfast as they resume their conversation.

>   LIGHTNIN
>   After that, I decided to hit the road, see
>   the world and boy am I seeing it, huh?

>   JO MAMMA
>   I'm kind of surprised your father let you
>   go so soon.

>   LIGHTNIN
>   I think he knew how frustrated I was, the
>   only Negro in this one horse town.

>   JO MAMMA
>   Negro? You're black, baby.

>   LIGHTNIN
>   What about you? Why did you decide to
>   become a woman?

>   JO MAMMA
>   That, child, is a *long* story.
>   (a beat)
>   Hey, after breakfast let's get you settled.
>   Don't worry 'bout a thang, sugar. You
>   call Ronald and tell him you're okay.
>   Just leave out the transsexual thing.

>   LIGHTNIN
>   How did you know his name was Ronald?

>   JO MAMMA
>   (quickly)
>   Why, you told me.

>   LIGHTNIN
>   I did?

They look at each other for a moment.

DISSOLVE TO:

A SERIES OF SHOTS

Lightnin and Jo Mamma looking over Lightnin's NEW APARTMENT. Lightnin opens the blinds. Outside, a view of The Strip.

The SARAH HOTEL PARKING LOT. A COP checks out an abandon car. It's Lightnin's Chevy.

OUTSIDE BENNY'S RESTAURANT. TOURISTS file in for their MORNING fix of bacon, eggs and coffee. A sign on the front door reads:

SATURDAY'S - EAT UNTIL YOU BARF SPECIAL $5.00

INSIDE A BUSY KITCHEN, Lightnin, a short order cook, sets two hot plates under a heat lamp. He burns his fingers.

> LIGHTNIN
>
> Cock sucker!

A WAITRESS picks up the plates with a towel.

> WAITRESS
>
> Who told?

LIGHTNIN'S APARTMENT. He's on the phone.

> LIGHTNIN
>
> Don't worry Dad, things are great. They
> found my car. I have an apartment and a
> job. Don't worry. Tell Jen I lover 'er. Bye.

OUTSIDE, in the back of lightnin's apartment building, a makeshift basketball hoop above the laundry room door serves as a recreational outlet. Lightnin wears his special knee brace. He practices his dribbling and hook shots. He runs in for a lay-up.

A large, attractive, Caucasian woman, age thirty, exits the washroom with a basket of folded clothes. Lightnin slams into her. They both hit the ground, Lightnin on top. The basket topples and clothes fly all over. It takes a moment for them to recover. Lightnin is face to face with the woman. She smiles. Lightnin is smitten. She is FLO NAZE.

> FLO NAZE
>
> Good technique.

> LIGHTNIN
>
> Are you alright?

                          FLO NAZE
          I've been worse.

Lightnin scrambles up and helps Flo Naze to her feet.

                          LIGHTNIN
          Oh, I'm terribly sorry.

                          FLO NAZE
          That's okay. Back in the wash, I guess.

Lightnin recognizes her.

                          LIGHTNIN
          Hey, aren't you one of the dancers in Jo
          Mamma's show?

                          FLO NAZE
          In deedie do. Most of the "girls" live here.
          The name's Flo Naze.
                          (extends hand)
          And you must be lightning.

                          LIGHTNIN
                          (correcting)
          Lightnin. How'd you know?

                          FLO NAZE
          Jo Mamma told us about you.

Lightnin helps her gather up her clothes.

                          LIGHTNIN
          So, you were a man once?

                          FLO NAZE
          Umm hmm.

She bends over to pick up some clothes, exposing a bountiful cleavage.

                          LIGHTNIN
                          (smiles)
          They did a great job.
                          (a beat)
          May I ask you a personal question?

                          FLO NAZE
          Sure.

                    LIGHTNIN
Why did you change?

                    FLO NAZE
That is a *long* story.

                    LIGHTNIN
Sorry.

They put the last of the clothes in the basket.

                    FLO NAZE
Do you like Chinese?

                    LIGHTNIN
Sure.

                    FLO NAZE
I'm off tonight. I'll take you to my
favorite place and we can get acquainted.

                    LIGHTNIN
Okay.

INSIDE of CHINKCHOW RESTAURANT, Lightnin and Flo Naze share some
dumplings as Flo Naze continues her story.

                    FLO NAZE
Careful, these are spicy. Anyway,
she was my high school sweetheart
and we got married. But something
was missing. I didn't realize it, but
I was gay.

                    LIGHTNIN
In the closet

                    FLO NAZE
Honey, I was in the closet so long,
I smelled like moth balls.
                    (laughs)
We divorced soon after. I wanted a
relationship with a man, but I wasn't
comfortable with the social stigma,
so I decided to become a woman.

LIGHTNIN
Are you *all* woman?

FLO NAZE
Oh, yeah. I even went to Sweden for
the operation.

LIGHTNIN
Are all transsexuals gay?

FLO NAZE
Pretty much. But some people are
confused. I knew a man who became
a woman, hated it and then had another
operation to go back to machismo. He
was Mexican.

LIGHTNIN
What about Jo Mamma? And why the
weird names?

FLO NAZE
Oh, a two parter. Well, first, baby. I
believe deep down that Jo's a man. Jo
was deeply hurt by his first love. A
woman. He also went to prison for
eight years and I think that's when he
did his sexual paradigm. Secondly, not
all transsexuals have "weird" names. It's
a dancer thing. My real name is Frank.

LIGHTNIN
Frank. *That* would be weird. Why Flo
Naze?

FLO NAZE
Because when I'm done with a man,
he'll have clear nasal passages.

LIGHTNIN
(sighs)
God, I wish you were really a woman.

FLO NAZE
Mr. Lightnin, I do believe you're flirting
with moi.

Flo Naze rubs Lightnin's leg.

                    FLO NAZE
          Well, I'd be a liar if I said, I wasn't
          attracted to you.

The NEXT MORNING OUTSIDE OF LIGHTNIN'S APARTMENT. Flo Naze slips out
of Lightnin's apartment as she buttons up her blouse. Jo Mamma is just getting in as
she opens up her door.

                    JO MAMMA
          Flo, what in hell are you doing?

                    FLO NAZE
                    (surprised)
          I, ah, well, I was visiting Lightnin.

                    JO MAMMA
          Are you crazy? He's just a boy.

                    FLO NAZE
          Eighteen isn't exactly a boy. So what?

                    JO MAMMA
          I don't think his father would approve!

A realization hits Flo Naze like a diamond bullet.

                    FLO NAZE
          Oh, my God. No wonder the resemblance.
          You're his daddy, mamma, whatever. Why
          didn't you tell me? I would've run from
          him. Now, I think it's too late.

Lightnin is standing outside the door. He looks as if he's seen a ghost.

MORNING - PIONEER UNIVERSITY CAMPUS. STUDENTS and FACULTY enter
and exit the MAIN ADMINISTRATION BUILDING.

INSIDE THE DEAN'S OFFICE, Harvard Coleman is on the phone.

                    HARVARD
          Yes, send them up.

From the LOBBY, Blaine enters a STAIRCASE with his old school chum Arnie. Blaine's gait seems quite normal as he and Arnie ascend the stairs. They race up the steps. Arnie is first to hit the top. As they walk down a CORRIDOR.

                    ARNIE
                   (winded)
          Dude, you've come a long way from
          the spaz you were last year.

                    BLAINE
                   (winded)
          Hate has been an instrumental part
          of my convalescence.

In Harvard's office, the Dean shares his aspirations as Blaine and Arnie listen intently.

                    HARVARD
          This University has a good football team.
          Now we need a basketball team. It needs
          direction and public relations. Blaine,
          your recovery has been nothing short of
          miraculous. However, I fear you're not
          prime for the rigors of the sport anymore.
          I see you coaching and promoting my
          dream: A champion, college basketball
          team here at P.U.
                   (looks out window)
          The football team is ninety percent black.
          Let's try and keep the basketball team
          homogenized. Arnie can help coach.

                    ARNIE
          When can we get to see the town?

                    HARVARD
          We'll be busy until the weekend. And
          then I guess you boys can wallow with
          the element.

LATE AFTERNOON - Benny's Restaurant PARKING LOT. Lightnin has finished his shift and is about to get in his car when Jo Mamma pulls up in her big Caddy. From her car window.

                    JO MAMMA
          You've got to stop running from me. I know
          I wasn't there for you when you were a child,
          but I'm trying to make it up to you. Give me
          a chance, please.

Lightnin jumps in his car and speeds off. Jo Mamma yells out.

                    JO MAMMA
          You can run, but you can't hide from
          yo momma, daddy, whatever.

At LIGHTNIN'S APARTMENT, he falls on the couch. There's a KNOCK.

                    LIGHTNIN
          Who is it?

From outside.

                    FLO NAZE
          It's me, Flo.

Lightnin gets up and let's her in. They hug. Lightnin breaks away and sits. She sits
next to him.

                    FLO NAZE
          Listen, baby, you're gonna have to
          deal with your father, ah, mother,
          whatever, eventually. Jo cares for
          you, deeply.

                    LIGHTNIN
          It's hard to warm up to a father who
          left me on a doorstep, to do time in
          the slammer for manslaughter. And
          then a has a *sex* change.

                    FLO NAZE
          Well, I had one too.

They kiss. Lightnin pulls away.

                              .

LIGHTNIN

This is sick. If my father, the one with
testicles, found out about all this, he'd
croak. Not to mention my sister. They
are my *real* family. What am I going do?

FLO NAZE

I know what you need.

LIGHTNIN

What?

FLO NAZE

A decongestant.

Lightnin laughs. Flo unzips Lightnin's pants. Lightnin's FACE lights up as he reacts
to Flo Nazes medicine. He begins to breathe deeply. Just then the phone RINGS.
Lightnin is unnerved and loses his strength. He gets up from the couch, zips up his
pants and answers.

LIGHTNIN

Hello. Dad!

INSIDE Ronald's kitchen.

RONALD

Lightnin. Hey, Jennifer and I are
coming out to see you.

INTERCUT - RONALD AND LIGHTNIN ON PHONE

LIGHTNIN
(covering)
Great. When?

RONALD

Next weekend.

LIGHTNIN

My place is kind of small…

RONALD

No, no, we're staying at the
Flamingo.

                    LIGHTNIN
        Flamingo!
                    (covering)
        Oh, great. I guess I'll see you next
        weekend. Bye, Dad.

Lightnin hangs up. He looks shocked.

                    FLO NAZE
        Are you okay?

                    LIGHTNIN
        No.

SATURDAY MORNING - McCARRAN AIRPORT

It's a busy airport. AIRLINES landing and taking off. OUTSIDE of BAGGAGE CLAIM,
Ronald and Jennifer are in line for a CAB. One pulls up. The DRIVER gets out and
helps them with their BAGS.

OUTSIDE of the FLAMINGO HOTEL.

INSIDE of Ronald and Jennifer's adjoining ROOMS, they unpack.

                    JENNIFER
        Wow, Las Vegas. Just the way I
        pictured it. The Strip, the casinos
        and poker. I can practice my
        chops, pops.

                    RONALD
        Easy, young lady. You have a couple
        of years to go before you're legal.

                    JENNIFER
        Can we at least watch some poker?

                    RONALD
        Let's do something as a family.

That evening, from Ronald and Jennifer's room we see the NIGHT LIGHTS. There's
a knock at the door. Jennifer opens and exuberantly jumps on Lightnin.

                    JENNIFER
        Lightnin!

He steps in and Ronald joins them for a group hug.

> LIGHTNIN
> Okay, what do you want to do?

> RONALD
> I hear that they have a thing called
> the sports book. Let's check that
> out.

> JENNIFER
> Sports! This is Vegas, dad. Let's see
> The Strip, the shows. Let's watch
> poker!

Lightnin takes a quarter out of his pocket. He flips it and cups it.

> LIGHTNIN
> Heads, sports. Tails, poker.

He peeks at the quarter and without showing it.

> LIGHTNIN
> Tails, poker.

DISSOLVE TO:

The CASINO. As they pass by the TABLES and SLOT MACHINES, Jennifer gawks like a typical tourist.

> RONALD
> So, you like Vegas, huh?

> LIGHTNIN
> Yeah, I do.

> RONALD
> Have you made any friends?

> LIGHTNIN
> Ah, yeah.

> RONALD
> What about college and basketball?

> LIGHTNIN
> I guess I should start thinking about
> that, huh?

> RONALD
> What about Indiana University?

> LIGHTNIN
> Naa. I'm going to check out some
> schools here in the West.

> JENNIFER
> Dad, look!

A sign that reads POKER TOURNAMENT.

Jennifer rushes over to the TOURNAMENT AREA, which is roped off. PLAYERS and DEALERS have commenced playing. SPECTATORS surround the tournament.

> RONALD
> Watch your sister, I've got to hit the
> John.

OUTSIDE, TRAFFIC is thick. INSIDE BLAINE'S CAR, Arnie ogles some girls walking by.

> ARNIE
> Hey, sweetheart, let's play Army. I'll
> be a soldier and you can blow the shit
> out of me.

Arnie laughs insidiously, while Blaine rolls his eyes.

BACK TO THE CASINO

Lightnin watches the game with Jennifer when they hear a commotion. A MAN in the crowd cries out.

> MAN
> Someone's taken my wallet!

Lightnin looks over at the man. A few feet away he sees Eli slithering away.

> LIGHTNIN
> Eli!! Jennifer, wait here.

327

Lightnin is in pursuit as Eli scurries off. Lightnin pushes his way through the crowd.

LIGHTNIN
Eli, you son-of-a-bitch.

Eli has made it to the exit and starts running down the street.

OUTSIDE, Lightnin is close behind and soon catches up with Eli. Lightnin grabs his collar and spins him around. Eli swings at Lightnin. He blocks the punch and swings back. He connects, knocking Eli down. Just then, BLAINE'S CAR passes by.

INSIDE CAR

ARNIE
Blaine, two fudgies are kickin' the
shit out of each other.

Blaine pulls over, they get out and join a SMALL CROWD already assembled. They push through.

ARNIE
Blaine, it's Lightnin!

Blaine and Arnie grab Lightnin and hold him. Eli takes this opportunity and slips away.

LIGHTNIN
You idiots! He's getting away!

Lightnin tries to shake them off. Arnie holds Lightnin while Blaine poises himself for some fist-a-cuffs.

BLAINE
Seems like old times.

He socks Lightnin in the face.

From the street, JO MAMMA'S CADDY pulls up to the employee parking structure ramp and stops. INSIDE the car, Jo Mamma and Flo Naze notice the ruckus and stop.

FLO NAZE
My God, it's Lightnin!

328

They both exit the vehicle ON THE SIDEWALK and run to Lightnin's aid.

JO MAMMA
Don't worry, baby, daddy's comin for ya.

FLO NAZE
(correcting)
Momma.

JO MAMMA
Whatever.

Jo Mamma spins Blaine around knocking him to the ground, while Flo Naze attacks Arnie. Just then, Ronald and Jennifer exit the hotel and spot Lightnin.

JENNIFER
Lightnin!

Ronald gets a hold of Lightnin who's nursing a bloody nose. Ronald notices Blaine and Arnie.

RONALD
What the hell's going on?

He and Jennifer pull Lightnin aside while the four (men) continue battle. Suddenly, FOUR SECURITY GUARDS enter the scene, contain the fight and bring them inside.

DISSOLVE TO:

INSIDE THE GUARD STATION - Blaine and Arnie are cuffed and sitting. Jo Mamma and Flo Naze try to explain the situation. Lightnin, Ronald and Jennifer stand off to the side. Jo Mamma addresses one of the guards, JOHNNY, whom she knows.

JO MAMMA
Johnny, these two thugs were roughing
up my boy.
(corrects)
I mean, this boy.

Ronald recognizes his old friend.

RONALD
Joe? Joe Favreau? Is that you?

JO MAMMA
(embarrassed)
Mmm-hmm.

RONALD
You've changed.

Flo Naze intervenes.

FLO NAZE
Can we continue old home week, later.
Jo, we've got a show in fifteen minutes.

Johnny addresses Lightnin.

JOHNNY
Do you want to press charges?

Lightnin looks at Ronald. Ronald shakes his head, "no."

LIGHTNIN
I guess not.

One of the other guards uncuff Blaine and Arnie.

JOHNNY
If I ever see you two near this place
again, you'll spend the night in jail.

LIGHTNIN
(to Blaine)
What are you doing in Vegas?

BLAINE
(smugly)
My dad's the Dean over at P.U.

As they exit, Blaine looks at Lightnin and Jo Mamma and smirks. Ronald addresses
Jo Mamma.

RONALD
We need to talk.
(to Lightnin)
Let's get you home. And I do mean
home.

330

                    LIGHTNIN
          I'm not going back to Indiana!

                    FLO NAZE
          How ya' gonna keep 'em down
          on the farm after they've seen…

Jo Mamma interrupts.

                    JO MAMMA
          Flo!

THE NEXT MORNING in Lightnin's apartment. He and Flo Naze are having coffee
at the kitchen table.

                    LIGHTNIN
          My dad'll be over soon. He and Jo are
          having a pow wow.

                    FLO NAZE
          Do we have time…

Lightnin interrupts.

                    LIGHTNIN
          No. May I be frank?

                    FLO NAZE
          No, I'm Frank, silly.

                    LIGHTNIN
          We can't do this anymore. This is wrong.
          For eighteen years I was a virgin, and
          within one week, I had sex with a nympho
          in Nashville and a transsexual in Vegas. I'm
          a normal guy, Flo. I just want a normal
          relationship with a normal girl.

                    FLO NAZE
          Someday you'll find out that *normal*
          ain't all what it's cracked up to be.

Flo Naze slides under the table. Lightnin grows weak.

LIGHTNIN
Alright, just once more.

DISSOLVE TO:

OUTSIDE of the apartment building, Ronald ascends the stairs with a piece of paper looking for Jo Mamma's apartment. Upstairs, Lightnin's door opens as Flo Naze leaves, half dressed. She gives Lightnin a quick kiss.

FLO NAZE
Thank you, sugar.

Just then, Ronald walks by.

RONALD
Lightnin?

Flo Naze scurries off.

FLO NAZE
Ah, thanks for the sugar.

LIGHTNIN
(mortified)
Dad, it's not what you think.

Ronald steps in.

RONALD
A half dressed transsexual, kissing
you is what I'm thinking.

There's a KNOCK at the door. It's slightly open. Jo Mamma peeks in.

JO MAMMA
Hello. May I come in?

She steps in.

RONALD
Well, Joe, it's been a long time. I
trust you know my son.

JO MAMMA
My son, actually.

332

RONALD

Alright, I'm not going to mince words,
Joe. What the hell's wrong with you?!
You were one of the manliest men I
ever knew. What's with the gay crap?

JO MAMMA

Gay! Ronald, you're such a square.
I'm not gay. I'm a woman, now. Look,
I know this is a lot to swallow and I'm
sorry. But you haven't seen me in
eighteen years. You never came to see
me when I was in prison. You never
answered one letter. And I sent a lot.

RONALD

I didn't. Ah, shoot, Joe, I'm sorry. I
guess I felt a little pissed-off. You go
and kill a guy, then you leave me with
your child. Now, I'm an unmarried man
with a black kid and a white kid in
Indiana! Do you think that's easy?!!
(a beat)
Regardless, I'm happy to see ya' old
friend, but Goddamit, why the sex
change?

JO MAMMA

It's complicated. Please accept this. Both
of you. I'm still your friend, Ronald. And
Lightnin, I have a lot to make up to you.
Please let me.

RONALD

Joe, this is not an ideal situation for
an eighteen year old kid.
(to Lightnin)
Are you and that Flo, person, doin' it?

LIGHTNIN

No.

RONALD
(not buying it)
Where in hell did I go wrong? You had a
good home and I did my best to coach you
in life and on the basketball court.

LIGHTNIN
Yeah, but where were you when Blaine
and his guerrillas were knockin' me
around? You turned the other way, dad.

RONALD
I'm sorry Lightnin. I could have done
better. Look at the position I was in. I
couldn't show favoritism towards you.
My job and our security were on the line.

LIGHTNIN
You were a good father. But, now I need
to see the world, do things I could never
do in Kucaision, Indiana.

RONALD
Oh, you're doing that, okay.

LIGHTNIN
(embarrassed)
Well, that's over. In fact, what I really
wanted to do in the first place was to go
to New Orleans and check out my roots.

Jo Mamma waves.

JO MAMMA
Well, here's one of 'em.

LIGHTNIN
What about my real mother? Where is
she? Dad, all you've ever told me were
lies.

Ronald's at a loss. Jo Mamma intervenes.

334

JO MAMMA

It's time you knew the truth. Your mother
was running with the wrong people. I
stepped in and well, a man died. When I
was away I never heard from her. I tried
calling her. All of her friends have probably
OD'd by now. I wouldn't even know where
to look.

LIGHTNIN

Was her name Jasmine?

JO MAMMA
(to Ronald)
Oh, you did mention her name.
(to Lightnin)
Yes, Jasmine. She took my surname,
Favreau. But who knows if she still uses
it. I know I don't, ha ha.

LIGHTNIN

There's only one way to find out. I'm
going to try and find her.

RONALD

You're not going by yourself. I can't
go with you. I have responsibilities at
school.

JO MAMMA

I'll go with him. Is that okay with you,
Lightnin?

LIGHTNIN

What about your show? You're the
"Queen of The Strip."

JO MAMMA

Flo can sub for me. I have vacation
time coming anyway. Pack your bags
baby. You and Jo Momma are gonna
find yo' momma.
(a beat)
I just hope it's not at a cemetery.

                                   RONALD
               Thanks, Joe.

                                   JO MAMMA
               And thank you, ol' friend.
                                   (to Lightnin)
               Who's your daddy?

Lightnin looks at Ronald.

                                   LIGHTNIN
               He is.

Lightnin and Ronald hug.

THE NEXT DAY - Lightnin and Jo Mamma are on the road. An AERIAL SHOT of the
Caddy as it passes by HOOVER DAM. INSIDE of the CAR, Lightnin is driving as he
and Jo Mamma are catching up.

                                   LIGHTNIN
                         I would often ask Dad who my real
                         parents were and he'd come up with
                         some lame story. Why Lightnin?

                                   JO MAMMA
                         When your mother and I first laid eyes
                         on each other a bolt of lightnin', literally
                         filled the night sky with a radiant light.
                         Soon after, you were conceived.

DISSOLVE TO:

As the SUNSETS, the car passes a highway sign that reads: LOUISIANA STATE
LINE 10 MILES.

NEXT MORNING - INSIDE of the car we SEE a sign that reads. NEW ORLEANS 30
MILES. Jo Mamma is driving.

                                   JO MAMMA
                         When your mother left me, I was
                         devastated. I idolized her and
                         admired the power she had. And
                         all of those years in prison, I
                         became confused and lost my soul.
                         When I was released, I decided to
                         become like Jasmine.

                                      336

LIGHTNIN
A stripper? Do you have relations
with men?

JO MAMMA
It's funny, I don't. *Or* with women.
A psychiatrist told me that I'm so
afraid of being hurt that I avoid both
sexes. I should've become a nun.

LIGHTNIN
The first black, transsexual, stripper, nun.

They both laugh.

JO MAMMA
Since I changed, life hasn't been bad.
I love my friends and my life in Vegas.

LIGHTNIN
Isn't it expensive getting a sex change?

JO MAMMA
Some medical schools do it for nothing.
It's sort of a trophy operation. I had mine
done in Tittsburgh.

LIGHTNIN
Don't you mean Pittsburgh?

JO MAMMA
Oops, Oedipal slip.

LIGHTNIN
Don't you mean Freudian?

JO MAMMA
Not if I can pass as your mother.

Lightnin sees a sign BOURBON STREET.

LIGHTNIN
Hey, Bourbon Street!

They pull up to a HOTEL.

Later that EVENING, Lightnin and Jo Mamma stroll down the OLD BLOCK. They approach the place where Club Seal used to be. It's now CLUB FOOT, a dance club. At the door, Jo Mamma sees a familiar face.

                    JO MAMMA
          Butch? Is that you?

                    BENNY
          No, I'm his son, Benny.

                    JO MAMMA
          No wonder you look so young. Where's
          the big man?

                    BENNY
          He's inside.

As they head inside.

                    BENNY
          I need to see some ID.

                    JO MAMMA
          Why, thank you.

                    BENNY
          No, him.

                    LIGHTNIN
                    (covering)
          I left it in my car.

                    BENNY
          Sorry.

                    JO MAMMA
          Okay, wait here. I'm going inside
          to talk with Butch. Maybe he knows
          where Jasmine might be.

Jo Mamma enters the club.

                    LIGHTNIN
          That's my dad.

Benny gives Lightnin a look.

INSIDE THE CLUB - Jo Mamma goes to the bar. It's early. Just a FEW PATRONS are sitting at the bar. Jo Mamma approaches Butch.

> BUTCH
> What'll it be?

> JO MAMMA
> Make it a club soda.

Butch looks at Jo Mamma as if he's had a déjà vu.

> JO MAMMA
> The place hasn't changed much.

Butch opens the club soda and pours it in the icy glass.

> BUTCH
> Do I know you?

> JO MAMMA
> Yes. I used to date Jasmine, one of
> your dancers, back in the day.

> BUTCH
> (surprised)
> You did? I didn't know she swung
> both ways.

> JO MAMMA
> She didn't. I had a sex change. Back
> then I was Joe Favreau. We had a kid
> together.

> BUTCH
> (startled)
> Get the fuck out of here!

He looks Jo Mamma up and down.

> BUTCH
> It *is* you. Nice work. Hey, didn't you
> go to the slams for a while?

JO MAMMA
Eight years. For pimpslaughter.

BUTCH
(recalling)
Rodrigo. He was a piece of shit.
(still amazed)
I'll be damned.

JO MAMMA
What ever happened to Jasmine?

BUTCH
Jeez, I donno. She was a junkie. She
got fired shortly after Rodrigo bought
it. She'd stop in once in a while. She
started looking bad. For all I know
she's either homeless or dead.

JO MAMMA
Hey, do you want to meet our kid?

BUTCH
He's here?

Butch looks out the window and signals to Benny to let Lightnin in.

BUTCH
That's my kid.

JO MAMMA
The acorn didn't drop far from the tree.

As Lightnin walks in, Butch sees the resemblance.

BUTCH
Amazing. So now you're the mother?

JO MAMMA
Father.

LIGHTNIN
Whatever.

340

The next MORNING in their HOTEL ROOM, Jo Mamma is on the PHONE. Lightnin sits on the bed listening intently.

                    JO MAMMA
          Jasmine Favreau.
                    (a beat)
          How about Jasmine Cowin?
                    (a beat)
          Okay, thank you.

Jo Mamma hangs up the phone.

                    JO MAMMA
          The Hall of Records has no
          documentation of any death
          certificate.

Jo Mamma looks in a mirror and straightens her hair.

                    JO MAMMA
          Let's go.

                    LIGHTNIN
          Where to?

                    JO MAMMA
          Playin' a hunch.

SERIES OF SHOTS - NIGHT - MUSIC - JOHN SCOFIELD'S *NOW SHE'S BLONDE*

The Caddy drives by different locations.

In the SEEDY PART OF TOWN, they cruise down a street where the local junkies hang out. Different MEN and WOMEN, sitting, standing and lying on the sidewalk.

In the RED LIGHT DISTRICT, STREET WALKERS of every variety strut their stuff, pose and beckon to Lightnin. TWO BLACK HOOKERS catch Jo Mamma's eye. They stop. Jo Mamma gets out of the car and approaches them.

                    JO MAMMA
          Jasmine?

                    HOOKER # 1
          Honey, you on the wrong block.
          We don't do bitches.

                         JO MAMMA
Oh, a woman with scruples.

                         HOOKER # 1
Huh?

                         JO MAMMA
Listen, honey. I'm lookin for my
sister. Her name is Jasmine. She
used to be a dancer, back in the day.

The hookers confer for a moment.

                         HOOKER # 2
Yeah, I know Jasmine.

                         JO MAMMA
Where can I find her?

                         HOOKER # 2
Oh, that's classified, baby.

Jo Mamma reaches in her bag and pulls out a TWENTY.

                         HOOKER # 1
Hmm. You gonna need Mr. Grant
for dat information.

                         JO MAMMA
Mmm?

                         HOOKER # 2
     A fifty.

Jo Mamma pulls out another TWENTY and a TEN.

                         JO MAMMA
A Jackson and a Hamiton. Where is she?

                         HOOKER # 1
She hangs out at the park, down
off Fifth Street.

She goes to take the money. Jo Mamma pulls it back.

                              JO MAMMA
                    What's she look like?

                              HOOKER # 1
                    Skinny, light skinned little sister
                    with a bad, blonde dye job.

                              HOOKER # 2
                    Be careful, she got the AIDS.

Jo Mamma hands her the money.

                              JO MAMMA
                    You better not be jivin' me. If you
                    are, I'll be back.

                              HOOKER # 2
                    Strait up, baby. I'll be waitin' here.

She looks over at Lightnin.

                              HOOKER # 2
                    How 'bout you sugar? You wanna date?
                    I'll suck you 'til your head caves in.

The hookers laugh it up as Jo Mamma gets in the car and drives off.

A PARK where the local dregs of society hang out. There are several BUMS sitting
and sleeping on the grass. Lightnin spots two BLACK WOMEN, poorly dressed and
sharing a cigarette.

                              LIGHTNIN
                    Dad, over there.

                              JO MAMMA
                              (misty)
                    You called me dad.

They pull over, park and get out. Lightnin gets a better look. One of the women has
blonde hair.

                              LIGHTNIN
                    It's her!

                              JO MAMMA
                    Let me handle this.

He approaches.

                              JO MAMMA
                    Excuse me. Do you know where I can
                    find Joe Favreau?

The Blonde perks up. It's Jasmine.

                              JASMINE
                    Who wants to know?

She begins coughing.

                              JO MAMMA
                         (to Lightnin)
                    Oh, my God. It's her! Talk to her.

                              LIGHTNIN
                    That's a pretty bad cough you've got
                    there. Can I get you a throat lozenge?

                              JASMINE
                    No, but I'll take drink.

                              LIGHTNIN
                    Maybe later. Is your name Jasmine?

                              JASMINE
                    Yeah.

She gets a better look at Lightnin.

                              JASMINE
                    Who are you?

                              LIGHTNIN
                    I'm Lightnin, your son.

She looks at him and begins to tremble. Tears well up in her eyes.

                              JASMINE
                    Lightnin?
                         (weeping)
                    Oh, God. I don't want you to see
                    me this way.

                                344

                        LIGHTNIN
                That's alright, mamma.

They embrace.

                        JASMINE
                Your father took you from me and
                then he went away. I loved him very
                much, but I got hung up, baby. I'm
                so sorry. There ain't a day that goes
                by that I that I don't think about you.

She pulls away and wipes her face.

                        JASMINE
                God, you got so big and handsome.
                You look just like your father.

She looks at Jo Mamma.

                        JASMINE
                And so do you.

                        JO MAMMA
                Jasmine, It's me, Joe.

She looks at him again.

                        JASMINE
                Is it Marti Gras?

                        JO MAMMA
                No.

                        JASMINE
                Then why are you dressed up like
                a woman?

                        JO MAMMA
                That's because I *am* a woman.

Jasmine is totally perplexed. She comes up to Jo Mamma and feels her breasts.

                        JASMINE
                Oh my God!

She begins to laugh. The laughter turns into a coughing spell. The woman with Jasmine speaks up.

                    WOMAN
          She's pretty sick.

                    JO MAMMA
          We're going to take care of you now,
          Jasmine.

                    WOMAN
          Can you spare some change?

Jo Mamma takes some money from her bag and gives it to the woman.

                    WOMAN
          Bless you.

DISSOLVE TO:

MORNING - LAS VEGAS - OUR LADY OF THE TABLES HOSPITAL

INSIDE - HOSPITAL ROOM

Jasmine is lying in bed with an IV hook-up. A NURSE comes in and checks her vitals.

                    RONLAD (V.O.)
          The good news: Jasmine didn't have AIDS.
          The bad news: She was diagnosed with
          Hepatitis, Tuberculosis and Mononucleosis.

INSIDE - CRAZY PONY

Flo Naze and company are on stage.

                    RONALD (V.O.)
          Jo Mamma quit the show.

INSIDE A HOSPITAL ROOM, Joe is recovering from his operation.

                    RONALD (V.O.)
          And Joe Favreau is recovering from
          his reversal operation.

346

Ronald and Jennifer are sitting and sweating on their FRONT PORCH drinking Kool Aid. Jennifer looks bored and yawns.

> RONALD (V.O.)
> Jennifer and I are back in our beloved
> Kucaision.

Lightnin, sitting at his desk in a CLASSROOM.

> RONALD (V.O.)
> Lightnin enrolled at Pioneer University.
> He's trying out for the basketball team.
> Against my advice. He seems to think
> that, even Dean Coleman would want
> the *best* on his team.

INSIDE the BASKETBALL COURT, Lightnin is trying out for the newly formed Pioneer University's basketball team, THE WAGERES. He wears his special brace. There are some FIFTY YOUNG MEN trying out for the team. Half of the team is white, some Hispanics and the rest are black. All are wearing their own gym clothes with numbers stapled on their shirts.

In the STANDS, there are no public spectators. At the OFFICIALS TABLE, Harvard Coleman, Blaine, Arnie and FOUR SCHOOL OFFICIALS conduct the event. Blaine makes an announcement.

> BLAINE
> Good afternoon and thank you for
> participating. We'll start with some
> preliminary tasks. We'll see how
> well you can perform. From there,
> we'll choose up sides and have an
> actual game.

The participants form a line. Arnie pitches to each of them as they dribble down the court and perform a lay-up into the basket. Lightnin performs this feat with ease.

DIFFERENT SHOTS of the players performing fouls shots. Lightnin sinks everyone.

Arnie chooses up sides.

> ARNIE
> It'll be skins and shirts. Number nine,
> twelve, six...

DISSOLVE TO:

The game is in progress. Half the players are wearing shirts, half are not. Lightnin is on the Skins team and is playing extremely well. He bonds with an Hispanic player, RAUL.

From the officials table, Blaine and Arnie are conferring.

> BLAINE
> I thought we put this guy out of
> business. His knee has shown no
> sign of stress.

DISSOLVE TO:

The Skins win the game. Lightnin and Raul HIGH FIVE one another. It's the end of the tryouts. Blaine makes an announcement.

> BLAINE
> Thank you, men. We'll make our
> decision tomorrow.

THE NEXT DAY in the campus HALL OF ADMISSIONS, on the BULLETIN BOARD, the list of players who made the team are posted. SEVERAL PARTICIPANTS gather around, one of which is Raul. Lightnin arrives and checks out the list. Neither of their names are on the list. They're both perplexed.

> RAUL
> Dude, this is wrong. You played
> an excellent game.

> LIGHTNIN
> And so did you.

DISSOLVE TO:

Back at his apartment, Lightnin is on the phone with Ronald.

INTERCUT - LIGHTNIN AND RONALD

> LIGHTNIN
> I don't get it, dad. I did everything
> right, I didn't miss a shot and our
> team won the game. Something's
> funny.

                              RONALD
Well, you know how Blaine feels
about you. He's prejudiced and for
that matter, so is his father, the Dean.
Sometimes politics beats talent. How's
everything else?

                              LIGHTNIN
Good. Joe and Jasmine are recovering
Nicely. How's Jennifer?

                              RONALD
She wants to move to Vegas. I told her
as soon as she's twenty one.

OUTSIDE OF PIONEER UNIVERSITY CAMPUS - It's Friday EVENING as PEOPLE
file into the SPORTS DOME. A sign above the entrance reads: THE WAGERERS
VS THE RAMBLERS.

INSIDE, a packed stadium. Lightnin and Raul take their seats as an announcement
comes over the P.A. SYSTEM.

                              ANNOUNCER (V.O.)
Welcome to the first game of the season
and the Wagerers first game. And now let's
meet out new team. Our first player. A
native of Las Vegas, guard, Barry Kimmel.

CHEERS from the home audience.

DISSOLVE TO:

                              ANNOUNCER (V.O.)
And finally, from Kucaision, Indiana,
Brad Winchell.

Lightnin and Raul look at each other.

                              RAUL
You notice anything?

                              LIGHTNIN
Everyone on the team is white.

The NEXT DAY at THE LAS VEGAS SUN HEADQUARTERS, Lightnin's Chevy pulls in the parking lot, followed by a VAN. Lightnin and Raul exit the car. Some FIFTEEN GUYS pile out of the van.

INSIDE an OFFICE, Lightnin and Raul are sitting at a desk with a middle aged woman, named MRS. STEINBURG. She is one of the papers chief editors.

                    MRS. STEINBURG
          And you say you're both victims of blatant
          prejudice at Pioneer University.

                    LIGHTNIN
          Yes, Mrs. Steinburg.

Lightnin presents a list.

                    LIGHTNIN
          This is a petition signed by all of the
          players who were rejected by the coach.
          Most of whom were qualified and all of
          them are minorities.

She examines the document.

                    MRS. STEINBURG
          That's interesting. Strange, too, because
          most sports these days are minority
          dominated. So this could be a case of
          reversed, reversed discrimination.
          Hmm. It could also be a great story. I'll need
          to verify the other names on this petition.

                    RAUL
          No problemo.

He motions to the corridor outside of the office. Through the plate glass window we SEE other players wave at Mrs. Steinburg. Mrs. Steinburg gets on her intercom.

                    MRS. STEINBURG
          Phil, get me Dennis over at Channel Nine.

INSIDE THE P.U. SPORTS DOME - NIGHT - A game is in session. The stands are packed. The scoreboard reads:

WAGERERS 57 BOULDERS 68

Harvard Coleman sits at the officials table with his four officials. Blaine and Arnie are on the home bench. Arnie barks out at a PLAYER.

                    ARNIE
          What do you have lead in your ass?
          Move it!

HALF TIME BUZZER

A CAMERA CREW has been taping the game. ACHMAD KABOB FURLONG reports the game, now gone into half time. Achmad wears a turban with a shamrock on it. Behind the crew, Lightnin and Raul and the other rejected players stand by.

POV CAMERA

                    ACHMAD
          Good evening, This is Achmad Kabob
          Furlong, Channel Nine News. We're
          live at The Pioneer University Sports
          Dome, where the newly formed
          Wagerers host the Boulders.

SHOT OF WAGERERS LEAVING THE COURT.

                    ACHMAD (V.O.)
          Allegations that this team is all white,
          isn't alright. Some students and qualified
          players at P.U. tried out for the team and
          were rejected because of their race. There
          seems to be a stench at P.U.

SHOT OF LIGHTNIN AND RAUL

                    ACHMAD (V.O.)
          With me now, two students that were
          rejected. Lightnin Sweeney and Raul
          Gomez. Can you substantiate these
          allegations?

                    LIGHTNIN
          After the tryouts, I noticed that most of
          white players were accepted and all of
          minority players were rejected. I have
          a signed petition from all involved.

SHOT OF THE OTHER PLAYERS WAVING IN THE BACKGROUND.

Achmad takes the petition. Lightnin grabs a basketball lying nearby.

POV CAMERA - MOVES TOWARDS THE LOCKER ROOM.

During the next speeches the, CAMERA PUSHES THROUGH A DOOR, DOWN A HALLWAY AND INTO THE LOCKER ROOM where Blaine, Arnie and the team have commenced the halftime proceedings.

> ACHMAD (V.O.)
> We're headed towards the locker room
> where we'll speak with coach…

> LIGHTNIN (V.O.)
> …Blaine Coleman.

CAMERA ON BLAINE who is pleasantly surprised by the news team. He fixes his hair. Lightnin, Raul and crew wait just outside the locker room.

> ACHMAD (V.O.)
> Blaine Coleman? Achmad Kabob Furlong,
> Channel Nine News. Is it true that one of
> the main qualifications of getting on your
> team is that you have to be white?

> BLAINE
> What?

He looks over at his players.

> BLAINE
> Well, these boys are all fine athletes.
> It's purely coincidental, that they're
> all white.

> ACHMAD (V.O.)
> We have a signed petition here.

Achmad waves the DOCUMENT in front of the camera.

> ACHMAD (V.O.)
> There are some seventeen students who
> tried out for your team and were rejected
> because they weren't white.

BLAINE
That's bogus. The guys who didn't make
our team, sucked.

Just then, Lightnin opens the door and he, Raul and crew wave at Blaine. Lightnin
spins the basket ball on his index finger as the CAMERA focuses in on them.

LIGHTNIN
Okay, boys. Let's show why you got
rejected from P.U.

They run out onto the court. Lightnin throws the ball mid court and SWISH. The
spectators don't quite know what to think, but there's a smattering of APPLAUSE.
Just then the other players spring into action, performing drills and maneuvers that
would rival the Harlem Globe Trotters. The crowd goes WILD. The camera crew is
on the sidelines catching all of the action.

ACHMAD (V.O.)
Look at these guys go. These are the same
boys that were rejected by coach Coleman
because they suck? A sucking of the likes
I have never heard.

Harvard Coleman and the officials are dumb founded. Harvard SCREAMS at TWO
BLACK SECURITY GUARDS who are enjoying the show. They ignore him. Blaine,
Arnie and the team enter the court and try to take the ball from the rejected players.
It's useless. The players out maneuver the team. CHEERS and LAUGHTER from
the crowd.

The camera crew goes into the stands to the officials table. Achmad tries to interview
Harvard.

CAMERA ON HARVARD

ACHMAD (V.O.)
Harvard Coleman, the Dean of P.U. Dean,
how do you respond to these allegations?

HARVARD
Can I speak off camera?

ACHMAD (V.O.)
Yes.

Achmad waves to the cameraman to back off. He does. Harvard gets close to
Achmad.

HARVARD (V.O.)
Allegations of racism? Allegations are for
Alligators. You can't prove racism. Now,
get lost you dune coon.

Harvard doesn't realize that he's still on mic. His comments are heard by the viewing audience.

CAMERA ON ACHMAD

ACHMAD
Dune coon? Hey, I'm also half mick. As
you've heard, this is an unprecedented case
of discrimination from a very bigoted man.
The minority players are far superior to the
Wagerers. I'll wager that there'll be a new
complexion on this basketball court in days
to come. A complexion of pimply spots of
different colors on a buttermilk canvas of
flesh. Okay, metaphors aren't my strong suit.
        (a beat)
Live from the P.U. Sports Dome, Achmad
Kabob Furlong, Channel Nine News.

ONE YEAR LATER

In the distance, the Vegas skyline lights up the EVENING sky. In the outskirts of Las Vegas at a strip mall, CARS pull in and out of the parking lot. Some PEOPLE enter a little BAR AND GRILL. A red and green neon sign reads LUCKY 13.

The CAMERA PUSHES INSIDE, to a PACKED HOUSE. Joe is tending bar while Jasmine waits on tables. At one table, Flo Naze and some of the other dancers from Transgression play video poker.

RONALD (V.O.)
Well, Joe and Jasmine finally tied the knot.
Joe bought a little joint on the west side of
town. Jennifer came up with Lucky 13.

INSIDE OF CAESARS PALACE CASINO - POKER TABLES. At one table, Jennifer is dealing to some CUSTOMERS.

RONALD (V.O.)
Jennifer has filled her life long passion
to play poker. But instead of losing
money, she can earn it, dealing.

354

INSIDE THE P.U. SPORTS DOME. During a game, Lightnin, passes the ball to Raul. Raul dunks the ball. CHEELEADERS CHEER. The scoreboard reads:

WAGERERS 98 HOOVERS 60

> RONALD (V.O.)
> Lightnin is the new captain of our team.

Coach Ronald is on the sidelines as Lightnin passes the ball to an ASIAN PLAYER.

> RONALD (V.O.)
> Lightnin is more generous with the ball
> and there's much more ethnic diversity
> on our team.

Meanwhile back in Kucaision. INSIDE the Greasy Platter, Harvard, Blaine and Arnie are at a table. They give their order to a WAITRESS.

> RONALD (V.O.)
> Harvard, Blaine and Arnie are back in
> Kucaision.

> BLAINE
> (to waitress)
> And I'll have the Crow Sandwich.
> Hey, where's Betsy?

A SHOT OF BETSY in her car as we SEE the DAYTIME Vegas skyline.

> RONALD (V.O.)
> And Betsy's going to be the head waitress
> at Bennies "Eat until you barf" Restaurant.

As she pulls into a GAS STATION, a SHERIFFS CAR pulls out. Inside the car, TWO SHERIFFS are in the front. In the back seat, handcuffed, Eli looks out of the window and notices Betsy as she bounces over to the gas pump.

> RONALD (V.O.)
> Hey, get your eyes off my girl, pal.

Eli seems to have heard that and looks around.

FADE OUT:

ABOUT THE AUTHOR

Pat Mulligan

Pat Mulligan started his career as a stand-up comic, which soon lead to an acting career. "My fifteen minutes of fame took twenty years to run its course in Hollywood." He was featured in sitcoms, commercials and films. Writing seemed to be the next progression. "If I want to act in a good movie, I'll write one." Another book by this author, *THE LIFE AND TIMES OF A HOLLYWOOD BAD BOY*, is also published by AuthorHouse. It chronicles Pat's life and the wild side of the Hollywood scene. During that period, he wrote five screenplays, three of which are compiled in this book: *APOCALYPSE LATER*, *DÉJÀ VU DÉJÀ VU* and *HOOSIER DADDY*.

DÉJÀ VU DÉJÀ VU came in tenth place in a national script writing contest, AMERICA'S BEST.